How Florida Happened

Florida Government and Politics

UNIVERSITY PRESS OF FLORIDA

Florida A&M University, Tallahassee
Florida Atlantic University, Boca Raton
Florida Gulf Coast University, Ft. Myers
Florida International University, Miami
Florida State University, Tallahassee
New College of Florida, Sarasota
University of Central Florida, Orlando
University of Florida, Gainesville
University of North Florida, Jacksonville
University of South Florida, Tampa
University of West Florida, Pensacola

University Press of Florida

Gainesville · Tallahassee · Tampa · Boca Raton

Pensacola · Orlando · Miami · Jacksonville · Ft. Myers · Sarasota

HOW FLORIDA HAPPENED

The Political
Education of Buddy MacKay

Buddy MacKay with Rick Edmonds

Foreword by David R. Colburn and Susan A. MacManus

FLA
B
MACK
EDMO

15 14 13 12 11 10   6 5 4 3 2 1

Library of Congress Cataloging-in-Publication Data
MacKay, Buddy.
How Florida happened : the political education of Buddy MacKay /
Buddy MacKay, with Rick Edmonds ; foreword by David R. Colburn
and Susan A. MacManus.
p. cm.
ISBN 978-0-8130-3484-3 (alk. paper)
1. MacKay, Buddy. 2. Florida—Politics and government—1951–
3. Lieutenant governors—Florida—Biography. 4. Legislators—
United States—Biography. 5. Legislators—Florida—Biography.
6. Diplomats—United States—Biography. 7. United States.
Congress. House—Biography. 8. Florida. Legislature. House of
Representatives—Biography. I. Edmonds, Rick, 1947– II. Title.
F316.23.M33A3 2010
975.9'063092—dc22 [B]   2009047972

The University Press of Florida is the scholarly publishing agency
for the State University System of Florida, comprising Florida A&M
University, Florida Atlantic University, Florida Gulf Coast University,
Florida International University, Florida State University, New College of Florida, University of Central Florida, University of Florida,
University of North Florida, University of South Florida, and University of West Florida.

University Press of Florida
15 Northwest 15th Street
Gainesville, FL 32611-2079
http://www.upf.com

This book is dedicated to my friend Bill Sadowski. Having retired from the Florida legislature after an outstanding career, Bill was managing partner of the Miami office of Akerman, Senterfitt, one of Florida's leading law firms. Lawton Chiles and I recruited him to serve as secretary of the Department of Community Affairs during the Chiles-MacKay first term, where he revitalized the department and dramatically improved the relationship between local and state government. Bill was killed in the crash of a state aircraft. He was an example to all who served with him.

Here are a few of Bill's thoughts about being a politician in a democracy:

Always respect another person's right to hold their own views, just as you want others to respect your right to hold independent views.

Don't question people's motivation; consider what they say on the merits. A good idea from a scoundrel is still a good idea.

Remember at all times that a legislator is merely a citizen who, for a limited period of time, is granted a modest portion of government's power. You are but a temporary part of the government. Moreover, never forget that the people in their Constitution retained all political power to themselves.

And don't forget that the people, in addition to granting power to the branches of the government, also declare certain protections for themselves. Be sensitive to those protections, such as their rights to be free from unreasonable government interferences and to freedom of speech and association and do not violate them.

Your family is a source of strength and a point of real world contact. Preserve and protect that strength at all cost. A legislative session is in many ways an artificial world. Don't lose touch with the real world.

You have two constituencies: one that elects you and one that you serve. The one that you serve consists of all the citizens of Florida.

Life is what happens to you while you are planning for something else.

—Gamble Rogers, Florida folksinger and storyteller.

Contents

Foreword

Florida has held a unique place in the American mind for over six decades. For many retirees, its environment has been like a healthy elixir that allowed them to live longer and more robust lives; for others, Florida is a place of renewal, where all things are possible; and for immigrants, it is a place of political freedom and opportunity. Historian Gary Mormino describes the state as a "powerful symbol of renewal and regeneration." It has been suggested that, if Florida had not existed in the post–World War II era, Americans would have been the poorer for it. Others who watched the 2000 presidential election wondered if that were so.

During World War II, Americans from all walks of life discovered Florida through military service, and it opened their eyes to the postwar possibilities. With the end of the war in August 1945, Florida veterans returned home, where they were soon joined by hundreds and then thousands of Americans who were ready to pursue a new life in the Sunshine State. In the sixty years between 1945 and 2005, 17 million people moved to Florida, increasing the state's population to 18.5 million people in 2005.

Florida's population growth, the settlement patterns of new residents, and their diversity had a profound effect on the state's place in the nation as well as the image Floridians had of themselves. Prior to 1940, Florida was the smallest state in the South and one of the poorest in the nation. Its society and economy was rural and agricultural, biracial and segregated, and most residents lived within forty miles of the Georgia border. These demographics and the state's history shaped the public's racial and cultural mind-set as well as its politics. Florida was a one-party state, controlled by the Democratic Party since the end of Reconstruction in 1876.

All that changed in the fifty years following World War II. By 2005—in less than an average life span today—Florida became the largest state in the region, the fourth largest in the nation, a senior haven, and a dynamic multiracial and multiethnic state. Most Floridians now reside closer to the Caribbean than they do to Georgia, and, for most of them, their image of themselves and their state has been significantly influenced by this new geographic orientation. By the twenty-first century, demographers viewed Florida as a microcosm of the nation because of its size and population complexity.

As Florida changed, so too did its politics. Voters threw out the constitution of 1885 in favor of a new document which would speak to the needs of a new state in 1968. They then gradually abandoned the Democratic Party in favor of a dynamic two-party system. By the 1990s, Republicans used their expanding constituency and control of the districting process following the 1990 census to take control of the state legislature and the congressional delegation. These were remarkable developments and reflected the dramatic changes taking place in the state's population and demographics. By 2008, Republicans controlled all state offices that were districted. However, in statewide races for governor, U.S. senator, and elected cabinet positions, as well as in presidential contests, Democrats frequently won and held a 6 percent lead over Republicans in registered voters (42 percent to 36 percent).

Such a politically and demographically complex and diverse population has made Florida today something other than a unified whole. The political maxim that "All politics is local" is truer of Florida than most other states. For example, those who reside in north Florida share little in common with those living in central or south Florida and vice versa. While those in southeast Florida see themselves as part of the "new America," those in north Florida view Miami as a foreign country. Ask a resident what it means to be a Floridian and few, if any, can answer the question. Ask a Floridian about the state's history, and even fewer can tell you that it has operated under five different flags, or that its colonial period began much earlier than that of New England or Virginia. Perhaps one in ten or twenty residents can tell you who LeRoy Collins was, despite Republican Jeb Bush's recognition of this Democratic governor as the model for all others who followed. It is literally a state unknown and indefinable to its people. Such historical ignorance and regional division become major obstacles when state leaders try to find consensus among voters and solutions that address the needs of all citizens.

An essential purpose of this series is to put Floridians in touch with their rich and diverse political history and to enhance their understanding of the political developments that have reshaped the state, region, and nation. This series focuses on the Sunshine State's unique and dynamic political history since 1900 and on public policy issues that have influenced the state and the nation. The University Press of Florida is dedicated to producing high quality books on these subjects. It is also committed to publishing shorter essays of twenty-five to fifty pages in this series that address some of the immediately pressing public policy issues confronting Florida. As part of this series, the University Press of Florida also welcomes book manuscripts on the region that examine critical political and policy developments that impacted Florida.

In this volume of our series, Kenneth H. "Buddy" MacKay describes his extraordinary political journey over twenty-seven years that took him from farm life in rural Ocala to the governor's mansion in Tallahassee. Along the way, he served as a state representative, state senator, congressman, lieutenant governor, the forty-second governor of Florida, and special envoy to the Americas for President Bill Clinton. Known for his honesty and integrity in service to the people of the state and nation, he focused his political career on working to improve the quality of schools, ensuring that families had access to affordable health care, making sure Florida's neighborhoods were safe, preserving and protecting Florida's environment and water supply, and transforming the state into the "Gateway to the Americas."

MacKay's political career in Florida unfolded as the "Pork-Chop" delegation—a group of rural politicians who fought to retain their region's control of the state legislature and state appropriations—gradually fell from power. The Pork-Choppers repeatedly blocked reapportionment of the state legislature to prevent south Florida residents from taking control of state politics. A U.S. Supreme Court ruling in 1967 led to their downfall and enabled the state to begin to modernize and meet the demands of a burgeoning population. Although MacKay was from rural Florida and thought initially by some to be a "Pork-Chop" ally, he was anything but. From the moment he took office, MacKay identified himself with the new leadership of the legislature which sought to address the numerous challenges facing Florida from education to race relations to the environment. Even though he cast his support with urban reformers, MacKay was well respected by many members of the rural delegation for his honesty and sincerity. In this volume, MacKay shares with us what those transitional days were like in Florida politics, the transition to a modern legislature and a professional staff, and the gradual passing of rural politics in the state. It is an incredibly entertaining and insightful examination of state politics during this critical transitional period.

MacKay also stood at the center of the political battle that saw the rise of the Republican Party to leadership in Florida. The shift from a "yellow dog" Democratic state to a red state is also a very important story, because it made possible the resurgence of the Republican Party nationally. MacKay, Reubin Askew, Lawton Chiles, and Bob Graham played pivotal roles in holding at bay the state's transition to the Republican Party. Their leadership and willingness to address difficult issues in a forthright manner to meet the needs of citizens and the state won them strong support among voters, and for most of the twenty-five year period from 1970 to 1995 they prevented the Republican Party from taking control of the state, even as state voters expressed frustration with the national Democratic Party. MacKay recounts these battles and the victories as well as the defeats that culminated in his loss of the governorship to Jeb Bush in 1998.

This is a remarkably frank autobiography that reflects the character of Buddy MacKay. His many friends and fans will welcome this book, and so will scholars who have studied this period, but whose firsthand insights have been limited because of the dearth of autobiographical accounts of this period. MacKay was at the center of it all, and he tells it extremely well. Without this book, one cannot understand the magnitude of the political changes that have taken place in Florida and what they all meant for the state and its citizens. MacKay tells the story as one would expect him to—with grace, wit, wisdom, and insight.

David R. Colburn
Susan A. MacManus

Introduction

More than a decade has passed since my political career came to a sudden end.

The results of my 1998 campaign to succeed Lawton Chiles as governor, while anguishing, had not been unexpected. Since July 1998, polls had consistently shown Jeb Bush with a lead that was big, but not insurmountable. In late August, though, just as voters were beginning to pay attention and we were starting to close the gap, the Republican-dominated Congress began an effort to impeach Bill Clinton. The charges had arisen out of a disgraceful sexual encounter in the Oval Office involving a young White House intern. The impeachment ultimately failed, but not before the resulting media spectacle had preempted every Democratic political campaign in America—including mine. Through heroic efforts and major sacrifices from friends and supporters, we narrowed the gap in my race against Jeb, but not by enough. In the end, I lost, and it wasn't close.

That was not the saddest part, however. On December 10, 1998, my close friend and the state's political icon, Lawton Chiles, died suddenly. I became governor of Florida for the final three weeks of our administration's second term. Not only was I a lame duck, but the legislature and much of the rest of state government had gone home for the holidays. So, I accomplished very little except to oversee an extended period of mourning.

I spent most of the next two years as President Clinton's special envoy to the Americas. I succeeded Mac McClarty, Clinton's close friend and former chief of staff, in the role. Presidential envoys are appointed for a specific purpose, in situations of special concern to a president. A recent example is President Obama's appointment of George Mitchell as special envoy for Middle East peace negotiations. The advantage to the parties is that the envoy speaks directly for the president, and also takes their messages directly back to the president, unfiltered by the State Department or other bureaucracies. In my case, as a special envoy, I was responsible for keeping the negotiations to achieve the Free Trade Area of the Americas, a hemispheric common market, on track. This had been a commitment of Clinton's at the 1994 Summit of the Americas. If we had been able to achieve a hemispheric common market, all of America would have benefited, but no state would have gained as much as Florida. But the effort lost steam in the Bush administration and ended in limbo—never officially killed but not accepted either.

After four years as an adjunct professor of law, I really retired. For me, that meant mainly spending time with family, managing a family farm, and volunteering. I also had time to reflect on forty years of public life in Florida and to pull together material from journals and sketches I had written while in office. The result is the book you have in your hands. I am not an academician, and this is not a neutral work of scholarly research. Rather it is one participant's recollection of events in the final four decades of the twentieth century—the period in which Florida became an out-of-control growth engine. With the brilliant exception of Governor LeRoy Collins and a few other progressive leaders, Florida was a politically backward state when I graduated from law school in 1961—only starting to free itself from the grip of segregation and the Pork-Chop Gang, a group of rural legislative "good old boys" whose main concern was to divide up the available pork. There were no "good old girls," as women in politics were a rarity. Ideally, in the forty-plus years that followed, Florida should have matured politically as its population soared and its economic muscle grew. In my view, that has largely failed to happen. Florida still suffers from the adolescent's inability to sacrifice short-term satisfaction to achieve long-term goals.

I was one of the leaders in the first successful effort to drag Florida away from its preoccupation with the Civil War and Reconstruction. This effort ultimately culminated in the reform of all three branches of Florida's government. With the aid of courageous citizens, prosecutors, lawyers, and grand juries, we dragged the institutions of Florida's government—kicking and screaming—from their position of intransigence (incompetent, segregated, and proud of it) to that of one of America's most reformed state governments. In less than a decade, Florida embraced what many now call the "Golden Age" of state government.

My thesis is that the political maturity to make those difficult changes in the 1960s and 1970s came out of the common experience of young men in World War II and the Korean War. By 1967, there was a bipartisan consensus and an emerging new generation of leaders, not only in the public sector, but in the private sector and in the press as well. These men championed the effort to reform and modernize state government.

A second struggle was under way at the time I entered political life. In this instance, the battles were not being fought in Tallahassee, but in places like Miami, West Palm Beach, Gainesville, and Ocala. This grassroots struggle was not initially led by men, but by two fearless, pioneering women. The first of these, Marjory Stoneman Douglas, was a writer and the daughter of Frank Stoneman, founder of the *Miami Herald*. At eighty years of age and almost totally blind, she founded Friends of the Everglades, one of America's first environmental advocacy groups, and proceeded to nag, bully, scold, and ultimately persuade Florida's political leaders to stop the destruction of the Everglades. I did not meet Douglas until later in my career, but I became acquainted with Florida's "other Marjorie," Marjorie Harris Carr, as soon as I announced for the Florida House of Representatives in 1968. My legislative district consisted of Alachua County, which opposed the Cross Florida Barge Canal as an environmental disaster, and Marion County, which supported the canal as an economic development bonanza. Campaigning in Alachua County, I got to know Carr and her advocacy group, Florida Defenders of the Environment. I also came to understand, early on, Florida's need to balance a concern for the environment with its desire for growth and economic development. I entered politics as an admirer of Marjorie Harris Carr and an opponent of the Cross Florida Barge Canal.

Politically, the growth equation, which has not changed since 1968, is much more complicated than it looks. So long as the national economy is healthy, Florida looks golden. New construction in Florida is like new oil fields in Texas. Everybody wins. When the national economy falters, however, Florida's economy goes into reverse. Or worse yet, when real estate prices collapse—as happened in the fall of 2008—we no longer get the revenue windfall associated with population growth and real estate booms, but the recession-related caseloads go up and massive budget cuts for schools and all other state programs become inevitable.

Much of my story is about these two parallel struggles. We were largely successful in reforming and modernizing Florida's outmoded government, but somehow we never succeeded in balancing environmental protection with the desire to stimulate growth and economic development. In many respects, this is the story of the paradox of Florida. It is all the more fascinating because no one knows yet how it will end. Variations on Florida's story have been told through the years by writers as different as Carl Hiaasen and Martin Dyckman. It is essentially the tale of how Florida's postwar reform consensus was overwhelmed by its growth mentality, and how Florida's tenuous political maturity of the seventies and eighties morphed into the naive and immature politics of today. If this sounds depressing, I'm misstating matters. I learned a long time ago that public life is not just a series of victories. Indeed it is a bad choice for those people who feel they always must win in order to be a success. Rather, politics is a mix of achievements and defeats, and the latter can come at considerable personal cost. Political involvement is more like a dialogue with advances, pauses, and setbacks. In my view, standing for something and joining the dialogue is the best way to participate, and a lot more satisfying than standing for nothing or simply dodging tough decisions in order to gain and hold office.

Besides, there is much fun to be had along the path. In my case some of the wilder adventures included campaigning in rural counties with their unusual folkways and methods of counting the vote. The wildest adventure of all was the Chiles-MacKay campaign in 1990, which was run from the sales floor of a Tallahassee car dealership. My bottom line on a political career of ups and downs in Florida is that I would still recommend it. In fact, some of the most important issues of my political life are still on the table in 2010, and I would be delighted if my stories help motivate at least a few readers to pick up the challenge and enter state politics.

Starting Out

The State Legislature

Where I Came From

According to family history, my grandfather, George MacKay, graduated from a distinguished Scottish engineering school before coming to the United States. But in point of fact, according to my father, George MacKay left Scotland at age seventeen as a journeyman carpenter, having completed a six-year apprenticeship to a master carpenter. The rest of his education was through correspondence courses which he took as an adult.

George MacKay married and, still in his twenties, moved to Central Florida in the 1880s when the first phosphate deposits were discovered. His success came early, when he invented the first rock crusher capable of separating phosphate ore from the flint rock to which it was bound. Nobody cared whether he was an engineer or a journeyman carpenter, so long as he could build rock crushers that worked. He quickly became the proprietor of a thriving construction company, then a foundry, and designed and built most of Florida's early phosphate plants. The business ultimately included the largest hardware and lumber supply house in Central Florida, as well as a funeral home and an auto parts store. In an age when few attended college, he encouraged all five sons to attend college and pursue a different specialty. His dream was that all would join George MacKay and Company and help expand its various engineering, construction, and architectural ventures, with my father, Kenneth MacKay, as the manager of the various retail businesses.

As with most family stories, the dream was beset with unforeseeable adversity. The oldest son, George, was killed in World War I, and the second son, Robert, was seriously wounded. Then in the late 1920s, the retail store burned to the ground. Insurance proceeds were inadequate, so the business relied heavily on bank credit when it reopened. At the beginning of the Great Depression, the bank which had financed the family business failed. Although the business was profitable, the family's credit lines were cancelled and all bank loans were immediately due and payable. The retail merchandise was subsequently sold at auction and the buildings of George MacKay and Company were also sold. Other family businesses were divided among those sons who had the stomach and fortitude to continue. Alfred MacKay took over MacKay Construction Company and MacKay Funeral Home. My father, Kenneth MacKay, purchased MacKay Lumber Company and MacKay Auto Parts. Their monthly payments provided the income, which supported my grandparents. For most Americans, the Great Depression began with the stock market crash of 1929 and the bank failures of the early 1930s. For Floridians, however, these were only the latest in an unbroken chain of disasters. Florida's problems had begun in 1926 with the collapse of its fabled land boom, and had also included deadly hurricanes and an infestation of the Mediterranean fruit fly which threatened the citrus industry.

I was born in the depths of the Depression in 1933. My father and mother, Kenneth and Julia, had married in 1930, just as the MacKay family's economic hardships were beginning. When I was born, my family was living in a boardinghouse. All available funds were needed for working capital and the monthly payments upon which my grandparents relied. It was a tough time, but our lives were not very different from those of our neighbors. MacKay Lumber Company was one of

Ocala's two retailers of lumber and building supplies. The competition was Todd Lumber Company, which was also locally owned. In both cases, the business included its own sawmill, its own land (valued at one or two dollars per acre), and its own timber cutting operations. Huge trees were cut by hand with two-man crosscut saws. The logs were dragged to a central spot with mules, oxen, or steam-powered skidders. Later in the thirties, the mules and oxen were replaced with worn-out trucks and tractors. Small sawmills known locally as "peckerwood mills" were designed to be disassembled and moved from one stand of timber to the next.

One of the consequences of the great land boom of the 1920s was that people had often bought Florida land without having seen what they were purchasing. When the bubble burst, many of these people had found themselves unable to pay property taxes, and much of Florida's land had been abandoned. For a person in the lumber business, it was less expensive to buy land with the timber on it than to buy the timber separately. By the end of the '30s, my dad owned thousands of acres of land, before becoming involved in cattle and citrus in an effort to earn enough revenue to pay his property taxes. There were no fences. It was not too different from the Old West portrayed in the movies, except that people were driving automobiles on paved roads where the cattle had the right of way. Good brakes were considered more important than powerful engines. There were stories of ranchers moving their cattle onto railroad tracks on moonless nights, knowing that the railroads were legally liable to pay for any cows hit by their trains. Whether or not these stories were true, more cattle were run over by trains during tax season than any other time of the year.

It was a great time to be growing up in Florida. Through the '40s, my brother George and I spent much of our boyhood hunting, fishing, and working outdoors. We had little understanding of the consequences of the Great Depression because it was all we knew. We thought we were a regular part of Dad's crew, although in retrospect, it appears much more probable that our Dad had figured out a way to use his field hands as babysitters and role models at no extra cost. My love of unspoiled, "undeveloped" woods, fields, lakes, and streams goes all the way back to those times. I know how beautiful Florida was and could still be. It saddens me to see people mindlessly destroy this beauty in the name of "development."

Florida's public schools, like its other institutions, were segregated, although I was raised—fed, disciplined, and nursed—by persons of color. Discipline at school was strict, and corporal punishment was expected for infractions of rules. There was no school lunch program. I walked home for lunch each day. From the first grade in Florida's public schools through my years as an undergraduate at Davidson College and the University of Florida, I never attended an integrated school or church, never ate at an integrated restaurant, and never stayed at an integrated hotel until I served in the Air Force.

In 1952, my dad was bitten by a rattlesnake. Because of the delay in getting medical treatment, he barely survived and his full recovery was in doubt for many months. Following his doctor's advice, he took steps to get his financial affairs in order. He sold much of his land to pay off his debts. As a family, we continued in the cattle, citrus, and timber business on a much-reduced scale.

My father and the legendary Ed Ball were occasionally involved in business deals together. On one occasion when I was home on leave from the Air Force, I was invited to sit in on the negotiation of a potential land swap. The meeting was at Ed Ball's mansion on Southwood Plantation, near Tallahassee. Much of the negotiation involved storytelling. One of my favorite recollections is Ed Ball's story of fleecing a Philadelphia lawyer. Unable to get the lawyer to reduce the price of a large tract, Ball had invited him to be his houseguest in Jacksonville, while personally inspecting the tract "to see how worthless it was." Ball had instructed the driver, a trusted employee, "to get stuck in the sand, and stay stuck all day. Make that Yankee lawyer help you dig out, and don't bring him home until black dark." That night, after a bath and several stiff drinks of bourbon whiskey, the sunburned, mosquito-bitten, and exhausted lawyer agreed that the land was essentially worthless. The price Ball paid was less than the value of the standing timber. In later years, as a new member of the Florida legislature, I met Ed Ball again.

His first comment was "I remember you. You're Kenneth MacKay's son. He was a real land trader." I took that as a compliment.

After graduation from the University of Florida, I served three years in the U.S. Air Force, which was racially integrated. My first attempt at direct political involvement occurred during this time. I was an Air Force pilot, and attempted to register to vote. I wrote the supervisor of elections, Miss Fan Pasteur, asking her for the document one needed to register as a Republican. What I received in the mail was the paperwork to register as a Democrat. I telephoned Miss Pasteur and informed her of the mistake. She said, "That wasn't a mistake. If you register Republican you will embarrass your family." This is the true story of how I became a Democrat.

When I returned to the University of Florida College of Law in 1958, I was startled to find that it was still as segregated as it had been when I left. The first African American law student, George Starke, who gained admittance by court mandate, had flunked out at the end of my freshman year. At the beginning of my senior year, a second African American, George Allen, was admitted. Like me, he had completed a tour of military service as a commissioned officer before entering law school. As law school student body president, I sought out George and introduced myself to him. I assured him that a group of us would do whatever was necessary to help him, so long as his goal was to be a serious law student. It was a tense meeting. Allen let me know in no uncertain terms that he "didn't need a damned bit of help." All he wanted was for us to stay out of his way! Despite this inauspicious beginning, George Allen and I developed a close friendship that has lasted to this day. When it came to academics, George was right: he didn't need our help. He had plenty of ability, and as a veteran, he had the respect of the faculty. Outside the College of Law, however, we were able to help George in a number of ways. He and his family were the first African Americans to attend movies on campus, eat at campus restaurants, and attend athletic events. Each of these "firsts" involved uncertainty, rumors, threats, and a great deal of hassle.

As time went on, the law school student body assumed the role of sponsor, guarantor, and protector, for George, his wife, Enid, and their children. Much of this occurred after my graduation, as Sandy D'Alemberte, Walt McLin, and other veterans who were members of the law school student body determined that George was not going to have to submit to the "Old Florida" rules in order to get the education he was entitled to as a student and an American.

Church Matters

Upon graduating from law school, I was employed by the law firm of Raymond, Wilson, and Karl, in Daytona Beach. Fred Karl, a partner in the firm, was a respected member of the Florida Senate. After two years, I moved back to Ocala and opened my own law office. Ocala, the county seat of Marion County, was only eighty miles from Daytona, but it might as well have been in a different state. Marion County's legislative delegation had consistently been in the forefront of North Florida Pork-Chop politics, while Volusia County's delegation, because of Daytona Beach and tourism, had been more identified with urban South Florida. Marion County's government was run by a colorful, rural, five-member board of county commissioners. The main issues in county government had to do with the location, construction, and repair of county roads. Blazing controversies raged over the best methods of road repair, with the sides divided fairly evenly between the traditional "cold patch" method and the more modern "hot patch" method.

The real issue that mattered in the early '60s was not patching roads, but racial segregation. Despite the U.S. Supreme Court's ruling in *Brown v. Board of Education*, Marion County's schools, public accommodations, and churches were still segregated. I helped my law partner, John McKeever, organize a group of educators and young community leaders who recruited and helped elect Dr. Edward Anderson and John Lane to the Marion County school board. Under their leadership, plus that of new school superintendent Mac Dunwoody, Marion County became one of North Florida's first integrated school districts.

I also led a study group for young adults at Ocala's First Presbyterian Church. The purpose of this class, named the Crossroads Class, was to study the moral dimension of political issues. Inevitably, we focused on segregation and concluded that First Presbyterian Church, being segregated, was on the wrong side of the issue. I was delegated to discuss the matter with the pastor, Rev. Fred Turner. He was sympathetic but felt strongly that if we pressed our case, the controversy would split the church. His solution was ingenious: First Presbyterian had already purchased land for a new chapel. Rev. Turner proposed that my group would become the initial members of the new church, which would be established as a mission of First Presbyterian, and which could establish its own policy on integration. From our point of view, it was a victory. Blacks who wished to worship as Presbyterians would have a church home. From Rev. Turner's point of view, peace was preserved, he got rid of a friendly group of malcontents, and First Presbyterian—while still segregated—was at least partially (if unknowingly) on the right side of the issue. The new congregation, named Fort King Presbyterian, opened without incident as an integrated church when a member, John Hankinson, invited a black teacher to our first service. My wife, Anne, and I are still members of Fort King Presbyterian Church, which is now almost fifty years old and recognized not as a typical neighborhood church, but rather as a center of concern on issues like child advocacy, poverty, and racial fairness. For many years, it was Marion County's only integrated Presbyterian church, and as a result, we now have a number of beloved and deeply committed Caribbean and African American members.

The Real World

The major lesson I took away from law school was an understanding of how Florida politics really worked. The surprise was that I had gotten all the way through Florida's public schools and university without understanding the unfairness, incompetence, and institutional corruption of Florida's legislature. Under the post–Civil War constitution, Florida's legislature had been apportioned under the infamous "county unit" system. Established in 1924, this system did not reflect the extraordinary population growth of the state after World War II. One common statement was that pine trees were better represented in the Florida legislature than human beings. What I didn't get was that county unit apportionment allowed the rural counties to band together and maintain control of the state legislature and through it Florida's purse strings and public policy as well.

One example of the ways in which rural counties dominated state politics was the decision to authorize pari-mutuel betting in 1931. The compromise that had made gambling acceptable in rural, church-going North Florida was that although racetracks could only be situated in counties that had approved them by a subsequent vote, racetrack revenues were to be distributed equally among all counties. So the sin was confined to the cities in South Florida, but the revenues from racing provided a majority of the money needed for roads and schools in most of the rural counties. This kept property taxes low, and thus disproportionately benefited Ball, the Lykes family, and a handful of other "family farmers" and mining interests, each of whom owned hundreds of thousands of acres of rural land. Those legislators and senators who were elected from rural counties understood that their most sacred duty was to protect the racetrack revenues. This so-called Eleventh Commandment was said to be somewhere in the Old Testament.

Like most schoolchildren (and their parents), I also didn't understand the implications of a legislature where the members had neither offices in which to work, salaries on which to exist, or professional staff on which to rely for information. As a practical matter, this meant that many if not most legislators were on retainer to corporations or interest groups. Most legislation was written by lawyers and paid for by groups interested in the issue. This also meant, among other things, that regulatory schemes ostensibly passed to protect Florida consumers actually functioned to prevent newcomers from coming in and competing. Later on, as a legislator, I found this to be true for industries as wide-ranging as banking, insurance, public utilities, trucking, small loans, telephones, funeral homes, and any place the government was "protecting" Florida's consumers. The interests actually being protected were not the consumers' but Florida's existing businesses. They were being protected from competition as well as potential liability.

Nowhere was this more apparent than in Florida's tax code. As a second-year law student, I started researching a law review article cataloging the exemptions in Florida's tax code. The project was far broader than I had expected, and my faculty advisor became increasingly unenthusiastic about the topic I had chosen. The project was abandoned, but not before I realized that I had stumbled on the master index of political power in Florida. Those people with political power, like businesses, lawyers, doctors, architects, and anyone remotely connected to agriculture, had simply seen to it that the products and services sold by them were exempt from the sales tax. As a result, the value of those products and services exempt from the sales tax was substantially larger than the value of goods and services actually covered by the tax. As of the time of this writing, this situation still exists. The problem that results from our narrow and exemption-riddled tax base is that the faster Florida grows, the quicker we run out of money. This is not just theory. After an extensive study, the Zwick Commission in the 1980s put the backlog of unmet infrastructure need—roads, sewers, schools, etc.—at 54 billion dollars. By now, it easily exceeds 100 billion dollars, and is growing with every new resident we add.

To make this Alice in Wonderland picture complete, our constitution prohibits taxation of income and inherited wealth. We have since passed laws eliminating taxation of intangibles—stocks and bonds—and artificially capping the taxable value of homesteads and agricultural property. Thus, whenever the national economy slows, the bottom falls out of Florida's budget. A disproportionate percentage of our newcomers are seniors entitled to Medicaid, which cannot be cut. This means that in bad times, the brunt of Florida's budget cuts is borne by schools, universities, and programs for children, the poor, handicapped individuals, and others whose needs, while pressing, are not entitlements.

By the time I left law school, I had come to realize that although Florida's outmoded government—with its narrow and unstable tax base—suited bankers, mine owners, major landowners, and their rural counties very well, it was unfair to a majority of Floridians. Without understanding all the implications of my actions, from the time I left

law school, I was part of a loose-knit second generation of young reformers who were rallying behind Chesterfield Smith, LeRoy Collins,
Sam Gibbons, Fred Karl, Ed Price, and others of Florida's World War II
generation. These early reformers—Republicans and Democrats alike—
had been raised in the backward-looking culture of the Old South, but
had been changed by their common military experience and shared a
vision of Florida not as part of the Old South, but as part of the new
America coming into being. In the early 1960s they were engaged in
an uphill battle to break the grip of the rural legislative bloc, which,
because of county unit apportionment, dominated Florida government.
These early reformers attracted others like me who had also shared a
common military experience and wanted to be part of Florida's new
leadership.

A major political earthquake occurred in 1967 when the federal district court in Miami ruled that the U.S. Supreme Court's 1965 doctrine
of "One Voter–One Vote" actually applied in Florida. At that time, the
Florida legislature was operating under an apportionment formula that
had been adopted in 1924. Each county elected one senator. That was
bad enough, but the House of Representatives was even worse. There,
each of the five most populated counties elected three representatives;
the next eighteen most populous counties each elected two representatives; and each of the remaining counties elected one. Now, because of
the U.S. Supreme Court, legislative district lines had to be redrawn to
give each Florida voter an equal vote. The year 1967 was the last stand
for the small-county ruling clique, the Pork-Chop Gang (so called because their main concern was to divide up all available government
pork). Most of the year was consumed by a colorful struggle by the legislature to *appear* to comply with the federal court's ruling, but actually
retain power in the rural counties.

Realizing that the chances of real reapportionment were small, the
court had retained jurisdiction. There was no realistic way for the legislature to obtain advance approval of a reapportionment plan. The result
was a game within a game. First, the rural-dominated legislature would
meet and redraw the district boundaries. Then it would adjourn and its
members would run for election to the newly constituted seats. While

the elections were in progress, urban interests would challenge the validity of the newly constituted districts. After the elections, with the court ruling still pending, the new legislature would meet for purposes of normal legislative business. Then the federal court would rule that the reapportionment plan was unconstitutional because it still unduly favored the rural counties. And the procedure would start all over. Normal legislative business would be suspended since the legislature was unconstitutional for all purposes except redrawing district boundaries. The still-rural majorities in the legislature would draw new boundaries. New elections would be held. New challenges would be filed by urban interests. The new legislature would meet, and the court would again declare the new apportionment unconstitutional. After three rounds of this game, the court lost patience with the legislature. Dr. Manning Dauer, a highly respected professor of political science at the University of Florida, was asked to draft a plan, and his plan became the basis for Florida's reapportionment. When this tortuous process finally concluded, some unfortunate souls had been required to run four times, in four separate districts, before actually serving a term as a legislator.

Following the reapportionment earthquake were a number of aftershocks, as Florida's political tectonics readjusted to the new reality of true democracy in which the majority actually ruled. The first aftershock was the overwhelming vote by the people of Florida to accept the far-reaching proposals of the Constitutional Revision Commission, chaired by Chesterfield Smith. This was the first rewriting of Florida's post-Reconstruction 1887 constitution. It literally set the stage for the restructuring of Florida's antiquated government. Sandy D'Alemberte and Jim Redman, both longtime friends of mine, were politically as different as night and day. Jim Redman, from Plant City, had been my roommate at the University of Florida. Jim was a strict Baptist and a plainspoken conservative. He saw the need for reform, but was a consistent voice for moving with caution. Jim worried that the new urban majority would turn a deaf ear to the legitimate needs of rural Florida. Sandy, from Miami, was a freethinking intellectual whose undergraduate education at the University of the South had been followed by the London School of Economics, and then law school at the University of

Florida where we had been classmates. After the marathon legislative sessions of 1967, both Jim and Sandy contacted me suggesting that I run for the newly created legislative district representing Marion and Alachua Counties.

The First Campaign

My opponent in my first race in 1968, for the Florida House of Representatives, was Angus Hastings of Ft. McCoy. Angus was a partner in real estate development with C. Ray Greene of Jacksonville, who was part of the political machine which had first elected Haydon Burns as mayor of Jacksonville and subsequently as governor of Florida. Ray was not particularly interested in reform. He understood full well what was at stake, and wrote a stump speech for Angus which portrayed Angus as the protector of private property rights and "traditional North Florida values" (i.e., segregated schools). Angus memorized the speech and delivered it verbatim to audience after audience. The speech was the generic, all-purpose North Florida political speech, and also very effective.

I argued that Marion County needed to be part of the reform process that was under way in the state. This went over reasonably well in Gainesville and Ocala, but not at all well in the rural precincts. I remember one night when I had to cover both a chicken pileau (pronounced "perlow") rally by the Marion County Democratic Party and also a countywide meeting of the White Citizens Council, a pro-segregation group that was particularly strong in rural areas of North Florida. Ed Cluster, a law school classmate, offered to speak on my behalf to the White Citizens Council so that I could be present at the Democratic rally. The next day we compared notes. While I was speaking to a crowd of thirty-five including the cooks at the Democratic rally, my opponent had given his "traditional North Florida values" speech to a crowd of several hundred people at the White Citizens Council.

My strategy was to make myself well known in Alachua County, while relying on my friends and respected family name in Marion County. Recognizing the influence of the University of Florida, Shands Teaching Hospital, and other public institutions, I set out to become knowledgeable about these institutions and their needs. This turned out to be important since more than half of Alachua County's total job base at that time was in the public sector. Historically, Gainesville and Ocala had been rivals, and I knew I would start out being regarded by faculty and others as an unsophisticated rural character whose main interest in higher education would probably be the Gator football team. In my first speech, I took pains to denounce legislative interference in higher education. The first and only Alachua County rally was at Gainesville High School, with an integrated audience of fewer than fifty people. Angus delivered his all-purpose stump speech, while I talked about the importance of education and the need for the legislature to quit meddling with our universities. A black man in the audience asked Angus what he meant by traditional North Florida values. The truth was, Angus hadn't thought about it, or he would not have included that particular line. The black man made it clear he knew what that meant—it meant segregation! Others inquired closely about adequate funding for higher education.

As we were leaving, Angus told me those were the university liberals. He added that if that was all there were of them, I could have them all. What I found out later was that the black man, Al Daniels, was a friend of George Allen's, my friend who had become the first black graduate of the University of Florida College of Law. George had called Al on my behalf. Al Daniels was also an influential voice in the political organization headed up by Rosa Williams, a diminutive woman with extraordinary leadership skills. Rosa and Al, working with Alachua County's African American churches, turned out several thousand black votes for me. The university community and the Alachua County schoolteachers, who had also been well represented at the single Alachua County rally, also supported me. Subsequently, Rosa Williams became a close friend and a trusted advisor throughout my career. I won the primary election by a margin of 65.5 percent to 34.5 percent, having carried Alachua County by a stronger margin than my home county. This pattern was to hold throughout my career, with Alachua County becoming my de facto political home county.

North Florida, the South

Like many other aspects of Florida, our geography is upside down. This unique situation is reflected in the culture of the Florida legislature. The further north you go, the further south you get. We got this way after World War II. Since that time, more than 15 million people have moved here from the North, settling mostly in South Florida. They live south of the 3 million people—mostly from southern states—who live in North Florida. We try to pretend Florida is a single state, but in reality, it is at least two. Rural North Florida is the southern end of Appalachia. Like rural Alabama, Arkansas, Georgia, Louisiana, and Mississippi, its main problems are lack of education, jobs, infrastructure, and consequently poverty. It is along the I-4 corridor where Appalachia meets the Northeast and Midwest. As the saying goes, rural North Florida is not only hundreds of miles apart from Miami, but hundreds of years as well.

The State Legislature

The Florida House, 1969

When I arrived in the Florida House of Representatives in 1969, Claude Kirk was in his third year as Florida's first Republican governor since Reconstruction. Kirk, a newcomer to politics, had defeated Robert King High, a liberal from Miami, with the support of large numbers of conservative Democrats. Expecting a conservative governor, Floridians were instead finding Kirk to be an erratic, self-promoting showman. Fred Schultz, a wealthy North Florida businessman who had been sufficiently progressive to be acceptable to urban South Florida, was Speaker, and an intense contest was under way to elect the Speaker of the House for the next term.

During my campaign, I had made it clear that I intended to be part of the legislative reform movement, which focused at that time on the campaign of Dick Pettigrew, of Miami, to become Speaker of the House. Pettigrew was supported by Alachua County's legislators, Ralph Turlington and Bill Andrews. From their perspective, his election would be a mandate to continue the massive effort to reorganize and reform Florida's government. In the remainder of rural North Florida, however, Pettigrew's election would mean the takeover of the legislature by urban South Florida. When contacted by Pettigrew, I had committed to support him before I was even elected. Upon arriving in Tallahassee, I was under intense pressure because Dick's rival was E. C. Rowell from Sumter County, which adjoined Marion County. Outside of Gainesville, the widespread expectation was that I would cast my vote with the North Florida rural bloc. The Speaker's race was closer than expected. Although the urban group held a clear majority of the seats in the House, it had only a tenuous majority within the Democratic caucus, and the only persons voting in the Speaker's race were Democrats. By the time it had concluded, I had my first real introduction to bare-knuckle politics. The real parties opposing Pettigrew were not the rural legislators, but the bankers, business interests, and agricultural leaders who had traditionally been protected by Florida government. One after another, they made clear the risk involved in supporting Pettigrew. It could end my political career, just as it was beginning.

The policy issues debated during my first term were historic in their impact. First the new, urban-dominated legislature professionalized its own House by authorizing and appropriating funds for professional staff and inaugurating annual sessions. My next political crisis took place over legislative salaries. At the outset, Governor Claude Kirk agreed with the Republican House leadership that legislative salaries should be increased from $100 a month to $1,000. After that bipartisan agreement had passed both houses of the legislature, Kirk vetoed it. The Republican legislators who had relied on Kirk's promised support for political cover were furious, and joined the urban Democrats in overriding the veto. I voted against the pay increase, arguing that although it was needed, it should not take effect until the beginning of the next term. I felt that we were morally obligated to serve the current term at the existing salary. We could then run for a new term at the higher salary. Jim Redman congratulated me but Sandy tactfully indicated that he thought I had chickened out. A second battle occurred over the consolidation of state government, which Dick Pettigrew led. The number of executive agencies was dramatically reduced, although the fragmentation of executive responsibility between the governor and the elected cabinet—a relic from Reconstruction—proved to be intractable.

Pettigrew's Governmental Reorganization and Reform Committee had also proposed streamlining public education by eliminating the separate Division of Vocational-Technical Education and making vocational education a part of the Division of Public Schools. Convinced that this would mean second-class status for vocational education, Senator Fred Karl opposed this. I had originally been employed by Fred Karl's law firm in Ormond Beach and had worked as Karl's associate. He was a friend and mentor, and I trusted his judgment. Thus, I led the opposition in the House (at this point, Redman agreed with my position and Sandy disagreed). To the surprise of everyone involved, Floyd Christian, commissioner of education, got caught up in the spirit of reform and supported eliminating the Division of Vocational-Technical Education. Senator Karl retaliated by proposing that the commissioner of education be appointed by the governor, instead of continuing to be an elected member of the cabinet. Karl's position was simple: if Floyd Christian wanted reform, we would give him *real* reform.

Claude Kirk, unpredictable as ever, agreed with our position. Suddenly I was in a much bigger fight, and found myself again on the side of the urban reformers. At this point, Redman was counseling me not to be led astray by those "Yankees from South Florida," while Sandy was giving me a lecture on the peculiarities of Florida's cabinet system. According to Sandy, a good way to appreciate the flaws of the cabinet system was to look at the realities of the elected office of comptroller, who nominally regulated banking, but also had to the power to determine who could receive a bank charter. This meant that, for persons interested in banking, having a friendly comptroller was a matter of economic life or death. If the office was no longer independently elected, the comptroller would be appointed by the governor, and thus much harder to control. The political risks to banking would go up immeasurably. So Florida's bankers were, in fact, the "army" defending the continuation of the independently elected comptroller. Similarly, the insurance commissioner had the power to set insurance rates. His political army consisted of thousands of local independent insurance agents. Knowing that making the commissioner of education an appointee of the governor meant that a second elected cabinet office would also be eliminated, opponents saw our proposal as a threat to the entire cabinet system. All the political interests took to the field, from bankers to insurance agents to farmers and county extension agents. It was as if Fred Karl and I had kicked over a nest of political fire ants.

In the end, Fred Karl's tactic won the day. Floyd Christian dropped his support for elimination of the Division of Vocational-Technical Education. And I had learned a major lesson about the politics of Florida's elected cabinet. No further effort was made to reduce the number of elected cabinet members until the 1990s. The armies disbanded and peace was restored, at least temporarily.

During the political effort to save the Division of Vocational-Technical Education, I became convinced that Florida's public schools were neglecting the needs of those students who were not bound for college. At that time, noncollege-bound students were a majority of all Florida's high school students. To my surprise, Speaker Shultz agreed that vocational education should be more closely examined, and appointed me chair of the Select Committee on Vocational Education. Unlike standing committees, select committees are appointed for a special purpose with separate staff, usually to develop expertise on a particular issue. In this instance, my committee was instructed to do an interim study of the effectiveness of vocational-technical education in Florida and report back to the next legislative session. Suddenly, as a freshman, I was a chairman. After interviewing vocational educators and visiting vocational and technical facilities, our committee found a high level of frustration in vocational education. The typical secondary school curriculum was designed to meet the needs of those students bound for college; the vocational curriculum was mainly courses in agriculture and home economics, neither of which met the needs of Florida's employers; and public school counselors had neither the time nor the training to do career counseling or job placement. This failure of the high school curriculum to meet the needs of a majority of the students was clearly a major factor driving Florida's high public school dropout rate. Vocational educators had been sounding the alarm, but felt that their concerns were being suppressed by the leadership of the Department of Education.

More controversial were our findings regarding apprenticeship training. Although more than 20 percent of all jobs were in trades like plumbing, electrician, and carpentry, where the training cannot be done in a classroom, Florida's Department of Education accepted no responsibility for apprenticeship training. This, they said, was the responsibility of the trade unions. In meeting with the unions, however, we found that no apprentice was accepted for training unless there was a specific job vacancy. As a practical matter, this meant that unions were training only relatives of union members. It also meant that there were no apprenticeship programs in rural, nonunion counties. In the entire state of Florida, only six minority students could be found in union apprenticeship programs. The report of our select committee resulted in the passage of a major legislative initiative to strengthen vocational education. Better funding and an expanded curriculum for vocational programs were provided and a new position, the occupational specialist, was mandated. This person was to specialize in career counseling and job placement for noncollege-bound students. Nonunion apprenticeship programs were mandated as a responsibility of the Department of Education, with guaranteed access for minority students. Today, more than thirty years later, vocational-technical education is a high priority in Florida's schools and colleges. I am proud that the turnaround started with our early effort in 1970.

Article V

While public attention was focused on the high profile struggles to reform Florida's legislative and executive branches, an even more intense battle was going on in the effort to modernize Florida's judiciary. Florida's courts were still operating under the outmoded revisions of the post–Civil War constitution of 1885, and the entire judicial system was fiercely resistant to change. As caseloads had increased, new courts had been added, but overall reform had been impossible. An example of the hodgepodge that had resulted was the court system in Miami in the 1960s with its large number of trial courts. An incomplete list includes circuit court, county court, county judges court, justice of the peace courts, small claims, metro, civil court of record, criminal court of record, and municipal courts. Each of these courts had different rules, its own bailiffs, clerks, and filing systems. To compound the confusion, there were overlapping jurisdictions with no centralized court administration. Plaintiffs could "forum shop," or select the court most likely to favor their claims. No one was in charge and no one was accountable.

Most people in the judiciary were opposed to reform because reform meant many people would lose their otherwise secure jobs. Many legislators were attorneys who practiced law in Florida's courts. As a practical consequence, this meant many legislators were reluctant to oppose judges, and Florida's judges had considerable political power. Much of the debate occurred outside the public arena.

In the constitutional revision of 1968 and again in 1970, reform of the judiciary was not put on the ballot because the legislature was unable to agree on the proposed wording. Those who wanted no change allied with those who thought the proposed compromises did not provide enough reform, and the result was stalemate. A famous line from an earlier reformer said it all: "Judicial reform is not a sport for the short-winded!"

After the 1970 election, Dick Pettigrew appointed Sandy D'Alemberte as chair of the House Judiciary Committee, with a mandate to develop a total revision of Article V, the judicial article of the constitution. As told by Sandy, the story of judicial reform is a fascinating study of the interplay of politics and policy. It began when D'Alemberte hired a young lawyer, Janet Reno, as his staff director. In an improbable turn of events, D'Alemberte and Reno developed a relationship of friendship and trust with Dempsey Barron, who chaired the Senate Judiciary Committee. Both committees held hearings around the state. By 1972, as the people of Florida heard stories of corruption in the J. P. courts and municipal courts, a consensus for reform began to develop. With the combined efforts of Governor Askew, D'Alemberte, and Pettigrew in the House, Dempsey Barron in the Senate, and Chesterfield Smith and the leadership of the Florida Bar, the proposed revision of Article V passed the legislature by the three-fifths majority required to put the measure on the ballot.

A final drama came with the decision to schedule the vote on Article V revision at the time of the presidential primary in March 1972. The early timing was critical because it meant that all of Florida's circuit judges would be running for reelection, and thus unable to focus their considerable influence on opposing Article V revision. The difficulty was that scheduling the vote at a special election required a three-fourths majority vote in both houses of the legislature. In the House, that meant corralling ninety votes over the opposition of lobbyists for justices of the peace, clerks, and judges, the same group that had kept previous reform efforts off the ballot. Finding ninety votes was an almost impossible challenge. At the last minute, the ninetieth vote came from Ed Blackburn, a veteran legislator who had previously served as sheriff of Hillsborough County. According to Ed, his wife felt strongly that he should put politics aside and vote for the special election instead of allowing judicial reform to be stalled by the interest groups opposing change. Blackburn decided to side with his wife and the reformers. This meant opposing many close friends from his former years in law enforcement. I always respected Ed Blackburn for his political courage in providing the ninetieth vote at the critical moment for judicial reform in Florida. The revision of Article V gave Florida one of America's most functional and least political court systems. Overlapping jurisdictions were eliminated, as were the so-called cash register courts—justices of the peace, county judges courts, and municipal courts whose fines had become a reliable source of revenue for many local governments.

The issue of doing away with the election of judges was politically impossible and thus omitted from Article V revision. Only after the Supreme Court scandals later in the 1970s (documented by Martin Dyckman in his entertaining book, *A Most Disorderly Court*) were Floridians willing to give up their right to elect appellate judges. To this day most trial judges in Florida must still run for election. Unfortunately, a cottage industry has emerged in judicial elections. Political "consultants" recruit judicial candidates, raise their campaign dollars, and manage their campaigns—all for a fee. With this exception, however, reform of Florida's judicial branch remains one of the greatest achievements of the "Golden Era" of government in Florida.

Askew, Chiles, and Pettigrew, 1970

During 1969, Reubin Askew, Democrat from Pensacola, launched a long-shot campaign for governor, and Lawton Chiles, from Lakeland, ran an equally improbable campaign for the U.S. Senate. Both of them had been leaders of the reform group in the Florida Senate. Like me, both were from counties that traditionally sided with the rural bloc, but both of them sided more often than not with the urban reformers.

Much has been written about their campaigns, both of which found ways to capture public attention by using free media to compete with the paid ads of their better-financed opponents. Chiles's walk across the state of Florida was a political classic, depicting as it did a vigorous young candidate walking though villages, towns, and cities, meeting with citizens on the street and seeking their advice while his opponent relied on the financial support of the state's traditional kingmakers. Askew took the unprecedented risk of proposing a corporate income tax, an idea originally developed in a master's degree thesis at Princeton University by Floridian Steve Pajcic. When faced with the charge by opponents that a corporate income tax would only be passed on to Florida's consumers, Askew found the perfect response. He began showing two identical shirts purchased from the same national corporation. One had been purchased in Georgia, which had a corporate income tax, and the other in Florida, which had no corporate tax. The shirts were priced the same, which meant that although Florida did not tax corporate income, the burden of the tax was *already* being passed on to Florida consumers. Until that point, not many voters had paid attention to the details of Askew's argument, but everyone understood the lesson of the two shirts. Moreover, in proposing to tax powerful national corporations, Askew positioned himself on the side of the ordinary citizen, just like Chiles. The two campaigns reinforced each other, and both Askew and Chiles won in 1970.

My second term in the legislature began in 1971, with Reubin Askew as governor and Dick Pettigrew as Speaker. It was as exciting as anything I have experienced in government. Askew was as different from

Claude Kirk as day is different from night. He was a strict Presbyterian who served nothing stronger than orange juice and disapproved of most of the things that had made Kirk interesting. He had a broad agenda of reform, starting with the proposed corporate profits tax, which was vigorously opposed by Florida's business community. He started things off in high gear by calling for a special session as part of his inauguration speech. Passage of Askew's ambitious agenda depended in large part on Dick Pettigrew. Askew had the vision and tenacity to see things through to a successful conclusion, but Pettigrew understood how all the pieces fit together, and had the leadership to keep the forces of reform united and motivated. He did this by developing an effective urban coalition with moderate House Republican leaders like the minority leader, Don Reed, from Palm Beach County, and Joel Gustafson, from Broward County, and by encouraging progressives from North Florida while also respecting the different demands of our constituents.

Under Dick Pettigrew, I was appointed vice chair of the House Insurance Committee, with Bill Gillespie of New Smyrna Beach as chair. Florida's automobile insurance rates had increased dramatically in the late 1960s. Adding to the controversy, several Florida auto insurance companies had failed, and were unable to pay the claims of persons who had bought their policies. Investigators found that the Department of Insurance had succumbed to political pressure, allowing companies to stay in business despite evidence that they were insolvent. Florida's consumer advocates charged that the elected insurance commissioner was a captive of the industry he regulated. The industry responded that the rate increases were not caused by lax regulation, but by the explosion of nuisance litigation arising out of minor "fender benders." Most of these cases were being settled, because the cost of litigation exceeded the amount of the settlement. After a year of mind-numbing hearings, Gillespie and I concluded that both sides were right. We proposed reforming the procedure for setting automobile insurance rates, coupled with tort reform known as No Fault Automobile Insurance. Gillespie's instructions to me were clear: my job was to figure out what to do, and his job was to get the votes. The concept of No Fault insurance was to take smaller cases out of the court system entirely. Each driver's insurance policy paid for injuries to occupants of his or her car, regardless of fault. In these cases, nobody had to sue anybody. The cost savings were dramatic, and the legislation mandated an immediate rate reduction of 15 percent. It was the most comprehensive tort reform in America at that time and still continues in Florida today.

The Third House Term

In 1972, my third term in the House, Terrell Sessums, an urban reformer from Tampa, served as Speaker. Terrell had been part of the reform coalition, and had emerged as a champion of better funding for education. I had supported him over a rural opponent, thus further cementing my role as a non–Good Old Boy. Sessums named me as chair of the House Education Committee, where I worked with (state) Senator Bob Graham in finalizing and passing the Florida Education Funding Program, known as the FEFP. Under the FEFP, each county is required to levy a specified millage, known as the "required local effort." For some wealthy retiree communities with high property values and relatively few students, the required local effort produces two or three times as much funding per student as the same millage in working-class counties like Hillsborough or Polk, which have lower property values and more students. State funds are used to eliminate this discrepancy. Poor counties receive disproportionately more state dollars per student than rich counties.

A number of the issues arising in fast-growing states like Florida cannot be accommodated within the traditional legislative committee structure, either because specialized staff expertise is required, or the time demands are too great, or both. In these instances, select committees are authorized with separate staff and a separate budget. I chaired the Select Committee on Utility Reform, which developed and passed a major legislative initiative in public utility regulation—including a mandated energy grid—as well as establishing a consumer advocate representing the consumer at proceedings to increase electricity and phone rates.

My most far-reaching project during my third term was chairing the two-year Growth Policy Project. Despite its dull title, the Growth Policy Project was an exciting, groundbreaking initiative. Convinced that Florida's governor and fragmented cabinet were institutionally incapable of producing a long-term plan capable of protecting Florida's natural systems, the Florida legislature undertook to develop its own Growth Policy. With Governor Askew's support and Speaker Sessums' strong direction, each committee worked on the areas within its jurisdiction, and then a considerable effort was made to transform the sum of these individual parts into a coherent overall policy. Concern about state growth and the need to limit its destructive impact on the state's environmental systems came up in committee after committee. The policy that emerged was that population growth should be limited to the carrying capacity of Florida's natural systems. The term "carrying capacity" had a distinctively academic ring to it. There were murmurs that I had been spending too much time around those pointy-headed professors at the University of Florida. As soon as I started showing slides of dried-up lakes and rivers, however, legislators began to understand and pay attention. As Mark Twain said: "Whiskey is for drinking; water is for fighting over!"

The Growth Policy Project received national recognition and added impetus to the effort, led by State Senator Bob Graham, to pass the 1973 Local Government Comprehensive Planning Act. This legislation was, in itself, a pioneering effort. By this time, however, intense opposition was building. The essential question—then as now—is whether the full costs of new growth are going to be paid by the developer, or continue to be included as part of the tax burden borne by existing residents, or worse yet, simply ignored. Water is for fighting over, and the battle for Florida's water intensified as people began to realize the implications of mandating any kind of limitations on Florida's potential population growth.

During my third term in the House of Representatives, I also served on the Joint Auditing Committee which was co-chaired by Rep. Jim Redman and Senator George Firestone, a leader of the reform effort and later secretary of state. One of the issues we considered was the proposal to impeach or otherwise discipline Tom Adams, who served as Reubin Askew's first lieutenant governor. Testimony showed that Adams had used public employees and equipment for his private benefit to the tune of $25,000. If he had been a bank president, he would have been fired. Like Jim Redman and George Firestone, I felt public sector officials should be held to the same standard as their counterparts in the private sector, and I voted for impeachment. Adams was dropped as lieutenant governor by Reubin Askew at the end of his first term and replaced by Jim Williams, who served with distinction. The end of this episode came the next year, when neither Jim Redman nor George Firestone was reappointed to the Joint Auditing Committee. Impeaching a member of our own party was a shocking proposal to old-time Democrats, and the House Democratic majority ultimately chose censure rather than impeachment.

As my third term began, I decided to run for House Speaker with Bob Hartnett, from Miami, as candidate for Speaker Pro Tem. Bob's assumption, based on written commitments he obtained, was that he could assure the support of the Dade County Democrats. My assumption was that I could extend the zeal for legislative reform, which was prevalent, to include reforming the internal political processes of the House. Both of our assumptions proved to be false. At the same time I was fighting to prohibit lobbyists and outside interests from influencing the selection of legislative leadership, the other candidate, Rep. Don Tucker, was raising money from lobbyists and donating it to legislative campaigns. My race against Tucker was competitive at first, and I felt I had a legitimate chance to win, particularly with the support of newly elected legislators. The press was not interested. To them, this was all "inside baseball." It was a political issue, and the only thing that mattered was who had the votes. The race suddenly swung against me as several members of the Dade delegation who had previously given me their written pledges now openly committed to Tucker. I subsequently dropped out of the race, partly from disillusionment and partly from the realization that my candidacy was not realistic. Lawton Chiles, quoting Senator Herman Talmadge of Georgia, later told me the mistake I had made: "Don't ever try to solve a problem that a man doesn't realize he's got."

The problem I was trying to solve still exists. Every two years, the new legislative leadership that takes office is already committed on major issues. Special interest money, funneled though "leadership funds" set up by each political party, now amounts to millions of dollars each election cycle. Unfortunately, in the absence of a scandal, the average Floridian still doesn't realize what a problem this is. As one cynical lobbyist put it: "Why try to buy a committee chair's vote when the same money can buy a commitment from the House Speaker?" The indictment of House Speaker Ray Sansom in 2009 showed that this problem still existed more than three decades later. In fact, as the Grand Jury pointed out, the use of "leadership funds" to allow special interests to contribute anonymously has expanded to the extent that it threatens to corrupt the entire legislative process ("It's the Whole Darned Barrel," by Howard Troxler, *St. Petersburg Times*, April 20, 2009).

Campaigning for the Florida Senate

Looking back, the year 1974 was a good time to leave the Florida House. Several of my closest friends had decided to move on, and for reasons spelled out above, I expected to be permanently sidelined as a member of the House. I had violated the first commandment of politics: "If you decide to shoot the King, don't miss!" My friend Jim Williams had been selected as lieutenant governor by Governor Askew, and his Senate seat was thus unexpectedly vacant in midterm. Jim had shared a sixteen-county Senate district with Bob Saunders, from Gainesville. Both of them urged me to run since the Senate had emerged as the focal point in the continuing reform struggle.

I announced at the last minute and found myself opposed in the primary by Marion Pettit, of Starke. Marion was the half brother of former governor Charlie Johns, and also had long-term relationships with all the elected county officials in the district. He was a thoroughly decent person who generically opposed "change for the sake of change" and framed the contest in terms of the interests of the small counties versus those of the large counties. The irony of his argument—focusing as it did on semirural Marion and Alachua as the "large counties"—went largely unnoticed. Bob Saunders, who had campaigned successfully in the same district, pointed out that in small county politics, you either played inside, if the courthouse officials supported you, or outside, if you had to run against the courthouse. In his campaign, Saunders had been forced to play outside, and he advised me to do the same. The outside faction controlled approximately the same number of votes as the insiders, and was less threatened by the idea of reform. The Saunders method was to load up a car with well-dressed, middle-class volunteers and campaign throughout the counties at fairs, livestock auctions, and population centers. Campaigning consisted of distributing pamphlets, introducing the candidate, asking for support, and moving on. This old-time campaigning turned out to be effective, and also a lot of fun. People in the rural counties tell great stories, and I learned that storytelling was an essential part of politics. I was able to win the primary without spending lots of money, and without negative advertising.

Dixie County Economic Development

Dixie County, situated on Florida's west coast at the mouth of the Suwannee River, was not unduly troubled by notions of political reform. One of the most fascinating Dixie County stories was told to me by a former senator, Etter Usher, who lived in adjoining Levy County. When Usher qualified to run in the Senate district that included Dixie County, he met with the courthouse insiders, who told him they would need $3,000 to assure that he would carry Dixie County. Having doled out $3,000 to the insiders, he was immediately confronted by the rival "outside" faction. Nothing personal, he was told, but since he had given $3,000 to the other side, they'd also need $3,000 since their faction controlled the remaining 50 percent of the vote. His financial arrangements completed, Usher overwhelmingly carried Dixie County. To his surprise, he was then invited by the rival factions to a joint barbeque. The congratulatory toast went something like this: "We don't know what kind of senator you'll be, but you sure made a fine candidate!"

My First Republican Opponent

After six years in North Florida politics, I finally had a Republican opponent. His name was Charles Curtis, and he was from Ocala. His technique was to come out swinging, and he did this by running full-page ads in all the small-county weekly papers, with the following headline: "Welcome Buddy MacKay. He brought you forced busing." He based this charge on my support of Reubin Askew's campaign opposing an anti-busing straw ballot. Although I felt strongly that my position was morally right, this was a highly inflammatory issue in North Florida. I remember feeling very lonely, as the ad had reached every county before I could respond.

Before the week was out, I received a telephone call from Smith Belcher, the head of the NAACP in Perry, Florida. Mr. Belcher invited me to a meeting at a Baptist church in Perry, which I attended. The crowd consisted of the black leadership from across North Florida. Smith Belcher held up the Republican ad, and said that since I had stood up for equal rights, it was time for the black community to stand up for me. I responded by saying that I thought segregation was wrong, and that I intended to continue to fight for fairness in North Florida. That was over thirty years ago. I am not sure Smith Belcher is still alive, but I will never forget his parting words: "I don't know what that ad will do in the white community, but it will get you every black vote in the Sixth District."

Curtis also hammered me for supporting Askew's corporate income tax, asserting that this vote proved I was an "Askew Liberal." Fortunately, I had taken Bob Saunders' advice, and had developed support outside the courthouse group in each of the small counties. If Curtis' allegations had been raised in the primary, I would have been in trouble, but in the general election, they failed to get traction. Most rural North Floridians still voted as Yellow Dog Democrats. Over the years, a number of the small-county leaders became my friends and loyal supporters. Rural politics is totally different from modern, urban politics, and a lot more fun.

The Lafayette County Manifesto

Of the fourteen small counties in my Florida Senate district, none was more distinctive than Lafayette (pronounced "La Fay' it"), which adjoined Dixie County on the east. Campaigning in Lafayette County was, in a word, different. Voters were clearly distrustful of people from big cities, and as far as they were concerned, Ocala was a big city. In addition, I was a *lawyer* from a big city, and they distrusted lawyers!

After the election, I was invited to come to a special gathering of the County Commission and the clerk, sheriff, and other constitutional officers. After the opening niceties, the clerk of the court gave the following statement: "Senator MacKay, here is what Lafayette County wants from you: Please don't help us any more!" I called that the "Lafayette County Manifesto," and to their credit, they lived by it. They never asked anything from the State of Florida—or anyone else, for that matter. All they wanted was to be left alone. It was a delightful place and a joy to represent.

Taylor County—Freedom of the Press

Taylor County, on Florida's west coast and immediately north of Dixie County, had two newspapers, one Democratic and one Republican. To my surprise, I got along with the Republican paper better than the Democratic, which was angry with me because I opposed Senate President Dempsey Barron, who also represented Taylor County. The Republican publisher was a curmudgeon named Miller Holland, with whom I frequently argued at public hearings. Despite our differences, he liked me because he thought I was honest, and also because I was willing to drive the 100 miles to attend their public hearings. It turned out that Dempsey Barron had represented Taylor County for eight years, and nobody could remember having seen him at a public function in that entire time.

On one memorable occasion, I was running for reelection after being the only North Florida senator to vote for the Equal Rights Amendment. This incensed the Florida Farm Bureau, which distributed bumper stickers all over North Florida that said: "Senator MacKay, please don't draft our daughters." As a dues-paying member of the Farm Bureau, I wasn't particularly repentant. Each time the issue came up, I made a point of asking what relationship the ERA had to agricultural issues. I also asked whether farm women shouldn't be entitled to equal rights in the job market. My local hearings were jam-packed, and unusually shrill. I could tell I wasn't making a lot of headway when the other members of the delegation kept moving as far away from me as possible. Every small-town newspaper and most of the Baptist churches were up in arms, except in Taylor County, where the hearing was genial and the ERA didn't even come up. At the reception after the hearing, Miller Holland, the Republican publisher, took me aside and asked if I had noticed that no one had mentioned the ERA. I expressed surprise that it didn't seem to be an issue in Taylor County. He responded: "They're not mad because they don't know how you voted on the ERA. They don't know because I didn't put it in the paper because I like you. You are a liberal SOB, but I like you." That's what I call freedom of the press, and a ringing endorsement as well!

The Florida Senate

My swearing in as a senator occurred on the same day as the selection of Dempsey Barron of Panama City as Senate president. Dempsey was a unique individual. He had dropped out of high school during World War II, lied about his age, and joined the Merchant Marine. After surviving the sinking of his ship by a U-boat and being honorably discharged, he had talked his way into Florida State University despite the absence of a high school diploma. At the end of his third year, he had been admitted to law school at the University of Florida despite the absence of a high school diploma or an undergraduate degree. Early in Dempsey's political career, he had been part of the reform group. When political power shifted to South Florida, Dempsey aligned himself more and more against the forces of change. As a House member, my final battles on insurance and utility reform had often been against Dempsey, who (it was delicately said) often "represented the industry point of view." On the other hand, he had provided significant support to Sandy D'Alemberte to modernize Florida's judiciary.

Shortly after being selected president, Dempsey made the speech in which he advised Governor Askew to "stay the hell out of my Senate." Things went rapidly downhill, as Dempsey made a major issue out of reconfirming O. J. Keller for a second term as Askew's secretary of the Department of Health and Rehabilitative Services. When Keller had first been hired, his challenge had been to transform Florida's various independent social services agencies into a single, coordinated agency. This had seemed relatively simple in the legislative debate—a matter of straightening out lines of authority on an organizational chart. In practice, however, it proved to be extraordinarily complex. Each agency had become accustomed to operating with its own separate and conflicting federal and state statutory authority, and had been answerable to its own independent board, which in turn had answered to one or more legislative subcommittees. To make things more binding, each of these independent fiefdoms was supported by a specialized group of private sector practitioners whose main function was to lobby the legislature, governor, and cabinet. What had gotten lost was the notion that the needs of families and children couldn't be divided into neat compartments on an organizational chart. Entire families would get lost in the bureaucratic morass, with the children being served by one agency while the parents were being denied services by another.

As a member of the House, I had become a friend of and advocate for Keller. He had taken on powerful and entrenched political figures, and had made enemies. Those of us who understood the magnitude of his challenges respected him for his courage, knowledge, and candor. As a brand new senator, I joined Bob Graham, George Firestone, and others in leading the effort to reconfirm him. It ended up as one of the most vicious battles of my entire career. The truth was that the only thing Keller had done wrong was to fire some of Dempsey Barron's powerful friends. My side lost, but only after Dempsey aligned a minority of Senate Democrats with the Senate Republicans. As a result, I accidentally emerged as one of the leaders of the "Doghouse Democrats," although I had only been a member of the Senate for a few weeks.

It was a strange experience being a permanent minority. The Doghouse Democrats were a majority of the Senate Democrats, and the Democrats were a majority of the Senate, and yet we were a permanent minority. Dempsey put together a coalition consisting of a conservative minority of the Democrats, and all the Republicans. He used this alliance with great effect to retain his influence over policy in the Senate. Dempsey was a tough opponent, and members of our group paid a price for our independence. All the unchecked power of the Senate president was focused against us, with no right of appeal. In my case, I was not initially assigned to any committees having to do with insurance, public utilities, or growth management. I was left with limited staff support, constant hassling over expense authorizations, and unfavorable bill references. Some of my bills were not even referred to committees for hearings until so late in the session that the committees were no longer meeting.

Under Senate rules, there was no provision for appeal of Dempsey's abuse of the power in the Senate presidency. Our only formal recourse was to call a party caucus and attempt to unseat him. We knew we lacked the votes to do this, so our only practical recourse was guerilla warfare. With the clandestine help of fellow reformers in the House, the essential elements of my unheard Senate bills were introduced as "friendly" amendments to House bills. My lack of staff was made up for by informal staff assistance from Governor Askew's office, as well as sympathetic Senate and House professional staff. All in all, I emerged almost unscathed. More importantly, my constituents, including the University of Florida, Shands Hospital, and most of Florida's prisons, were also unaffected. The Doghouse Democrats included Bob Graham, Betty Castor, George Firestone, Harry Johnston, Pat Neal, Ken Jenne, Edgar Dunn, George Stuart, Don Chamberlin, Pat Frank, and me. Not a bad group of which to be a member!

One major hassle was my inability to obtain authorization for an office in Gainesville, my largest city. In effect, my sole staff for a sixteen-county district was Samelia King in my Ocala office. This problem was solved by a group in Gainesville, led by Cornelia Hannah, a retired teacher, and Polly Doughty, then a leader in the Gainesville League of Women Voters. They obtained a donated office, provided furniture, phones, and organized a volunteer staff which ran an effective district office for two years. Cornelia Hannah became the first of my "Guardian Angels." There were many others—ordinary citizens who were unwilling to sit by silently.

Summing up the Seventies—Florida's Decade of Change

When I came into the Florida legislature, the "Old Guard" had been decimated as a result of the historic reapportionment battle. The iron grip of the rural legislators had been broken and the Pork-Chop Gang no longer existed. The special interests that had historically controlled Florida politics were reduced to fighting a series of holding actions, like a defeated army in retreat. Although I did not realize it at the time, it was not a single revolution, but a series of intertwined changes all taking place at the same time. The role of women in politics was beginning to change, and I was privileged to serve with Carrie Meek, Betty Castor, and Pat Frank, who were entering the ranks of political leadership and who were special friends as I was starting out. Carrie Meek, from Miami, was a true pioneer, being both female and minority. After serving with distinction in both the Florida House and Senate, Carrie went on to become a respected and influential member of Congress. Betty Castor first served as a member of the County Commission of Hillsborough County, and then the Florida Senate. In her later career, she was elected statewide as commissioner of education, and subsequently served as president of the University of South Florida. Pat Frank also began as a member of the County Commission of Hillsborough County, and was then elected to the Florida Senate before being elected again to the Hillsborough County Commission. At the same time, a number of talented minority candidates were being elected, usually from urban constituencies. It was an exciting time, and many of us naively thought Florida politics had permanently changed. Others, who had fought the reapportionment battles, knew differently and warned that the traditional political coalition of money and power would soon reemerge. Unfortunately, they proved to be correct.

As a Presbyterian reared in a strict Calvinist tradition, I entered politics having been taught that boasting was only slightly less sinful than having fun. In politics, I not only had fun, but also came to realize that political campaigns consisted entirely of speaking glowingly about yourself and your accomplishments. I remember hearing the need for self-promotion best framed by Baldy Strickland, a rough-hewn professional fisherman from Crystal River who was running for reelection to the Florida House in 1967. "I take pride in my accomplishments," Baldy began, "and most of all I take pride in my humility!" In that spirit, here is a summary of my major accomplishments in the Florida legislature during the '70s.

When I entered politics, I was a North Floridian representing a rural and semirural region. Ocala and Gainesville were growing, but the rest of my region was static. I was unique in rural North Florida politics in that I perceived Florida's challenges as predominately growth-related and urban in nature. We potentially faced the same problems as New York and California, but our government was more like Alabama and Mississippi. With our explosive growth, we were already behind. In 1971, my view was affirmed by a multistate study commissioned by the Southern Governors' Association. The chapter on Florida was entitled "The City of Florida." Its point was that, even in 1971, Florida was already more urban than New York. Based on that, with Terrell Sessums' support, I led the Growth Policy Project, which sounded the alarm. I also had a major part in the development and passage of the following initiatives:

Property tax reform (led by Sandy D'Alemberte), No Fault insurance (with Bill Gillespie), the Florida Education Funding Program (with Bob Graham), Workers' Compensation reform (with Bill Sadowski), vocational education reform, public utility reform, the public counsel, and trucking deregulation (with George Sheldon). I also chaired a select committee that passed the phosphate severance tax, and chaired the House committee (with Senator Phil Lewis's Senate committee) that developed Florida's Administrative Procedures Act. I have never tried to calculate the cumulative savings that resulted from my legislative proposals. No Fault auto insurance has saved billions since 1972. Workers' Comp reform has also saved billions, despite the fact that we never quite got it right. Each time we tried to stop one set of abuses, other problems would arise. Probably the biggest savings to the public came from an energy grid (mandating the interconnection of electric utilities), the public counsel (reduced utility rates), and trucking deregulation (reduced freight rates). I also served on the legislative advisory panel of the Southern Regional Education Board, a respected interstate compact created after World War II by the southern states as a cooperative effort to upgrade their lagging colleges and universities.

At another level, I strengthened the institutions in which I served by hiring highly qualified professional staff, several of whom happened to be minorities. Mario Taylor was the first African American ever to work for the Florida House at a professional staff level. Subsequently, as the chair of the Senate Education Committee, I hired Barbara Cohen Pippin, the first African American employed as professional staff in the history of the Florida Senate. I am extremely proud of Mario and Barbara, both of whom became highly respected legislative staff directors. Later, as lieutenant governor, my selection of Kendrick Meek to be responsible for my personal security resulted in Kendrick being the first African American promoted to the rank of captain in the history of the Florida Highway Patrol. After serving in several senior staff positions for the City of Jacksonville, Mario Taylor was selected in 2003 as northeast Florida regional director for the Department of Environmental Protection; Barbara Pippin is assistant to the president of Broward College; and Kendrick Meek, having served in both the Florida House and Senate, has now made his mark as a member of Congress.

Finally, I made an impact as one of the leaders of the second generation of reformers, following LeRoy Collins, Reubin Askew, Lawton Chiles, Dick Pettigrew, Sandy D'Alemberte, Bob Graham, Jim Redman, and others. Like our predecessors, our generation was bipartisan. Republican legislators like Curt Kiser and Bob Johnson could be counted on to support the reform efforts, and often paid a greater price than their Democratic colleagues.

Part of the challenge facing politicians advocating reform in Florida is being tagged as a "liberal." The technique—perfected by Ed Ball when the term implied sympathy to Communists and integration—is still widely used to intimidate Florida politicians who might otherwise be inclined to embrace reform. In this state, which is now changing more rapidly than any place in the United States, this intimidation is particularly costly. Consider this parable: *A farmer's well runs dry. Is it liberal, or conservative, to drill a new well?* In my view, ideological slogans don't make sense when applied to Florida's problems. Refusing to adapt to a changing environment is not conservative. It is just plain dumb.

Finally, to use Baldy Strickland's language, I take "humble pride" in having been chosen three times in six years for the *St. Petersburg Times'* award as the Most Effective House Member, and four times in six years as the Most Effective Senator.

The Equal Rights Amendment

In 1977, the vote to ratify the proposed Equal Rights Amendment to the U.S. Constitution came before the Florida Senate. Florida was a pivotal state. If we failed to ratify, the Equal Rights Amendment was doomed. I had initially opposed ratification, believing Florida's constitution and statutes provided adequate protections for Florida women. I changed my position after one of the most unique meetings of my entire political career. Anne Marston, wife of University of Florida president Robert Marston, called and invited me to a small, unpublicized discussion of the ERA to be held at her home. Upon arrival, I was introduced to a group of largely nonpolitical women. My recollection is that the group included, among others, a librarian, a teacher, a telephone operator, a nurse, several university professors, and Anne Marston. Several of the women were from the small rural counties north of Gainesville.

Anne said she and her colleagues respected my manner of analyzing political issues, and wanted only to be sure I understood the underlying reason why the ERA was important to Florida women. Each of these women had lived at least part of her life in a state—or states—other than Florida. Some had experienced discrimination in inheritance, others in employment, and others in divorce proceedings. The ERA did not affect them as Floridians, but none of them had any way of knowing when their career, their husband's career, or even family emergencies might require them, or their daughters or granddaughters, to reside in a state whose laws do not protect women from discrimination. At that time, Louisiana was the most egregious example, with divorce and inheritance laws that still reflected the influence of the Napoleonic Code, but several other states were mentioned as well. The discussion was non-ideological, and the examples were specific. They knew their position was unpopular in North Florida. In fact, they felt certain that I would be the sole North Florida senator favoring the ERA if I supported them. They did not ask for a commitment—only that I look carefully at the facts and take into account the situation of other North Florida women who supported the ERA, but found the situation too intimidating to speak out publicly.

I made no commitment, but a short time later, after some research of my own, I discovered that Anne Marston's allegations were accurate. Based on this, I changed my position and publicly supported ratification of the ERA. The vote was close and could have gone either way. The ERA failed in Florida, and that was the de facto end of the decade-long national effort. For me, however, the drama of the ERA was replayed in each of the sixteen counties I represented. Bumper stickers appeared overnight with the message "Senator MacKay, please don't draft our daughters." The Farm Bureau, with active chapters in each of my sixteen counties, as well as evangelical pastors in search of a rallying cry, proceeded to pack halls to oppose me whenever I spoke in the community. To their credit, and despite the defeat of the ERA, Anne Marston's quiet network did not abandon me. I will never forget the hush that came over a packed and hostile crowd when a well-known local nurse or telephone operator would take the microphone, obviously uncomfortable, and say something like this: "Senator MacKay did what was right, and you women and your daughters ought to be standing with him, instead of shouting at him."

The other real act of integrity which remains fresh in my mind today was a statement made by Senator Curtis Peterson of Lakeland at each local delegation hearing. Although he opposed the ERA, Senator Peterson was deeply offended by the local Farm Bureaus, each of which was trying to outdo the others in questioning my patriotism, judgment, and fitness for political office. Here, in essence, is what Senator Peterson said to them: "I always thought the Farm Bureau was interested in agriculture and farming. Senator MacKay is a third-generation family farmer. He is as good a friend as the Florida farmer has. Unless you can show me what the ERA has got to do with agriculture, I suggest that the Farm Bureau take this item off your official policy statement. You may defeat MacKay, but you're going to lose a lot of support in the Florida Senate, including mine."

Everybody's Got the Right to Vote

Dixie County

There's an old story that says it all about Dixie County. It is about a hotly contested sheriff's race "in the old days." The incumbent noticed that he was trailing as the ballots were manually pulled from the box and counted. He asked for a short recess, and retired with his chief deputy to the graveyard, where he allegedly obtained the ballots of a few more faithful constituents who had failed to vote because they were deceased. It was cold and rainy, and after a while, the deputy said: "Let's go, Sheriff. Its cold, and besides, we've got enough names." To which the sheriff responded with indignation: "Oh no! This is America! Everybody's got the right to vote."

There's no doubt that people feel strongly about voting in Dixie County. In fact, many people feel voting is a property right. Claude Kirk found that out soon after he was elected governor. One of his most amusing confrontations was his standoff with the county commissioners of Dixie County, all of whom had been indicted for buying votes. Kirk, a Republican, removed the entire board, calling a special election to replace them. All five former incumbents promptly ran and were reelected. I was told they got a steep discount on the same package of purchased votes as before. Then, having been reelected, a Dixie County jury acquitted them and tranquility was restored.

Because of my association with Reubin Askew, I was never offered the opportunity to participate in the mercantile aspects of Dixie County democracy. Everyone seemed friendly enough to me, although I never seemed to be capable of attracting much of a following at the ballot box. As luck would have it, when it came time to run for reelection, I was at odds with Louis Wainwright, the director of Florida's prison system. Because of this conflict, I had major problems in every county where a prison was located. Prison guards all came from big families, and Wainwright's ability to mobilize these voters and punish opposing senators at the polls was considerable.

On election night, I had the usual listening post at campaign headquarters, and the voting pattern quickly became clear. I was losing every one of the small counties that had a prison, but winning the large counties by a sufficient margin to assure reelection. In the absence of voting machines, Dixie County was unique. On the one hand, there was an inability (they said) to provide a definitive vote count. In lieu of that, they would say things like: "We're doing the best we can." But then, in a disconcerting way, my Dixie County chair, Hal Chewning, would allow how it would help if he could tell the ballot counters how I was doing overall. Finally I called and told him I had won in the rest of the district by more votes than the entire population of Dixie County, including the graveyard. His response was a Dixie County classic: "Hey, fellas, he's won. Can't we let him carry Dixie County?"

The Sheriff

One of the offices that has survived almost intact from medieval England is that of sheriff (Shire Reeve). Once elected to office in his "shire," or locality, the sheriff exercised sole responsibility to enforce the law. In Florida, this meant the sheriff was a commanding figure in local government. Many sheriffs have also served a full career in office and then passed the office along to a favorite son. Examples of families with successive father-son enforcement careers include the Halls in St. Johns County; the Muhrees in Clay County; the McCalls in Lake County; the Whiteheads in Union County; and the Reddishes in Bradford County. With the advent of illegal drugs, Florida emerged as the main highway for drug smuggling for the eastern half of the United States. Suddenly several sheriffs became central figures in America's new criminal network. Millions of dollars were quietly being made available to rural sheriffs in small coastal counties, to do nothing more than stay away from certain areas at crucial times. Politically, big money had suddenly and mysteriously been thrown into contests for the office of sheriff.

In the 1970s, in one of the toughest battles confronting the legislators, they approved the creation of the Florida Department of Law Enforcement, a statewide prosecutor, and a statewide grand jury. The legislature also adopted a RICO law to enable law enforcement to prosecute both organized crime and white collar crime. In what seemed to be a constant pattern, I was on the side of the urban reformers, and opposed by the rural North Florida residents who worried about excessive state government interference with their lifestyle. Some of my bitterest enemies over this legislation were Florida sheriffs.

The Happening: Baker County

All my memories of doing battle with the sheriffs are not negative. I recall one incident in particular that still leaves me smiling today. In the 1978 session, I supported the efforts of Speaker Hyatt Brown to reduce the benefits of Florida's "high hazard" retirement system, which covered law enforcement, firefighters, and prison guards. The issue seemed clear to me. Sheriffs and others with a total of thirty years in the high hazard pension system could retire with a pension in excess of their highest salary. Somehow this had slipped by legislators in prior years, and the actuarial projections of future costs were outrageous. After extended debate, the Florida Senate cut the benefits so that a thirty-year law enforcement official would retire with a pension of 96 percent of his highest salary. I was the deciding vote.

Six weeks later, I found myself running for reelection, with fourteen of the sixteen sheriffs in my senatorial district actively campaigning against me. My opponent was "Cap" Wilson, chief deputy of Alachua County. The charge was that I was "soft on crime," which, when added to my vote in favor of the ERA, convinced my opponents that I was a liberal. The irony of being attacked as a liberal as a result of my fiscally conservative vote to reduce spending would have been fun to think about if I had not been in such a tight spot. Only two sheriffs stepped forward and spoke up on my behalf, and I'll never forget them. One was Don Moreland, the sheriff of my home county. A tough, quiet, professional lawman, Don is one of the best elected officials I have known. The other sheriff who came to my defense was Dolph Reddish, a twenty-year veteran in Bradford County and a maverick of the first order. Dolph made it clear that he disagreed with my vote, but supported me because I wasn't willing to be intimidated by Sheriff John Whitehead and the "Good Old Boy" power structure of North Florida. Sheriff Whitehead's influence was legendary. As sheriff of Union County, he had developed a political partnership with Louis Wainwright, who ran the Florida Department of Corrections. At that time, the vast majority of Florida's prisons were in North-Central Florida. So, any time a person crossed swords with either Whitehead or Wainwright, he faced the opposition of the sheriffs as well as the prison guards and their families. Since jobs in the prison system were a source of patronage, the applicant from the largest family got the job.

In any event, when Dolph called and offered to publicly support me, I gladly accepted. He said the next time they had a "Happening," he would take me as his guest. I readily accepted his offer, although it occurred to me that I did not know what a "Happening" was. A couple of weeks later, as the campaign heated up, Dolph called and invited me to a Happening that night at the 121 Roadhouse. The address was 100 miles from Ocala, but Dolph said to come to Starke and I could ride the rest of the way with Dolph and Maxie Carter, the chairman of the County Commission in Starke. So, I showed up at Dolph's office at six o' clock, still not knowing what a Happening was. Dolph, Maxie, and I rode to the small town of Macclenny in Dolph's official car, complete with a sheriff's star on the door and a "popcorn popper" blue light on top. Maxie, a Baptist deacon in his late fifties, was a perfect contrast to Dolph: a trim, handsome, divorced, man of the world—the exact person that Baptist deacons warned their daughters to avoid.

It turned out that Maxie didn't know what a Happening was either, so I was spared the humiliation of having to ask. As Dolph explained it, a Happening was an informal meeting of the elected officials from all over North Florida, together with representatives of the more prominent, well-connected private sector business owners whose success depended on doing business with local government. In other words, it was a secret meeting, held without notice to the press or the public, at which public policy issues were discussed and decisions were reached— the very meeting that had become a crime because of the 1967 statute known as the Sunshine Law.

Trying to appear casual, I asked Dolph if he was aware of the recent incident in Broward County where county commissioners had been indicted, removed from office, and convicted of a crime because of a meeting just like this. He responded that the Sunshine Law only applied to meetings. The event we were attending was not a meeting; it was a Happening. Happenings were beyond the scope of the Florida legislature. Besides, the only person who could convene a Grand Jury and indict anybody was the state attorney, and he would be there just like all the other elected officials. Besides that, he said (rather pointedly, I thought), this was about the only chance I would have to overcome the stigma that now threatened my career as a North Florida senator.

I was not aware of it at the time, but the 121 Roadhouse had played a central role in the events that had led to Baker County's bawdy reputation. Baker County, situated on the Georgia border directly west of Jacksonville, was historically the center of Florida's moonshine industry, with a reputation for wide-open living and casual law enforcement. Taking its name from Highway 121, the Roadhouse was situated only a few miles from the Georgia state line. When we arrived at the 121 Roadhouse, folks were taking part in a traditional outdoor fish fry. Maxie and I were relieved that it was just a fish fry. At least we knew how to act at a fish fry. What we were expected to do was "work the crowd." This meant shaking every hand as we were eating fried mullet and hush puppies, and swatting away flies and gnats while simultaneously appearing totally at ease. After six years in small-county politics, I could do this, although not as well as Maxie. As it got dark, the crowd started thinning out and we assumed it was over. I was relieved. If we left right then, I could be home by midnight. "Oh, no," said Dolph, "the Happening is inside. It's just getting started."

Inside, the 121 Roadhouse looked just like a hundred other taverns I had seen in my Air Force years—dimly lit, with a dance floor and a country-and-western band, surrounded by booths on three walls, and a bar across the fourth. Through the haze, I saw that the crowd included the same people Maxie and I had "worked" outside, plus a number of other males, and a number of smiling, high mileage beauties who were aggressively working the crowd in a manner not at all typical of political fish fries. As Dolph matter-of-factly explained: "You always have Georgia Girls at Happenings. What you do is just grab one. They work by the night (as opposed to by the hour, or by the trick)." Dolph waded in, following his own advice, leaving Maxie and me standing by the door, each for his own reasons trying to figure out how to survive the next two hours without being detected. Finding a booth, we ordered soft drinks—Maxie because of his religion, and I because I still had to drive across a number of counties where the chief law enforcement officer was my strongest opponent. It quickly became apparent that everything was on the house—girls, liquor, band, and all. The benefactors were road and building contractors, suppliers, and generally people who did business with county and municipal governments, all of whom were in the surrounding booths.

Through the smoky gloom, I recognized Joe Newmans, sheriff of Baker County, and one of my adversaries. To my surprise, Joe smiled at me and was exceptionally cordial. That was because, as they say in North Florida, he had been taken suddenly drunk. Unable to resist a cheap shot, I said, "Joe, what are you going to do if there is a crime tonight?" Never at a loss for words, he responded, "You don't understand. I've got every criminal in Baker County hemmed up in this room!" At midnight, Maxie couldn't stand it anymore and demanded that Dolph disengage himself so we could go home. Dolph indignantly refused, informing us that Happenings never got over within just one night. In fact, he said, he didn't expect to go home for two or three days. That was the last straw for Maxie, who just said, "Dolph, give me the keys. I'm leaving whether you come with me or not." Something about Maxie's demeanor convinced Dolph, who tossed the keys to Maxie and resumed dancing without missing a beat. The rest of the story saw Maxie and me driving the sheriff's car back to Starke, trying to figure out the best explanation if we should have a wreck or get stopped by John Whitehead's deputies in Union County. We also tried to think how the newspaper headline would read if we got stopped. I got home at about three thirty, grateful to be alive.

A few days later I saw Don Moreland, my local sheriff, and told him I had been to a Happening at the 121 Roadhouse. His face assumed an Inscrutable Professional Law Enforcement Expression as he said, "I don't go to those." But I know he has always wondered whether I stayed for two days, or three.

Misfeasing: Franklin County

In 1978, the Florida Senate had occasion to exercise its constitutional duty regarding charges proffered against elected officials by the Governor's Office. The matter involved the sheriff of Franklin County, who had been removed from office by Reubin Askew for misfeasance in office. The Senate then had to decide a) what the facts were, and b) whether the facts constituted misfeasance. As it turned out, this case also involved a prior determination of what it takes to "*fease* in office," and whether "*misfeasing*" was the same thing in Franklin County as the rest of the world. Because of the publicity and conflicting testimony, the Senate appointed a hearing master, Steve Kahn, to hear the evidence and make a recommendation. At the hearing before the full Senate, this is the way the evidence was summarized by Kahn:

The sheriff, who had been in office twenty-four years, had only one deputy, and thus had no ability to staff the county jail at night or on the weekends. This required a cooperative spirit on the part of the Franklin County prison population. As it turned out, the sheriff accomplished this by a unique incentive system. He started out by allowing each prisoner two beers a night at the county's expense. On weekends, he allowed female overnight visitors. Pot was grown in the jail yard, although in fairness, it was never clearly shown that the sheriff took part in this agricultural endeavor (this led Senator Jack Gordon, of Miami, to dub the event as the episode of the "jolly jail"). Whenever he was hosting a fish fry, the sheriff would provide the inmates a county-owned pickup truck complete with fishing poles, bait, and a couple of cases of beer. The inmates were expected to drink the beer, drive the truck, catch and cook the fish, and then presumably check themselves back into jail. This came to a head when the Florida Highway Patrol apprehended the county's pickup truck one afternoon, full of freshly caught fish and happy drunks, who turned out upon investigation to be all the inmates of the county jail.

Having read the sworn testimony carefully, I concluded that this was an open and shut case of misfeasance. To my surprise, both the hearing master and all the senators from the Panhandle counties of northwest Florida disagreed vehemently. Senators Pat Thomas and Dempsey Barron, in particular, were upset that some of us seemed to feel that the sheriff's actions were somehow wrong. After all, they pointed out, there was no one hurt, no evidence of any prisoners ever abusing the situation, and no known way to keep a jail open in the absence of jailers except with the cooperation of the prisoners. When the vote was taken, only senators Castor, Chamberlin, Saylor, Zinkil, and I voted to sustain the governor. The sheriff was reinstated and reelected the next year. As a postscript, Pat Thomas confided to me (after the vote) that the fish being transported when the inmates were arrested "might have been" intended for a fish fry honoring Senator Dempsey Barron, the Senate president.

The High Water Mark

By the time I left the Florida Senate, Reubin Askew had served eight years as governor and Bob Graham had been elected to succeed him. A third generation of reformers had emerged as leadership in the Florida

House and Senate. These were people who shared the Collins/Askew/ Pettigrew vision of what Florida could become, and were prepared to take political risks to turn the vision into reality. In the House, Steve Pajcic, Lee Moffitt, Jon Mills, and Bill Sadowski were major players, as were Harry Johnston, Betty Castor, Pat Frank, the remaining Doghouse Democrats, and others in the Senate. The reform vision was not confined to the Democratic side of the aisle. Curt Kiser, Bob Johnson, and many other Republicans were indispensable to the effort.

Bob Graham's eight years as governor—from 1978 to 1986—represented in many ways the high water mark of the reform and modernization effort which began in the '60s with reapportionment and the historic constitutional revision of 1968. Graham set ambitious new goals in education, protection of environmentally sensitive land, and growth management. Backed by strong legislative leadership, he moved Florida decisively forward in these areas. He made a courageous effort to broaden Florida's laughably narrow tax base, which ultimately failed in the face of unified opposition from Florida's business interests. This failure convinced Harry Johnston and Jon Mills—then the incoming Senate president and House Speaker—and other leaders in Florida's government and private sectors that the only way to achieve meaningful tax reform was to sunset, or repeal, all the sales tax exemptions, effective at a future date. In effect, this technique shifted the burden of proof, requiring each exempt business or entity to come forward and explain why continuing its exemption was beneficial to the public. Steve Pajcic, one of Florida's most visionary leaders, was the Democratic nominee for governor in 1986, having defeated Jim Smith in the Democratic runoff. Smith changed parties, taking many of the more conservative Democrats with him. Smith's action assured the election of Bob Martinez, a Republican, as Florida's next governor, and left the Florida Democratic Party in a shambles.

Bob Martinez and the Services Tax

Having run on a promise of no new taxes, Martinez immediately found himself in a box on taking office. On the one hand, there was a major revenue shortfall at a time when Florida's legitimate revenue needs had expanded dramatically. On the other hand, Harry Johnston, Jon Mills, and other legislative leaders, through the wholesale sunsetting of unwarranted tax exemptions, had set the stage for a major overhaul of Florida's tax base. Two of my friends, John Edward Smith and Jim Apthorp, aggressively pushed the proposed reform in the private sector. The proposed services tax also had the support of many of Florida's more progressive business leaders. The key feature was the extension of Florida's sales tax to the sale of services, like lawyers' and architects' fees and yacht brokers' commissions, as well as products. By closing these loopholes, the tax base could be significantly broadened. Since everybody, including the rich and powerful, would be paying, it would have then been possible to cut the sales tax rate from 6 percent to 4 percent while still raising the amount of revenue Florida needed. To his credit, when confronted with the facts, Governor Martinez had the courage to reverse his position and support passage of the services tax.

Incredibly, Florida's Department of Revenue was caught off guard when the services tax passed, and proved unable to develop regulations or explain how businesses should comply before the effective date of the new tax. The media industry (whose advertising services would now be taxed like any other service) predictably saw the tax as a threat to freedom of the press. A firestorm of opposition developed. The problems could have been addressed by delaying the effective date of the tax while regulations were finalized, and by exempting the media industry from the tax. Legislative leaders were prepared to do both things, but Bob Martinez was not. When confronted by an open rebellion from most Republican supporters, he reversed his position and advocated repeal. Democratic supporters could not withstand the opposition to the services tax by themselves, and many broke ranks to vote for repeal. That was the end of the services tax, and also the end of the political career of Bob Martinez.

The defeat of the services tax marked the continued failure of Florida's leaders to address the many needs of the state and its citizens. So long as new flocks of snowbirds continue relocating to Florida, real estate and construction projects boom, and tourists flock into the state, Florida's tax structure produces adequate revenues. But periodically, things go awry as they did in the Arab oil boycott of 1973 or the economic recession of 1991–1992, or more recently the housing collapse of 2008. When that happens, there are literally insufficient funds to meet legitimate state needs, and our "real" tax policy rises up and bites us. What we tax is only products, and even then we exempt many things that rich people buy. The majority of what we sell—services—remains exempt. This formula resembles some aspects of a nuclear reactor. So long as there isn't a mishap, things go well, but even a small misstep can cause a chain reaction. When that happens, the whole thing melts down.

Medicaid stands as a major point of vulnerability in Florida's budget. Congress mandated the program as an entitlement for seniors, but Florida is required to pay more than half the costs. When a recession occurs, Medicaid costs escalate, even as state revenues decline. We are at the top of all states in Medicaid exposure by virtue of our large retiree population. At the same time, we are at the bottom of all states in education funding at all levels. Mentally ill inmates are kept in jail cells for lack of mental health facilities. There is not much left to cut. This chain reaction is what devastated Bob Martinez, and it almost destroyed Lawton Chiles and me less than a decade later. Lawton survived by making greater budget cuts than any previous governor in Florida history, and eight years later left the state of Florida with a budget surplus. Jeb Bush happened to govern during a time when things went well fiscally, but not because of anything he did. The surplus funds accumulated by our administration were not reserved to help in bad times, but were instead squandered in the form of tax cuts for the wealthy.

As Governors Martinez and Chiles found out, when housing goes bad in Florida, government finds itself in a double bind: revenues collapse, while demands for services remain constant or increase. Governor Charlie Crist found himself facing this same double bind, and realized toward the end of his third year in office that things would probably not improve politically in Florida until the national crisis in housing finance had run its course. Unless he had somehow summoned the courage to raise taxes in an election year, he would have found himself running for office after having been forced to slash the state budget in four consecutive years. Faced with this reality, Crist prudently decided that it was time to run for the U.S. Senate. Everyone in Florida politics—conservative and liberal—knows what needs to be done, but actually doing it is another matter. What Florida needs is another Reubin Askew—someone willing to treat Floridians like adults.

Running for the U.S. Senate, 1980

My First Statewide Campaign

In 1979, Dick Stone was nearing the end of his first term in the U.S. Senate. Stone's voting record stood in sharp contrast to that of Lawton Chiles, Florida's senior U.S. senator. After the Watergate scandal, Chiles had emerged as a leader in the group of young reformers in the U.S. Senate, particularly on budget issues. Following Jimmy Carter's election as president in 1976, Chiles had worked closely with Carter to implement his legislative reform proposals. Stone had not been part of the reform effort during his years in Florida politics, and had a reputation for putting politics above policy. He was regarded by the press and many others as unduly cautious and unwilling to take a position without first testing to see which way the political winds were blowing. From my point of view, Stone was not an asset to Florida in his Senate position.

After extended discussions with my wife, Anne, my siblings, and my law partners, I decided to run against Dick Stone in the Democratic primary. If I won the race, I would be in position to make a real difference on issues of much greater importance than those decided by the Florida Senate. By early 1979, I had also become increasingly restless as a member of the Florida Senate. The district I represented consisted of sixteen small rural and semirural counties—almost one-fourth of the geographical area of Florida, but sparsely populated. My legislative salary reflected that the state legislature met only two months each year, with occasional committee meetings in between legislative sessions. In reality, however, as a committee chair and a member of the Senate leadership, I found myself occupied year-round with legislative matters. Not having independent means, it was necessary that I practice law full time to support my family. In essence, I had two full-time jobs. The result was that my law practice was increasingly jammed into the remaining weekdays I was not traveling, plus every Saturday and Sunday. At the same time, after the death of my father, I had assumed the responsibility— along with my brother, George MacKay—of managing the family agricultural ventures. This meant even greater stress on Anne, who now was raising our sons more or less on her own. In fact, I was borrowing (actually stealing) time from my family, business, and church, in order to meet the challenges of being the kind of Florida Senator I wanted to be.

Politics Trumps Policy

My decision to run for the Senate was based on two assumptions: First, I assumed I could persuade Floridians that they and their families would benefit from my policy-oriented approach to governance. The U.S. Senate was the premier policy forum in the world, and I had proven that I was a leader on issues of policy. Out of a field of more than a dozen candidates (one of whom was the incumbent), I was endorsed by the editorial boards of every major newspaper in Florida except the *Jacksonville Times-Union* and the *St. Petersburg Times*, which endorsed Dick Pettigrew in the primary. I took the position that the *St. Petersburg Times* knew a real liberal when they saw one. Even though I had little or no name recognition outside the North Florida counties I had represented, I assumed I could find a way to win in a statewide race. This was more of a challenge than I had anticipated. Because of its growth and complexity, Florida is not a state where old-fashioned grassroots campaigning works. Winning statewide in Florida requires television. Candidates without money must find a "gimmick," like Lawton Chiles's 1970 walk across Florida, to get on television. Otherwise, the ability to raise money is an important qualification. Despite the fact that I had alienated many of Florida's biggest political contributors, my initial fundraising went reasonably well, and I was fortunate to be able to hire Bob Squier, whose television ads had helped elect Bob Graham. Squier's theory was that he could get voters sufficiently interested in my policy-oriented campaigning that the press would start covering my public events. In effect, my paid media would lead to free media. He had followed much the same theory in Bob Graham's successful "workdays" campaign for governor. Unfortunately, after I had been campaigning for several months, Bill Gunter entered the race. My fundraising was significantly diminished at the very time my need for television advertising intensified.

The Gunter Misunderstanding

In 1979, Bill Gunter was Florida's state treasurer and insurance commissioner. He had previously served in the Florida Senate and the U.S. Congress, and he and I had joined forces on issues involving insurance reform. Several of my supporters in the business community were also friends and supporters of Gunter. Their advice was to check with Bill Gunter before committing to the U.S. Senate race. There was a possibility that Gunter would also decide to run against Dick Stone, and the two of us would cancel the effectiveness of each other's candidacy. Stone had narrowly defeated Gunter in the U.S. Senate race in 1974, and a number of observers felt that Gunter would ultimately be drawn into the 1980 race in a rematch. I asked for a private meeting with Bill Gunter, and laid out my plans to announce against Dick Stone. I told Gunter that if he intended to run, I would stay out of the race. I listened carefully to Gunter's answer, and understood him to say he was happy in his relatively new position as state treasurer, and that he would not get into the U.S. Senate race.

Months later, as polls indicated that Dick Stone was clearly vulnerable, Bill Gunter announced his candidacy. He said I had not listened carefully enough. His recollection was that he had said he had "no present intention" to run. It did not matter whose recollection was accurate. Gunter's entry into the race dried up my ability to raise money. A number of my supporters in the business community could not afford to alienate Gunter in his role as state treasurer and insurance commissioner, and withdrew their support for my candidacy. I was faced with the decision of whether to drop out or continue regardless of the dramatically increased risk. I made the decision to continue, even if it meant reducing my purchases of paid television and paying most of the cost out of my own resources. This ultimately turned out to be the case. Polls showed me on track to be in a runoff against either Gunter or Stone, but I ran short of funds and had to reduce the final media purchase. In order to continue, I had to raise $300,000. I raised this money by selling several parcels of land. This decision was hard enough, but after the race was concluded, I discovered that I owed a significant amount in capital gains taxes as a result of the land sales. I narrowly lost out to Bill Gunter in 1980. Gunter went on to defeat Dick Stone in a runoff, but then lost to Paula Hawkins in the 1980 Reagan landslide.

Following my defeat, I spent the next two years as a full-time husband, father, lawyer, and private citizen. Our two oldest sons, Ken and John, were finishing high school and starting college. Son number three, Ben, was entering high school, and son number four, Andy, was entering kindergarten. It was a good time to be home. My law practice flourished and I started paying off my campaign debts. I enjoyed private life immensely. There was only one problem: after the first year, I was restless.

The Vertical Counties

Miami-Dade, Broward, and Palm Beach Counties—Florida's Gold Coast—have roughly one-third of Florida's total population. Flying along the coastline, this hundred-mile strip is an unbroken expanse of high-rise condos. Walt Young, a senior Florida legislator from the Ft. Lauderdale area who was a close friend, introduced me to condo politics in 1978. At that time, my Florida Senate district consisted of sixteen

North Florida counties, a majority of which had populations of fewer than 10,000. "Think of these high-rise condo developments as vertical counties," Walt said. "Each group of buildings is a voting precinct, with its own voting machine in the lobby of the main building. They vote 95 percent Democratic, so your only challenge is to get them to come downstairs to vote. Precinct captains sit in the lobby and check off the residents as they vote. They assume those who haven't voted by 3 p.m. either died overnight, or else forgot what day it was. Either way, someone needs to check on them, so turnout teams start knocking on doors of those who haven't voted."

"These people are Roosevelt Democrats, who learned their politics in the Democratic machines of Chicago, Tammany Hall, New Jersey, and Boston," Walt continued. "They vote from palm cards containing lists of names selected by local party leaders, and your challenge as a candidate is to be sure your name is on the list. To get on the list, you've got to spend time working the crowds around the swimming pools and community rooms. You've got to convince these people that you are one of them, despite the fact that you appear to be a redneck from North Florida with a southern accent."

From that beginning, I came to know and love the condo commandos. I tend to see Florida's problems from an urban perspective, and found myself actually looking forward to campaigning in South Florida. By the time of Florida's 1988 Senate race, I was as strong in the Gold Coast region as any statewide Democratic candidate. This support was critical since the Gold Coast is the place where Democratic primaries and runoffs are decided.

The Congressional Years

Getting to Washington

There is a one-liner that expresses the traditional North Florida view of Washington:

Q: How do you get to Washington?
A: It's easy. Just go north and turn left.

As a practical matter, you traditionally had to be a Democrat to win in North Florida. All this changed following passage of the Civil Rights Act. By the time I ran for Congress, most North Floridians—although still nominally Democrats—were hostile to the policies of Jimmy Carter and the liberal Democratic leadership of Ted Kennedy and Tip O'Neill from Massachusetts. During this time, southern moderates like Sam Nunn and Lawton Chiles were fighting a lonely battle for survival as constituents turned increasingly to the ideological politics of Ronald Reagan and the Republican Party.

My first campaign for Congress took place in 1982, when I ran in a district that had no incumbent because of reapportionment. My platform called for a balanced federal budget and morality in foreign policy.

A couple of newspapers pointed out that this put me simultaneously on Reagan's left in foreign policy, and on his right in economic policy. One pundit went so far as to say that I had Reagan surrounded. Although this observer agreed with my proposals, he thought they were overly complex when contrasted with Reagan's simplistic slogans. It was particularly frustrating to advocate fiscal discipline when President Reagan was arguing that balancing the budget was unnecessary. Under a new economic theory nicknamed "Reaganomics," if tax rates could be cut sufficiently, the result would be a dramatic expansion of economic growth, so that tax *revenues* would grow even after *rates* had been cut. This theory, which had originally been diagrammed on the back of a cocktail napkin, was named after its inventor, Arthur Laffer. Reagan had first latched on to Laffer's theory two years earlier in the Republican primary when his opponent (George H. W. Bush) had derided it as "Voodoo Economics." Now, two years later, the cocktail napkin diagram—called the Laffer Curve—was America's economic policy.

For most of his first two years as president, it had appeared that Reagan could make no mistakes. Armed with simplistic images of "welfare queens" driving up to food stamp offices in their Cadillacs, Reagan had convinced a sizable bloc of southern Democratic members of Congress, called Boll Weevils, to side with the Republican minority and make major across-the-board cuts in social welfare programs. My opponent, Ed Havill, was not unduly troubled with complex ideas. "I support President Reagan" was his answer to every question. To my frustration, this approach proved surprisingly effective. Reagan had made a virtue of ignorance. It was widely understood that he did not understand the implications of his own proposals. Indeed, his disdain for complex intellectual ideas was a major part of his charm. Somewhere during that magical political time for the president, he made one mistake. In an unguarded moment, he proposed privatizing Social Security. If he had understood how Social Security works, he would have known that it is a pay-as-you-go system, which means that if current workers stop paying in, there will be no money to pay benefits for current retirees. Fortunately for me, my opponent also didn't understand how Social Security works. When asked about privatizing Social Security, he simply said, "I support President Reagan." Claude Pepper, champion of the senior citizen, campaigned all across America to be certain all retirees and midcareer workers understood that President Reagan was proposing to bankrupt Social Security. The issue resonated beyond all expectations. The result was that I was elected, along with fifty-one other Democratic candidates from around the country in the fall of 1982. We were the largest class of freshman Democrats since the Watergate scandal. Claude Pepper, who became a mentor and friend, was the patron saint of our class of '82.

Heavy Lifting

My congressional district was roughly the same size as my former Florida Senate district. As a state senator, I had been supported by a staff of three. As a member of Congress, I had a staff of sixteen. Half of my staff concentrated on constituent casework, the effort by every congressional office to protect citizens from senseless bureaucratic actions by agencies of their own elected government. Casework also involved protecting members of Congress from their constituents, their interest groups, and their lobbyists. This work involves promptly answering thousands of e-mails, letters, and phone calls. The arrival of computers had not reduced the burden of communicating with constituents, but had actually expanded it in manifold ways. Despite my quaint attitudes about political fundraising, I was quickly made aware that I had a cadre of Washington lobbyists at my disposal. I was assured that they were too sophisticated to want commitments on specific votes. What was expected (they said) was that they would get personal input before any vote critical to their interests. Not many months passed before the "understanding" was put to the test. My Steering Committee member, who lobbied the Committee on Science and Technology and represented the interests of defense contractors, was retired admiral Spence Matthews. Somewhat shaken, Admiral Matthews reported that I had received a rating of "zero" on my first votes on defense appropriations. I reminded him that I had informed him from the outset that I favored a stronger conventional military, but opposed President Reagan's nuclear buildup. My first votes had all been

"No," as the White House had pressed for multiple nuclear warheads on everything from aircraft to submarine-launched ballistic missiles. To his credit, Spence Matthews didn't quit my Steering Committee. I was told, however, that he warned other lobbyists that Congressman MacKay was "hard to steer."

In comparing the congressional schedule to that of the Florida legislature, I came to realize that the workloads and time demands were not terribly different. The major difference was that while the Florida legislature was in session for only sixty days each year, the congressional schedule spread the required work over the entire year. Parkinson's Law states that the amount of time required to accomplish a given task will expand to meet the amount of time available. The congressional schedule is an excellent example of Parkinson's Law run amok.

As members of Congress–elect, we were sworn in two weeks after the November election, although our official duties did not begin until early January. This time delay was beneficial, since we needed time to hire staff, get organized, and adjust to living part-time in Washington, and part-time in Florida. In Congress, each member is given a lump sum budget to cover staffing needs in Florida and Washington, as well as the cost of traveling back and forth. Many members rent an apartment in Washington and commute back to Florida for weekends and district work periods. Such travel is essential, and office budgets are adequate to cover this cost. I was fortunate to have highly capable and experienced senior staff with whom I had worked in the Florida Senate and my law practice. Greg Farmer, my friend and campaign manager, moved to Washington and became my administrative assistant, or staff director. Samelia King stayed in Ocala, organizing and managing district offices in Gainesville, Ocala, and Leesburg. Nancy Cowart, my legal secretary, became my personal assistant, and Julie Fletcher, who started as an intern, became manager of my Washington office. I was extremely fortunate to have this experienced leadership available. They had lived with me through the unsuccessful 1980 U.S. Senate campaign as well as my congressional campaign. They knew how to cope with the stresses of politics and functioned well without supervision. Indeed, most people thought my office functioned far better when I was not present. When I got to Washington, the constituent mail started pouring in even before I had an office. Sam Gibbons, a senior member of Congress from Tampa, generously made an office and telephone available to me, and that was all I had for several weeks.

Compared to many of my colleagues, my staffing was heavy on policy, although this meant our district staff in Florida was stretched thin. Mike Troy, a talented young person who had worked for several years as a policy analyst in Bill Nelson's congressional office, became my policy director. Gainesville, with a VA hospital, Shands Teaching Hospital, and the University of Florida, had need of a sophisticated office. Fortunately, I was able to hire Jean Godwin, who had previously managed Congressman Don Fuqua's Gainesville office.

It quickly became apparent that it would be impossible for me to meet with everyone who wanted to see me, or, for that matter, to go to all the events to which I was invited. Even reading the letters which were flooding in proved to be more than I had time to do. After talking to senior members, I decided to set aside time to develop expertise in certain areas, and then divide the remaining time according to my priorities. Otherwise, they advised, the political demands of the office would overwhelm any attempt to focus on policy issues. This led to regular Monday night dinners, where my senior staff and I met with people who had expertise in areas of interest to me. This plan proved to be very valuable to me, and as word got around, established an early reputation that my staff and I were serious and knowledgeable. As a result, we were later given opportunities to expand our policy staff at no cost by using graduate students on fellowships. When we ran out of space, we operated a "night shift." To the amazement of my colleagues, my office was staffed twenty-four hours a day for extended periods. This innovation enabled me to staff the Democratic Budget Group and other initiatives, and established our reputation as a different kind of congressional office.

After getting organized, our first real duty as new members of Congress was to listen to the State of the Union address and depart for a ten-day President's Day district work period (recess). At some point in February or March, we began attending sporadic committee hearings, where we were only expected to stay awake, look interested, and be quiet. This period was followed by another recess for Easter. The committees then resumed work from mid-April until the Memorial Day recess, another district work period. The serious work of the Congress began after the Fourth of July district work period. From July 10 until August 5, pressure mounted to complete the initial budget work before the month-long August district work period, which was followed immediately by the Labor Day district work period. From mid-September until Thanksgiving, there was an intense drive to complete the eleven separate appropriations bills, and then reconcile the total spending to the limits specified in the previously adopted budget resolution.

Newly elected members of Congress were expected to spend most of their first term back home to maximize their chances of reelection. For senior members, the district work periods were occasions for overseas travel and rest, but for the rest of us the district work periods were the times when the true heavy lifting took place. Town meetings, interest group politics, and face-to-face meetings with individual constituents dominated most of our time.

The Congressional Reception

It is impossible to appreciate the extent to which the action (or inaction) of the Congress affects everyday life until one experiences the phenomenon of the congressional reception. Every organization in America interested in issues dependent on congressional action (or inaction) has at least one of these events each year, usually timed to bring the maximum number of local leaders to Washington just before votes critical to the organization's interests. The pressure for receptions is so great that members of Congress are expected to attend at least one each night, and sometimes three or four. To reduce time demands, receptions are typically held in a congressional office building. If this happened in Tallahassee, someone would be indicted. In Washington, however, no one seems to notice the impropriety of using congressional office buildings to make it more convenient to lobby. It is all part of America's full-service Congress.

As a Presbyterian and an introvert, I found congressional receptions, with their crowds, superficiality, and noise, as close to hell as I ever want to get. One cannot fully appreciate the hypocrisy without actually experiencing it. A close approximation would be the tightly packed shuttle bus at the Los Angeles airport. Everyone is in a hurry to get someplace else, but in order to get someplace else, it is necessary to talk to the stranger most immediately jammed up against you. In order to talk, it is necessary to shout. The most disconcerting part is that everyone is trying to appear to make extended eye contact with his or her member of Congress, while actually looking around to see if anyone has come into the room who is more important. To cap off the bedlam, everyone has at least one camera, and is willing to kill—if killing is necessary—to have a picture shaking hands with a dazed, glassy-eyed member of Congress.

Upon hearing me express this view, a seasoned lobbyist explained it to me: "Your problem is that you're too self-centered. This doesn't have anything to do with you. This is about me! The way my members judge my clout is by counting the number of members of Congress who come to our reception."

Bed Wetters

Many of my colleagues, like me, were former state legislators accustomed to a system where hard work was rewarded. Guided by past experience, they aggressively tried to take responsibility. In the Congress, these members were known as overexcited "bed wetters" and viewed by senior members as having missed the essential point. The way to get ahead in the Congress was not to work hard or come up with new ideas, but to prove you could be reelected. Until you had done that, no one took you seriously.

Knowing from the outset that I had a bleak future as a House insider, I was not a bed wetter. Having run on a platform of congressional reform, I knew that whatever I accomplished would be over the objections of the House leadership. To make matters worse, with a southern accent and Buddy as my political name, I was targeted from the outset as probably already collaborating with the Boll Weevils, the southern conservatives who were providing critical votes to President Reagan. The "leadership" wouldn't be comfortable with me no matter how hard I tried, so I decided to relax and do what I thought was right. I was in the ironic position of having been labeled too liberal in Tallahassee, and now being tagged as too conservative for Washington.

By my definition, a political bed wetter is one who is afraid to vote his conscience. Under this definition, the real bed wetters in the Congress are not the newcomers, but the senior members.

The Red Light District

Television cameras were everywhere in the Congress. At hearings of major committees like Ways and Means or Commerce, front row space was provided so that banks of camera crews could operate without interfering with each other. I was a member of the Committees on Science and Technology, Foreign Affairs, and the Budget. Much of the routine work of these committees was not covered by television. When a crisis occurred, however, like the shuttle disaster at NASA or the discovery of President Reagan's illegal Iran-Contra war, I became accustomed to multitudes of television cameras in my committee meetings. When the red lights on the television cameras came on, this meant that a segment of the evening news was being filmed. Everybody acted differently when the red lights came on. Members, prodded from behind by staff, looked alert and played their assigned roles. Democrats tried to look knowledgeable, while Republicans looked skeptical. The testimony had been supplied days earlier in written form, along with suggested questions for members to ask. Congressional staff, network reporters, and lobbyists had reviewed it line by line. There were no surprises. Everything was scripted.

I found myself fascinated by the faces on the other side of the witness table. Every seat was taken. People stood in line for hours to be assured of a seat. I had been surprised at first to see the same people in the audience at every hearing. Then it became clear. They were representing corporations or groups whose interests were affected by the actions of the committee. I was surrounded by staff, witnesses, and audience, all of whom were being paid to be there. Everyone in the room was working off the same script, and programmed to play a role when the red lights came on. That part would be on the evening news. Nothing else was of any great significance, except that the testimony would become part of the official record.

Sweet Thursdays

For me, like most members of Congress, Thursday was the finest day of the week. It usually began with a work schedule that wound up early, included a dash to Reagan National, a flight to Atlanta, the trauma of changing planes in Atlanta, a flight to Gainesville or Orlando, and finally the drive to Ocala.

Friday was a political day, when each member of Congress did his best to be seen "back in the District." Ocala, Gainesville, and other Central Florida cities were no different than Washington. The rule was: "If it wasn't on television, it didn't happen." The entire goal was to be captured on local television while doing some kind of spontaneous good work. As in Washington, everybody played to the red light on the camera. Preschools, kindergartens, Habitat construction sites, and particularly nursing homes were all accustomed to visits by members of Congress accompanied by staff and local press . . . and sometimes even picketers. Each event was an opportunity for a press interview, plus two minutes on the local evening news. For many members of Congress, this was all just part of the job—necessary to stay in touch with constituents. For me, it always left a bad taste in my mouth. The temptation was to worry more about the red lights on the cameras than the real-life problems of my constituents.

Leaning Yes

One of the first lessons I learned in Congress was how to count. The incident that led to this insight is still fresh in my mind. In early March 1983, my chief of staff, Greg Farmer, my colleague, Congressman Tim Penny, and I had undertaken to host an organizational meeting of the

Class of '82 Budget Group. To assure a good crowd, I had agreed to provide pizza and beer. Between us, we had personally contacted all fifty-two Democrats in our class. The response had been enthusiastic. "I'll try to come," "I'll put it on the schedule," and "I'm glad you're doing this" were the most common responses.

Encouraged, we had decided we would probably have at least forty in attendance. That translated into 120 cans of beer and twenty pizzas, paid for out of my pocket. At the appointed time, Tim, Greg, and I found ourselves alone in the room, with the exception of one colleague, Jim Moody, a member of Congress from Wisconsin. Jim said he didn't think our ideas for budget reform were realistic. He had come for the pizza, beer, and fellowship. What I had learned—at the cost of 120 cold beers and twenty pizzas—was how to count, or the importance of distinguishing between "Leaning Yes" and "Yes." Our colleagues had all decided, for one reason or another, that their other "Leaning Yes" opportunities were more enticing than beer, pizza, and balancing the budget.

Under the system used in Congress to count votes, there are five separate categories:

No   Leaning No   Undecided   Leaning Yes   Yes

No member of Congress is ever counted as a "Yes" until the direct question is asked: "Can we count you as a Yes?" Even then, the answer is not considered final. It is prudent to go back at frequent and regular intervals and ask: "Are you still a Yes?" At first glance, this vote counting system seems to epitomize everything that is wrong with the Congress. On reflection, however, it is simply an acknowledgment that, when difficult decisions are an everyday occurrence, people will inevitably keep all options open until the last minute.

Through the Looking Glass

Like several other congressional colleagues in the Class of '82, I had led many of the state legislative reform efforts of the 1960s and 1970s. Like my colleagues, I was surprised to find that in key areas, I was better informed than senior members, for whom legislative reform was only a word—and an unwelcome word at that. The one area of total mystery to all of us, however, was the newly enacted Congressional Budget Act. For those of us with budget expertise, it was straight out of Alice in Wonderland. It did not even faintly resemble any other budget procedure we had ever seen.

Before the end of our first ninety days in office, a group of us decided that if we were to have any hope of becoming effective members of Congress, we had to develop an understanding of the Congressional Budget Act. We also concluded that the congressional leadership had absolutely no interest in educating us on budget procedures. If we were to gain this information, we would have to dig it out for ourselves. In partnership with Tim Penny, a newly elected member from Minnesota, I cofounded the group which did the digging and which became known as the Democratic Budget Group. By the end of our freshman term, the Class of '82 knew as much about the Congressional Budget Act as anyone in Congress. What we learned was that congressional budget reform had been a decade-long effort led by budget experts like Lawton Chiles, Sam Nunn, and Pete Domenici, and had been supported by the huge Watergate Class of 1974 that had been elected on a platform of congressional reform. The basic idea was to superimpose separate House and Senate budget committees on the appropriations process, with authority to propose overall spending limits at the beginning of each budget cycle. These limits, if approved by a majority vote of the House and Senate, became binding on the appropriations process. This cumbersome layer had been superimposed on the process because the Appropriations Committees of the House and Senate had refused to change or give up any control of their respective cumbersome and archaic procedures. As we subsequently discovered, senior members of the House Appropriations Committee still had no intention of abiding by the discipline of the Budget Act and would not do so unless shown by a vote each year that the membership of the House would force compliance.

After the early vote on overall spending limits, the eleven appropriations subcommittees would each develop its own separate bill, each of which would be debated and passed as a separate spending bill by the whole House. Invariably, the sum total of the eleven separate bills would exceed the Budget Committee's imposed spending cap and a process known as Reconciliation would begin. As anyone with common sense could anticipate, each house would reconcile differently. All of this would culminate in the traditional Appropriations Conference Committee to adjust the differences between the House and Senate. It was cumbersome and confusing, and worked to maximize the power of the appropriators—and the opportunities for enterprising lobbyists to slip in special interest tidbits known as "earmarks."

The Budget Act was still in its infancy in 1983, and chairs of the appropriations subcommittees (known informally as the "College of Cardinals") were nominally cooperating, but actually resisting this new restriction on their power. In 1983, all eleven bills were finally passed, but in the meantime we ran over into the new fiscal year, which started the first day of October. This delay required passage of a Continuing Appropriation Bill and was much like putting the federal government on cruise control to allow spending in the new fiscal year to continue at the previous year's level while the Reconciliation debate continued. As Thanksgiving approached, the Class of '82 joined the debate with enthusiasm. Our finest hour was our amendment proposing a 1 percent across-the-board cut on all spending. We lost the vote, but the combination of strong press support and a respectable vote on the proposed 1 percent cut meant the issue could not be ignored. The spending cap set by the Budget Committee had to be met. As soon as we demonstrated enough strength to be taken seriously, the debate ended. Cuts were miraculously approved, and the appropriations bills were passed in time for adjournment by Thanksgiving.

The Class of '82 also established the tradition of meeting early each Wednesday morning to keep up-to-date on budget actions. At first the senior leadership tried to ignore these meetings, but when experts like Paul Volcker and Alice Rivlin started attending, the leadership found it prudent to show up as well. These meetings are still the only place where members of Congress can be briefed each week by the Budget Committee, Congressional Budget Office, Federal Reserve, and others with budget expertise. The Class of '82 played a significant part in the effort to hold Presidents Reagan and George H.W. Bush accountable on their pledges to reduce the deficit, and later became the leaders in President Clinton's successful effort in the '90s to balance the federal budget. The Democratic Budget Group, which Tim Penny and I originated, became today's Blue Dog Democrats, a group of more than fifty moderate and conservative Democrats which now is the swing vote in the U.S. House of Representatives, insisting on fiscal discipline on issues like health care reform.

The Dire Emergency

When Congress reconvened for the 1984 session, one of the first issues scheduled for debate was the Dire Emergency Supplemental Appropriation Bill. During this period, the Class of '82 came to understand the true nature of the problem confronting us. In order to achieve a compromise and adjourn in time for Thanksgiving, the chairs of the various appropriations subcommittees had arbitrarily reduced appropriations for 1983. The effort now, at the very beginning of 1984, was simply to restore these cuts by passing a "Dire Emergency" Supplemental Appropriation. By doing this at the very beginning of the next session, the supplemental appropriation was not counted as part of the prior fiscal year's spending. The Budget Committee's proposed spending cap for the next fiscal year had not yet been established, so the supplemental appropriation was not included in the new fiscal year. The intended result would have been that the resulting increase in the 1984 deficit would have literally dropped between the cracks.

All of this came to light when members of the Budget Group happened to notice that part of the 1983 Dire Emergency was the failure to include funding for the twelfth month of the U.S. Postal Service. Bizarre as it seemed, the prior year's miraculous cuts had been achieved by omitting the final month of the budgets of the Postal Service and other "nonessential" agencies. The "Dire Emergency" was that unless these cuts were restored, the Postal Service and other "nonessential" agencies would run out of money at the end of eleven months.

The chair of the Appropriations Committee was Jamie Whitten, the senior Democrat from Mississippi. As a fellow southerner, I was one of the few members of the class of '82 who could understand Whitten, particularly when he purposely mumbled his comments. My innocent inquiry concerned the circumstances which could have led to the omission of the twelfth month of mail service and other "nonessential" federal programs. The answer was a lengthy and passionate denunciation of the Budget Act as well as the failure of new members to appreciate the value of land, farming, and traditional American values. Exactly how all this related to our failure to fund the Postal Service for its twelve months of operation was unclear to me and everyone else in our congressional group.

Whitten wasn't the only person I embarrassed by exposing the fraud in the annual Dire Emergency Supplemental Appropriation. The majority leader, Jim Wright, sent a staff member to lecture me on the importance of being a team player. My response was that teams only work when there is a huddle or some effort to include team members in the decisions. I had not seen a single huddle in my entire one-year career, and thus assumed that what we had was not a team, but a dictatorship. Anytime Jim Wright wanted me to vote as part of his team, all he had to do was signal for a huddle, so that I could take part in the actual decision leading to the vote. Having battled Dempsey Barron for six years in the Florida Senate, I knew firsthand the difference between a team and a dictatorship. Jim Wright subsequently became House Speaker. His brief tenure is the topic of the book, *The Ambition and the Power*, by John M. Barry. Barry's book gives an accurate picture of Wright's dictatorial ways, and outlines my continuing unwillingness to play by Wright's rules.

"De-Authorize De Barge Canal"

Aside from the budget fight, my biggest triumph in my first term in Congress was the deauthorization of the Cross Florida Barge Canal. As it turned out, the entire uncompleted part of the canal was in my congressional district—a district that had, before reapportionment, been represented by Bill Chappell, the leading congressional supporter of the canal. Upon arrival in Washington, I discovered that the authorization of the canal was contained in a mammoth public works bill which reauthorized all of America's public works projects. The multi-year authorization was scheduled for 1984, my second year in Congress. The good news was that the Public Works Bill was automatically open for amendment. This meant that I would at least be allowed to be heard on the subject. The bad news was that Bill Chappell (sixteen years' seniority), Charlie Bennett (thirty-four years), Claude Pepper (eighteen years), and Jim Wright (twenty-five years) were all strong supporters of the Barge Canal.

Since I was in my first term, I literally had no responsibilities other than to vote and take care of my constituents' problems. As environmental activist Marjorie Carr pointedly reminded me, this meant that I could devote considerable time to the Barge Canal. After gathering the facts, I became absolutely convinced that Marjorie Carr was right. The proposed canal was a boondoggle which would be cut into the Floridan Aquifer, Central Florida's main water source. Any major industrial spill would be an environmental disaster, with the chemicals flowing directly into Central Florida's primary water supply. On top of that, the economic studies justifying the canal had been totally unrealistic in the real world, and it would take more than 100 years before the cumulative benefits of the canal would justify the costs. I set out to visit all 435 members of the House to be certain everyone had the facts. In the process, I advised almost every single member of Congress of my vehement opposition to the canal. Despite my lack of seniority, my opposition was taken seriously because of the strong tradition that gives each member a veto over location of federal projects in his home district. Mike Troy, a member of my staff, designed a campaign button that said "De-Authorize De Barge Canal," which we liberally distributed to House members and their staffs. The buttons became a popular item, so that Mike had to come out with several editions. Buttons were everywhere in the halls and in committee rooms. So, when the day of the vote finally arrived, I had reason to feel confident that I would get substantial support for my position.

The debate became not only emotional, but surprisingly extended. Several senior members confided that they had never actually seen a member trying to kill a pork-barrel project in his own district. One or two even asked rhetorically if "the distinguished gentleman from Florida" (me) understood what the job of a member of Congress involved. It seems you're supposed to bring projects home, regardless of their merit or effect on the environment, not fight them off. Because Chappell, Bennett, and Pepper were strong supporters of the canal, other senior members from Florida couldn't bring themselves to side with me in the debate, although they freely told other members individually that the canal was a boondoggle. Jim Wright, the majority leader, was making it clear that he was taking notes. Anyone siding with me ran the risk that his own projects might be looked at with disfavor. Wright had the power to make this happen. To cap it off, it turned out that the original sponsor of the Cross Florida Barge Canal, back in 1941, had been none other than the beloved Claude Pepper, then a U.S. senator. Forty-three years later, Claude Pepper was now a senior member of Congress, still passionately committed to the canal.

On the "straight" fifteen-minute vote count, my side clearly won a majority of the votes. Jim Wright was presiding, however, and the clock was simply held open until the canal proponents could twist enough arms to make it a tie vote. At that point, the vote was recorded, and the chair heatedly instructed "the distinguished gentlemen from Florida" to get together and decide what they wanted for their fair state. In other words, I had to help develop a compromise to deauthorize the canal without making my senior colleagues lose face. It turned out to be an easy matter. We agreed to leave the canal authorized from Jacksonville to Palatka, but deauthorize it from Palatka to the Gulf of Mexico. In that manner, the Cross Florida Barge Canal could still exist in the part of Florida represented by Congressmen Chappell and Bennett, but it would no longer be authorized from Palatka to the Gulf of Mexico, the area represented by Congressman MacKay. As a practical matter, this meant that although the canal was useless for a cargo ship or barge, you could paddle a canoe or kayak from Jacksonville to Palatka, transiting the Buckman Lock at Palatka, and you would have been in the canal the whole way. The Cross Florida Barge Canal was deauthorized west of Palatka, however, so the Buckman Lock is actually a useless artifact. The cost of operating and maintaining the Buckman Lock for Florida's canoeists, however, is something on the order of $1 to 2 million per year.

The deauthorization battle continued after I left the Congress. Congressman Charlie Bennett emerged as the hero of the next phase. The State of Florida and the counties through which the canal would have run wanted to get their hands on the federally owned canal lands. In their hands, the right of way could be used for schools, equipment sheds, ballparks—perhaps even new real estate developments or industrial facilities. Congress had to first pass legislation transferring these lands to the state, however. I was not in public office at the time, but I felt strongly that the canal right of way should be preserved as a linear park or greenway, running from Palatka all the way to the Gulf of Mexico. When I contacted him, Charlie Bennett agreed, and blocked the legislation which would have transferred the land until language was included to prevent counties and cities from "cherry-picking" the canal land for free sites for local projects. The Cross Florida Greenway, appropriately named after Marjorie Carr, is the result. As Florida continues to urbanize, the Greenway will be the focal point of one of America's finest systems of greenways, parks, and trails. Charlie Bennett deserves credit for stepping up at the critical moment.

Unlike the story of the Cross Florida Greenway, the last chapter of the battle to deauthorize the Cross Florida Barge Canal has not been resolved, and the fiasco continues to the date of this writing. State Senator George Kirkpatrick led a multiyear effort to save Lake Ocklawaha. Lake Ocklawaha, located southwest of Palatka, is actually that part of the Ocklawaha River which was dammed up to make the reservoir necessary for the operation of the lock, which was renamed the Kirkpatrick Lock in recognition of Senator Kirkpatrick's efforts to prevent its elimination.

Creating Lake Ocklawaha meant the destruction and flooding of thousands of acres of pristine wetlands and also the flooding of miles of the winding, canopied Ocklawaha River. "Free the Ocklawaha" is the battle cry of Marjorie Carr's group, Florida Defenders of the Environment, as well as an energetic, feisty new group, the Putnam County Environmental Council. The fight centers on the Florida Senate, which somehow manages, year after year, to prevent taking out the Kirkpatrick Lock and dam. Like many other intractable struggles, the real issue is different from the political issue. In this case, however, the real issue is so superficial as to be embarrassing. What is really at stake is the bass fishing in Lake Ocklawaha. The irony is that the bass fishing would be just as good in the restored Ocklawaha River, and the fishermen could be surrounded by a unique wilderness wetland instead of an ugly, swampy, man-made lake.

Ollie and Me

Confronting Jamie Whitten and the House leadership during my first term was a piece of cake compared with opposing President Reagan, the CIA, and Colonel Oliver North. This occurred during my second term, after I had been reelected with only token opposition. I was appointed to the Foreign Affairs Committee in January 1984. At this time, the mistrust of the CIA's covert activities in Central America was so great that Congress had adopted the Boland Amendment, prohibiting the CIA from spending any money on covert activities aimed at overthrowing the Sandinista government of Nicaragua. In April 1984, the press broke the story that, despite the direct congressional prohibition—and in violation of international law—the CIA had mined the harbors of Nicaragua. In the House, this controversy centered on the Foreign Affairs Committee, and committee members from Florida were under extreme pressure to support President Reagan in his battle against Fidel Castro and Castro's communist friends, the Sandinistas.

I opposed Reagan's policies in Central America, including aid to the Contras. All of Central America was engulfed in an undeclared war. Thousands of innocent civilians were being killed, maimed, and tortured, and no effort was being made to seek a lawful, diplomatic solution. Much of the training, armament, and financing of the Contras was coming from the Reagan White House, in direct contravention of the congressional prohibition. It was patently in violation of the U.S. Constitution, and nobody seemed to care. Haynes Johnson, in his best-selling 1991 book, characterized the 1980s and the Reagan administration as *Sleepwalking Through History.* In my view, the sleepwalkers were in the Congress. President Reagan, through Oliver North and the CIA, had illegally sold missiles and other armaments to our enemy, Iran. The proceeds had been deposited in secret Swiss bank accounts and were being used to finance an illegal effort to overthrow the government of Nicaragua.

My First Junket

My friend Mike Andrews, a member of Congress from Houston, Texas, also opposed Reagan's unlawful actions in Central America, and was getting the same political heat. Mike and I decided to go to Central America to get a firsthand look, but quickly realized our trip could not be an ordinary congressional fact-finding tour put together by the State Department. Other members opposing Reagan who had done this warned us that the only "fact" they found was that the tour had actually been put together by the CIA. Information provided to them had been carefully censored. And the administration circulated information on their return that was designed to embarrass them with their constituents. Mike and I nevertheless decided to go, but arranged to travel on a trip sponsored by the Universalist Unitarian Church, which vigorously opposed the Reagan policy in Central America. The tour leader was a career military officer who had resigned his commission in protest of the unlawful Reagan/Ollie North actions. As an expert on Central America and a patriotic citizen, he did everything he lawfully could to try to expose the actions of the Reagan administration.

Since we were not traveling in an official capacity, Mike and I decided that each of us would invite a trusted friend to go along. The assumption was that we would probably be attacked politically when we returned home, as the others had, and it would be helpful to have a nonpolitical local person to confirm what had really happened. My close friend, Dr. Ed Anderson, agreed to go with me at his own expense. Since we were not sponsored by the State Department, we could not travel on U.S. government aircraft. The only airline flying into Nicaragua was owned by the Sandinistas. They were out of money, and this plane showed it. The Sandinistas had acquired the plane from a Greek airline. It had not even been repainted, and the logo it carried was in Greek. The two-man crew looked like they had come from Greece with the plane as part of the deal. Our fellow passengers were a motley mixture. The only thing they had in common was that many of them had not washed recently. Our plane left Mexico City uneventfully. There was a shortage of fuel in Nicaragua, so the plane stopped for fuel in San Salvador, so that it would have enough fuel for the return trip. No one was allowed to deplane, since El Salvador was technically at war with Nicaragua. When the engines shut down for refueling, the air conditioning ceased. That was difficult enough, but then the crew couldn't get the engines restarted. At the end of the first half hour, the captain reported that the starter on engine number one would not function. At the end of the second half hour, he reported that they had solved the problem, and we would be airborne shortly. They started engine number three. While engine number three was running, they took its starter off and put it on engine number one. The other engines started, the air conditioner resumed its efforts, and we departed, although many of us wondered if we shouldn't have stayed in El Salvador.

In Nicaragua, we found—as the State Department had warned—that the Sandinistas were not the kind of people one would want for neighbors. While they treated Mike and me with respect because of our opposition to U.S. aid to the Contras, they were reluctant to provide us with much information. Our tour guide knew his way around, however, and we were able to talk with ordinary citizens as well as Sandinista troops. The people we interviewed were under no illusions about Daniel Ortega and his top commanders. They viewed them as little better than thugs but still saw them as an improvement over the CIA-sponsored Contras. We went into the field and visited a troop of Contras who were digging in for an expected attack. Despite the patriotic rhetoric of the Cold War, these were not "freedom fighters," but ordinary peasants. Like their counterparts in the Sandinista army, they and their families were caught up in an ideological battle they didn't understand. In each instance, if the head of the family remained neutral, both sides automatically assumed he was sympathetic with their opponents. This meant the chances that he and his family might escape without being tortured or killed were minimal.

We next visited El Salvador, which was in the throes of a long-running civil war. The insurgency, the FMLN, was an umbrella group named after Farabundo Marti, the original leader of El Salvador's revolt against the military junta which had seized power in 1932. In 1984, the FMLN consisted of five center and left of center factions. It included Communists, but the Communists were not the dominant faction. There was evidence of assistance from Castro, but even the CIA briefing officers said that the FMLN was not a front for Castro, or anyone else.

Unlike the Contras in Nicaragua, the FMLN fighters were highly disciplined and motivated. Here, the CIA supported the right-wing government and the insurgent army was the FMLN. They were holding their own, even against modern airpower supplied by the United States.

The Catholic Church in El Salvador was a major force for peace and was trusted by both sides. We were shown two initiatives by the Catholic Church, both of which were profoundly moving. The first was a hospital where people were brought whose legs had been blown off by land mines. Most were children. Both sides were using land mines indiscriminately. After a battle, nobody took the trouble to remove land mines or even document their location. Thousands of people on both sides of the conflict had lost one or both legs, but there were no artificial limbs available in El Salvador and no money to purchase them. U.S. aid only went to fight the insurgents. The church organized an effort, within the hospital, to fabricate rudimentary prosthetic legs. The second church project we visited was a partially completed cathedral which was being used as a sanctuary for displaced families whose villages had been destroyed in the fighting. These families had no place else to go when local church records were destroyed in the violence. Displaced families had no way to prove who they were or where they had lived, and they were automatically suspected by each side of being sympathetic to the opposition. Some families had literally lived in this sanctuary for years, with no hope of survival beyond the boundaries of the church until peace returned. One of my vivid recollections is meeting with groups of children, many of whom had never been outside the walls of the cathedral since the time of their births.

As a postscript, after the conclusion of Reagan's second term, the conflicts in Nicaragua and El Salvador were peaceably concluded. Both the Sandinistas and the FMLN disarmed, and their fighters registered to vote. As of this writing, more than two decades later, Daniel Ortega is now the elected president of Nicaragua, and the Sandinistas are now the governing party. To complete the transition, the candidate of the FMLN was elected president of El Salvador in 2009.

In 1984, when Mike Andrews and I returned to Washington, the next chapter in this story was like a bad dream. Rumors spread that we had traveled in Central America with a group of people who favored Fidel Castro over Ronald Reagan. We later discovered that, unbeknownst to our hosts, the interpreter who accompanied us had been on the payroll of the CIA. My opposition to Reagan's Central American policies earned me the enmity of the Cuban American National Foundation, which spoke for Florida's large Cuban exile community. It also put me on the hit list of such fictitious political action groups as the Friends of Democracy, Friends of Reagan, etc. Full-page newspaper ads began running in my congressional district accusing me of being soft on Communism and friendly toward Fidel Castro. The headline was: "Whose Buddy is he?" Similar ads also ran in districts of Mike Andrews and other congressmen who opposed the illegal covert activities in Central America.

Ollie North Meets Larry Gallagher

Suddenly I found myself running for reelection against a strong opponent, a Republican city commissioner from Leesburg named Robert Lovell. As soon as Lovell announced, well-known national Republican fundraisers started helping him. Within days, he had $50,000 in his campaign account, with more in the pipeline. I could see the hand of

Ollie North everywhere I looked. There was a second Republican candidate, Larry Gallagher, but nobody took Gallagher seriously. Thus far, he had raised only $450, most of which had been spent on pencils to hand out at campaign events. On one side they said, "Elect Gallagher/Buy American." The other side, in small print, said, "Made in Taiwan."

Lovell didn't bother to campaign in the primary. Gallagher was a joke, he said. On the night of the primary vote, Greg Farmer and I were watching election returns. I had been unopposed in the primary, and our main interest was in the governor's race. On the Republican side another Gallagher, Tom, was involved in a hotly contested primary. Tom Gallagher, the candidate for governor, had saturated the Tampa and Orlando markets (the south half of my congressional district) with television ads. Tom Gallagher's ads inadvertently helped Larry Gallagher defeat Bob Lovell for the Republican nomination in Florida's Sixth Congressional District. Many voters thought Larry and Tom were one and the same person. So instead of facing an attack from the right by Bob Lovell, I was facing Larry Gallagher, who still had half his pencils to give out and came at me from the left.

Gallagher's first press interview revealed he was strongly pro-choice. He also volunteered that he had no problems with any kind of sex between consenting adults. As his pencils indicated, he advocated higher tariffs to protect American jobs. He opposed President Reagan's free trade initiatives, and didn't think we should be involved in Central America. In other words, he was as opposed to Reagan and his leadership as I was, although for different reasons. I did my best to keep a straight face during the campaign. I was actually closer to the Republican position than the party's own nominee. Gallagher was indeed a joke, but the butt of the joke was Ollie North. The Republican Party acted like Gallagher did not exist, while Gallagher issued a steady stream of press releases blasting the Republicans for not supporting him. It was a political circus, and I was having a great time watching it.

The final chapter in the strange story of Larry Gallagher began with a full-page newspaper ad paid for by his four children. The headline, in bold letters, said: "Don't vote for Larry Gallagher. He abandoned us and he will abandon you." The text of the ad alleged that Gallagher had been married twice and had abandoned both families. His four children, having been raised in orphanages, felt strongly enough to pay for the anti-Gallagher ad. Gallagher immediately sued the newspaper for publishing the ad. He quickly came to realize that a politician should "never get into a public argument with someone who buys ink by the barrel." The newspaper, of course, followed with a series of stories about the Gallagher lawsuit and about his abandonment of his children. I sat on the sidelines watching this fiasco unfold, knowing full well I would be reelected.

Presbyterian Picketers

One day during my second term, I was scheduled to make comments at the Sunrise Workshop in Lake County and cut a ribbon dedicating a new building. As I got there I realized fairly quickly that I was the target of an anti-abortion demonstration. Rather than disrupt the ceremony, I walked over and introduced myself to the picketers, who were obviously upper-middle-class retirees. One gray-haired lady took me aside and whispered, "We're Presbyterians. We've never picketed anybody before, and we're very nervous. Are we doing it right? Do we look okay?"

Caught off-guard, I said, "I'm Presbyterian, too. I've been picketed quite often. You look fine, and your signs look really good." She said, "What do we do now?" I said, "Just turn around and look at the camera and say whatever you want to say." She looked tremendously relieved, and I was beginning to feel pretty good about the whole affair. But then, she turned to face the camera, pointed her finger at me and shouted "Murderer!"

What made it so bad was that I couldn't even laugh!

Flag Day at Masaryktown

Masaryktown, in Hernando County (population 920), was founded in 1926 by Dominic Voscinar as a center for first generation Czech retirees, and was named after the first president of Czechoslovakia, Tomas Masaryk. I had heard about Masaryktown's unique culture, but now that Hernando County was part of my congressional district, I had the chance to experience it firsthand.

There were two specific times each year when Masaryktown expressed its unique heritage. The best known was the annual Czech folk festival, which culminated in the Chicken Plucking Contest. As congressman, I was fortunately not expected to be part of the Chicken Plucking Contest, but I was an essential part of the second festival, Flag Day, when residents of Masaryktown celebrated their allegiance to their new home, the United States.

The ceremony was to begin with a parade, in which I was to march alongside Uncle Sam and Miss Liberty. The three of us were to be followed by the Knights of Columbus, who had the most splendid uniforms I had ever seen. Each Knight wore a tuxedo with a cape and a hat with plumed feathers like the Three Musketeers. The finishing touch was a ceremonial sword in a silver scabbard, hung across the shoulder of each Knight from a red, white, and blue sash. The first problem on this particular Flag Day was that the parade was rained out. The entire ceremony was to be held inside, beginning with the Knights' formal presentation of the flag. This was done with the Knights standing at attention with swords drawn. Trying to get the long swords out in the narrow corridor without skewering each other involved much of the same lunging, bobbing, and weaving that probably took place back in the days of real sword fighting. Even without enemies, the risk of injury to the Knights was high.

I learned that there is essentially only one message appropriate for Flag Day at Masaryktown. Old Glory proudly waves, reflecting the hopes, dreams, ideals, work, sacrifices, and unity of America. Anyone who doesn't feel the thrill and challenge of this message is an unworthy American, and probably a Communist sympathizer as well. Although that was the only theme at Flag Day, the program featured eleven speakers, and I was the eleventh. By the time I started speaking, even Uncle Sam and Miss Liberty had had enough.

Veterans Day, 1985

One November night in 1985, my wife, Anne, and I attended a candlelight service for POW/MIAs in Belleview. To me, the Vietnam Vets—even with all their problems—were the most touching part of the entire veterans' movement. The thought occurred to me at this ceremony that although their rhetoric was a call to remembrance for their missing comrades, they were the ones being saved by this ceremony. For some of them, their passion for their missing comrades gave them reason to keep on living. In fact, while we were bowed in prayer, I found myself praying for the troubled, bearded, tattooed veterans around me, instead of their missing comrades. What a vivid demonstration of the scars and lasting consequences of that Godforsaken war.

Those guys had been damaged for life, and so had the lives of the people who loved them. And they were really only able to communicate with each other—their colleagues who shared the same experience. Veterans Day used to be the day when we honored our veterans. Because all of us shared in the sacrifice (the theory goes) all of us get to share in the glory. Vietnam was our first war where our young people had to go through the suffering alone, and were then denied the honor of being acknowledged as heroes. What a horrible thing—to literally have to go though hell before you really reach adulthood—and then to come back to a nation that is trying to put the whole experience behind it, like a person trying to get his or her life back together after a nervous breakdown.

Maybe this had to happen to take the glory out of war, leaving nothing but the suffering. For better or worse, we produced a generation of veterans who were rejected by society. Perhaps it was a necessary step in the transition to a nation of peacemakers, but what a loss for these men and women who did nothing wrong but serve their country in an unpopular war.

Each of us defines the people we relate to. We do this subconsciously. When we tell a veteran he is highly honored, we help set him free from the demons of having lived through the hell of modern combat. We aren't able as a nation to set our Nam Vets free, because the only way to do this would be to admit we sat by and allowed our leaders to sacrifice their lives in our names.

Don't Single Anyone Out: Offend Everyone

By the time I ran for my third term in 1986, a high voltage Christian fundamentalist television station affiliated with Pat Robertson had begun broadcasting in my part of Florida. During the campaign, I was picketed throughout my congressional district by a coalition of Right to Life groups. "Christian" picketers were joining hands and praying for my death and the death of my supporters, even at Fort King Presbyterian Church, where I regularly attended. Some of my supporters reacted harshly to the picketers and tried to prevent them from attending my meetings. It was Christian against Christian. My colleagues in Congress marveled. Not many people could start their own holy war.

During this period, the FBI grew concerned at the number of death threats I was receiving. Suddenly, Anne and I had to cope with round-the-clock FBI protection during the ongoing political campaign. I complained to the agent-in-charge that the bureaucratic restraints of the FBI were harder on a candidate than the risk of being shot. His response was classic: "If you get yourself killed on my watch, it will hurt my career!"

In addition to my conflicts with the Right to Life advocates, I was beginning to face opposition from the Washington lobbyists for AARP, who purported to speak for retirees. The tension resulted from my continuing efforts to reduce the budget deficits. Specifically, I had joined with Lawton Chiles to try to reduce the growth in the cost of entitlement programs like Social Security and Medicare. CBS News got interested in this unlikely effort by a member of Congress representing a large retirement population. A crew headed by the well-known CBS reporter, Lesley Stahl, attended my town meeting in The Villages, one of the largest retirement communities in the state. The topic of the discussion, announced in advance, was constraining entitlements. My argument was that the attendees were almost all grandparents, and I assumed they were interested in not leaving their grandkids stuck with an unfair financial burden. The discussion at the town meeting was more positive than I had expected and Lesley Stahl's nationally televised interview was my "fifteen minutes of fame" as a member of Congress. Ironically, while my local constituents appreciated what I was trying to do, the Washington lobbyists for AARP and NARFE (National Association of Retired Federal Employees) saw the interview as proof that I was opposed to the interests and concerns of retirees.

My friend Ted Phelps commented that I was compiling quite a record. Thus far I had offended the White House, the congressional leadership, the Christians, the Cubans, and the retirees. Not bad for a mere two-termer.

The Lincoln Memorial

Most mornings in Washington, I ran or walked on a route from my apartment on Capitol Hill past the Reflecting Pool to the Lincoln Memorial and the Vietnam Memorial. This particular August day was so smoggy that I could barely see the aircraft taking off from National (now Reagan) Airport. As I stopped for a breather at the Lincoln Memorial, it occurred to me that the brooding figure of Lincoln provided a sense of perspective amidst the traffic, tourists, construction, and generally chaotic urban scene around me. In fact, the figure of Lincoln and the Reflecting Pool were the only places of peace as we faced another day in this urban metropolis. The contrasts were so stark that I was amazed I had moved past them so often without noticing.

New construction was everywhere, alongside trees dying from pollution and smog. Lavish expenditures were being made on things of concrete and steel, while homeless people were still there from the previous night sleeping on the grates. Inscribed in large letters inside the Lincoln Memorial are the Gettysburg Address, and also the Second Inaugural Address. Perhaps my education in an Old South public school system had kept me from studying the Second Inaugural. But what a remarkable speech it is. The Civil War had not been concluded, but the Union side was clearly on the cusp of victory, with surrender by the South only a few weeks away. Lincoln concluded his speech with these unforgettable words:

With malice toward none;
with charity for all;
with firmness in the right,
    as God gives us to see the right, let us strive on
to finish the work we are in;
to bind up the nation's wounds;
to care for him who shall have borne the battle,
and for his widow,
and his orphan,
to do all which may achieve and cherish a just, and a lasting peace,
among ourselves,
and with all nations.

The crowd at Lincoln's inauguration had expected arm-waving, tub-thumping triumphalism. When Lincoln was finished, they were stunned. It was the only inaugural address in American history where there was no applause. Another hundred years would pass before Americans would fully appreciate what Lincoln had said.

Congress—The Conclusion

One of Shakespeare's greatest images is that of the tide: "There is a tide in the affairs of men. / Which, taken at the flood, leads on to fortune; / Omitted, all the voyage of their life / Is bound in shallows and in miseries." In politics, riding the tide involves risk, whether the decision is a single vote or an entire campaign. Not every tide leads to greatness. Indeed, from the monumental tides of Brutus' day down to the modest, restrained, cautious tides of modern times, many more adventurers have ended up hurled against the rocks than lifted to the heights of greatness.

Each member of Congress takes considerable risk getting there. Soon, however, we discover that the real life of a member of Congress is not as demanding as it appears. Then, as small increments of institutional power come our way, we discover that we have something to lose by taking a risk. As we gain seniority, the temptation to avoid risk grows each year. Newer members constantly want to try out new ideas. In many cases, their proposals are based on programs that are already working successfully in other settings. Senior members, on the other hand, are risk averse, generally resistant to new ideas, and tend to look with suspicion on programs that originated at the state or local level. The process has a subtle but definite corrupting influence, and one can watch colleagues slowly abandon their idealism, accepting in exchange a minor but secure role in an institution which becomes, as a result, risk averse.

Seniority is thus a paradox. On the one hand, it insulates senior members from pressure. During my time in Congress, no one could take away their chairmanship if they refused to go along with the crowd. But at the same time, seniority becomes an increasingly comfortable cocoon with many perks that provide endless justification for members to avoid risky decisions. The role of the leadership is to balance these conflicting goals. Inevitably, the leadership responds to the senior members. The result of these internal dynamics is an institution mired in the shallows.

Some grow to appreciate the finer aspects of life in the Congress. Good salary, unlimited perks, universal homage, unlimited travel, and cultured and entertaining companionship are important to happiness, and in the eyes of many, goals worth compromising to attain. Others increasingly find it impossible to remain satisfied in a role that looks important, but really lacks in substance. Finally the contradiction becomes so stark they find it impossible to respect either the role they play or the institution which creates and demands the role. I grew disillusioned by relationships which were totally transactional in nature—affection from people who are paid to develop personal relationships and affection for congressmen. Doing favors, and making it appear to be a pleasure, because they need reciprocal goodwill. For me, it was time to move on.

Tough times: the MacKay sawmill in 1936. Courtesy of the author.

Swearing in as a member of the Florida House of Representatives "back before the Earth cooled." Courtesy of the Florida State Archives.

Above: Senator Phil Lewis and Buddy MacKay. Together with Senator Curtis Peterson, we made up the "Select Committee on Ignorance." Courtesy of the author.

Left: Senator MacKay speaking with passion in 1976, while seatmate Pat Thomas reads constituent mail to stay awake. Courtesy of Florida State Archives.

Candidate Bob Graham sings (off key) the Graham Cracker Song. (He governed better than he sang.) Courtesy of the *Ocala Star-Banner*.

MacKay, with trucking lobbyist E. C. Rowell and Jon Shebol after they had been defeated by MacKay and George Sheldon. (Deregulation of trucking.) Courtesy of the author.

Candidate MacKay in the ill-fated 1978 campaign for the U.S. Senate. Courtesy of the author.

Campaigning in the 1978 Gasparilla parade in Tampa. Would you vote for this man? Courtesy of the author.

Campaigning in 1979 with Rosalyn Carter, America's most gracious First Lady. Courtesy of the author.

Campaigning for Congress in a 1982 Fourth of July parade with two other clowns. Courtesy of the author.

Celebrating victory in the 1982 congressional race with Anne and my hometown Guardian Angels. Courtesy of the author.

Making an inspirational speech at the Flag Day in Masaryktown with Uncle Sam and Miss Liberty. Courtesy of the author.

Announcing my candidacy for the U.S. Senate in 1988, with the endorsements of Reubin Askew and Jon Mills. Courtesy of Florida State Archives.

Retiring Senator Lawton Chiles helps out in my 1988 campaign for the U.S. Senate seat he is vacating. Courtesy of the author.

Pushing out frozen citrus trees: a good way to get rid of frustrations after losing the 1988 Senate campaign. Courtesy of the author.

Reubin Askew does his best to make Lawton and me look respectable in 1990. Courtesy of Joe Reilly.

Lawton Chiles with MacKay, Graham, and Reno mystifies a South Florida audience with a "Cracker" saying. Courtesy of the author.

Walking with Lawton and lots of friends in 1990. Courtesy of Florida State Archives.

Watching the 1990 inauguration parade with family. This is as good as it gets. Courtesy of the author.

Campaigning with Meril Stumberger and condo commandos, capturing the straw poll at the 1991 Florida Democratic convention, and sweeping Bill Clinton from unknown to early front-runner. Courtesy of the author.

Chiles and MacKay campaign the old-fashioned way for reelection in 1994. (Lawton loved classical music.) Courtesy of Joe Reilly.

In 1996, our wives finally got both of us cleaned up at the same time. Courtesy of the author.

Celebrating the 104th birthday of one of Florida's heroes, Marjory Stoneman Douglas. Courtesy of the author.

Lawton Chiles with Bob Butterworth, Bob Montgomery, and Bob Kerrigan, announcing the 1997 settlement of the "Joe Camel" tobacco litigation. Courtesy of the *Palm Beach Post*.

MacKay and Dantzler campaigning for governor in 1998. Courtesy of the author.

Even the He-Coon can't salvage my disastrous 1998 campaign for governor.
Courtesy of the author.

Taking the oath as governor of Florida at midnight of one of the saddest days of
my life. Courtesy of Florida State Archives.

Inaugural cannons—pointed the wrong way. Courtesy of the author.

Running for the U.S. Senate, 1987

At the beginning of my third term, I found myself face to face with the realization that there was no way I was going to be a career member of Congress. I was already having to start fundraising for the next campaign, even though the current term had just begun, and the thought of having to run for reelection every two years was discouraging. Even more disheartening was my continuing friction with the Speaker, Jim Wright, and his staff.

Newt Gingrich and a group of "new" Republicans had launched an offensive to discredit Bob Michel, the Republican minority leader, as well as Speaker Jim Wright. They argued that Michel's collegial, nonpartisan style was outmoded and ineffective, and that Jim Wright was corrupt. Gingrich's eventual success led to the destruction of the collegial political culture in Congress. He showed how to win by demonizing anyone who disagreed with him. Both political parties began to divide ideologically. The Gingrich Republicans led the way by attacking and isolating the moderate and centrist Republicans of the Northeast and Midwest. Gingrich and his allies saw these Republicans as nonbelievers who would join with Democrats on issues that they thought would help the nation. Such views and voting patterns were anathema to the new

Republican leadership. As I continued working with Lawton Chiles, the Democratic Budget Group, and outside groups like the Committee for a Responsible Federal Budget, I increasingly felt the same polarizing pressure. In the U.S. Chamber of Commerce's annual ratings, I was shown as too liberal, while at the same time being rated by the AFL-CIO as too conservative. Each side attempted to put pressure on me and others by giving advance notice that certain key votes would be included on their rating charts. The days when moderates from both parties could work toward bipartisan compromise suddenly became a thing of the past.

In 1985, I considered running for governor of Florida. Polls at that time suggested that I would be a formidable candidate for the position. Charlie Whitehead, the chair of the Florida Democratic Party, and a number of other major Democratic players came to Washington to urge me to run. It may indeed have been the right time. Harry Johnston and Steve Pajcic had both already declared, however, and it was difficult to think about running against two of my best friends. I chose to stay out of the 1986 governor's race. Bob Martinez, a Republican, won the election in 1986. Now, in the last months of 1987, Martinez had run into major trouble. During the election, he had committed not to increase taxes. As governor, however, he had changed his position and supported the Democrat-sponsored services tax. When the services tax had become unexpectedly controversial, he had made things worse by again reversing his position and joining the effort to repeal it. Bill Nelson was already campaigning for the 1990 Democratic nomination. Once again, it appeared my chances of victory in the governor's race were promising, and offers of support came my way yet again.

In the midst of these developments, Florida's political world was turned upside down in the autumn of 1987 when Lawton Chiles, an odds-on favorite for reelection to the Senate for a fourth term, suddenly withdrew from the 1988 race. Reubin Askew announced his intention to run and immediately became the leading contender. I opted to support Askew, who I felt would make a major impact on the U.S. Senate.

The 1988 Senate Race

Early in April 1988, I received a phone call from Reubin Askew. He was profoundly disillusioned by the obscenely large amount of money required for the U.S. Senate campaign, and he had decided to withdraw from the race rather than engage in the fundraising that he recognized was essential but that personally offended him. He said he thought I should run, and offered to endorse me. He had already raised more than a million dollars. He intended to return these funds to his contributors with a letter of thanks, but offered to end the letter with a request that the money be contributed to my campaign. He concluded by saying he would delay announcing his plans for two days to give me an opportunity to talk things over with Anne. Needless to say, this was an extraordinarily generous act, as well as a vote of confidence from a person I placed on the same level as LeRoy Collins. Anne, like me, was overwhelmed by Reubin's generosity. We decided to enter the U.S. Senate race, although by this time I had taken preliminary steps to put together a statewide organization for the 1990 campaign for governor.

After the dust had settled following Askew's announcement, reality raised its head. There were fewer than five months before the Democratic primary. Initially, my strongest competitor was the respected congressman, Dan Mica, from West Palm Beach. Then I got a telephone call from insurance commissioner Bill Gunter, in which he informed me that he had once again decided to enter the race. That meant I was facing a vigorous primary campaign, which would culminate in a vote just after Labor Day. It was likely that none of us would win the nomination outright, requiring a six-week runoff campaign. If I emerged as the Democratic nominee, I would then face Republican congressman Connie Mack in a six-week general election campaign. Gunter's entering the primary also meant that after going on the air with television ads for the final four weeks of the primary, I would have to continue the television campaign during the entire period of the runoff. If I won the Democratic nomination, I would enter the six-week general election campaign with no money and a lot of animosity among Democrats from the bruising runoff. On the positive side, I would have considerable momentum and a fully seasoned campaign organization.

Because of the Republican fiasco with Larry Gallagher, the 1988 primary campaign was the first time my congressional voting record was put to the test in a political contest. I had opposed President Reagan's nuclear arms buildup, and had also voted with Lawton Chiles to reduce the rate of increase in the cost of Social Security and Medicare. I had also opposed Reagan's illegal and immoral CIA-sponsored wars in Central America. Now I was competing with Bill Gunter, who was strong in North and Central Florida, while also facing Dan Mica, whose base was in South Florida. Fortunately, the biggest concentration of Democratic voters was the retirees in the high-rise condos of Dade, Broward, and Palm Beach counties. These were predominately educated, well-informed mainstream Democrats who opposed President Reagan. They were comfortable with my voting record, although they found my southern accent hard to understand.

The temptation in Florida politics is to run as a conservative in North and Central Florida, while also running as a liberal in South Florida. The problem is that, although everyone knows the state has a split personality, it is not possible to be on both sides at the same time. Some candidates have tried, but sooner or later the media caught them in the act. Their South Florida speech was recorded and replayed by their opponent before North Florida audiences, and that was the end of their election hopes. Parts of my voting record fit well in each of Florida's geographic regions. Voting to cut budgets was conservative enough for North Florida Democrats, even though the budgets I had voted to cut were Reagan's increased expenditures for nuclear weapons. On the other side of the equation, my opposition to Reagan's illegal war in Nicaragua was taken by South Florida's condo dwellers as evidence that I was a mainstream Democrat. Dan Mica had supported Reagan in Nicaragua. I edged past Mica and into a runoff with Bill Gunter.

In contrast to the primary, where the tone of the campaign had been positive, the 1988 runoff against Gunter quickly turned negative. Having come from far behind to make the runoff, I had the momentum on my side. The Gunter campaign seized on my vote in favor of selling radar surveillance aircraft to Saudi Arabia, and spread the rumor that I was against Israel and probably an anti-Semite as well. AIPAC, the pro-Israel lobby, joined with Gunter, which made things worse. Instead of continuing with the themes from my successful primary campaign, I was suddenly playing defense with only three weeks before the runoff election. On the positive side, an AP writer preparing a story about the runoff asked former governor LeRoy Collins to comment on the race, and Governor Collins endorsed me in very positive terms. I called Governor Collins to thank him and he gave me this advice: "Buddy, you are like me: sometimes you get out so far in front that your troops can no longer see the flag."

My former law partner and close friend, Sam Dubbin, called Michigan Congressman Sandy Levin, one of my colleagues in the congressional class of '82. Both Sam and Sandy were upset that my record was being distorted, and they composed a letter documenting my strong pro-Israel record. It was completed, signed by a dozen well-known Jewish members of Congress, and distributed throughout the Gold Coast condo community, all within three days. Simultaneously, public forums were organized in Miami Beach, Ft. Lauderdale, and West Palm Beach. Congressmen Bill Lehman (Miami), Sandy Levin (Michigan), and Mel Levine (Los Angeles) personally appeared to endorse me and answer questions about the AWACS issue. Sandy and Mel had flown all the way across the country to appear on my behalf, although both were involved in their own reelection campaigns.

The result was that the anti-Israel charge backfired, and my ties to Florida's Jewish community grew stronger than ever. The friendship and loyalty of Sam Dubbin, Bill Lehman, Sandy Levin, and Mel Levine is something I can never repay, but will never forget.

The Dukakis Debacle

Our primary campaign took place alongside the presidential campaign of Democrat Michael Dukakis. Like it or not, in the general election, my name was on the next line down from his on the Democratic side of the ballot. Dukakis made every mistake possible, allowing the campaign of George H. W. Bush numerous opportunities to portray Democrats as ineffective, gutless liberals. Dukakis' opposition to the death penalty and Bush's blatantly misleading "Willie Horton" ad campaign magnified this portrayal. Horton was a convicted felon who committed an armed robbery and rape while on a weekend furlough program that was supported by Governor Dukakis. The Bush campaign attributed this tragedy directly to Dukakis, charging that he was soft on crime.

To cap things off, just as I was emerging bruised and penniless from the runoff, Dukakis' campaign manager held a press conference to announce that the Dukakis campaign was writing off Florida as "hopeless for Democrats" and relocating its Florida staff to Ohio where "things looked more hopeful." Michael Dukakis, a genuinely nice person, has personally apologized several times for this gratuitous act of incompetence on the part of his campaign manager.

One Fool at a Time

While I was slogging through my primary and runoff battles, Connie Mack was in the enviable position of having only one opponent in the Republican primary. That opponent, Robert "Mad Dog" Merkle, was totally ignored by Mack, who won the primary easily with nearly 62 percent of the vote. Having no runoff and money to burn, the Mack campaign began running anti-MacKay ads during the Democratic runoff. Asked by the press whether I was going to respond to Mack while still engaged in the Democratic runoff, I made the comment, "He'll have to wait his turn. I intend to deal with them one fool at a time"! "One Fool at a Time" became the title of a country-and-western song and expressed my frustration in more ways than one.

Compounding my situation, federal law permitted active duty military personnel stationed overseas to declare residency in the state of their choice. Unbeknown to most Floridians, our state, with no income tax and no estate tax, is the chosen "place of residence" for a great many of America's active duty soldiers, even though most of them have no intention of actually living here. During the autumn of 1988, several letters to active duty military officers were sent out over President Reagan's signature, pointing out the importance of the Florida senatorial campaign to America's security and urging Florida's nonresident soldiers to request absentee ballots and vote for Connie Mack. While I won the race among those citizens and active duty soldiers who actually resided in Florida, I lost the overseas military absentee vote by an unprecedented 80 percent to 20 percent margin.

The next set of fools, a group of foreign automobile dealers, raised the money for a last minute independent expenditure of approximately $600,000. They were upset over Democrats' attempts to impose tariffs on imported autos. As a free-trade Democrat, I had voted against these proposals, which meant I had actually sided with the foreign auto dealers. They didn't understand this, however, and opposed me even though I had supported their position. Their money was used to pay for a TV campaign in North Florida featuring the ad, "Hey Buddy, you're a liberal." I had no complaint about the "independent" ad, which had actually been produced by the Mack campaign, but the additional money came in after the deadline for new ads. This meant I had no chance to respond.

When the same ad had been run by the Mack campaign in South Florida, there was some indication that it may have actually helped me. This time, however, the ad ran only in North Florida. Moreover, the huge expenditure was not "independent" in any sense of the word, and this time the ad was concentrated in a relatively small market in the final three days before the polls opened. It really hurt. The only option available to me was to file a complaint with the Federal Elections Commission, which I did. The ruling, a tie vote, was handed down three years later.

One Fool Too Many

The final set of fools with whom I unknowingly had to contend were Florida's local supervisors of elections. Perhaps "fools" is too strong a term, although when we discovered what had happened, I confess I used other terms that were far stronger.

Like Al Gore twelve years later, I discovered this last problem only in the early morning hours following the election. Like Al Gore, I had been declared the winner in all three national news networks, on the basis of statistical analysis of exit poll data. Then, in the early morning hours, all projections were withdrawn, citing "statistical anomalies." The statistical anomalies came about because the voting machines failed to count all the votes that were cast. The next day, Connie Mack was declared the winner by 35,000 votes out of more than 4 million total. As with Al Gore, I was faced with a substantial undercount in Palm Beach, Broward, and Miami Dade, all of which were strongly Democratic counties. In all these counties, local elections officials trying to speed up the voting process had replaced their old, slow, but reliable voting machines with new computerized machines. These same machines in these same precincts were responsible for the same "statistical anomalies" twelve years later. Most recently, Al Gore was deprived of the presidency and America got George W. Bush—a disappointing president to say the least—who actually trailed Gore nationally by half a million votes, but still won the election.

In the Gore fiasco, with Florida's butterfly ballots and hanging chads, the final conclusion was that the machines had simply failed to count the votes. In the 1988 U.S. Senate race, however, that explanation had seemed too simple. In Florida's earlier U.S. Senate election in 1980—a comparable presidential election year—for every one hundred citizens who had voted in the presidential contest in these four counties, three had not voted for a Senate candidate. But in 1988, in these same four counties, fourteen out of every one hundred citizens who voted for president were not recorded as voting in the U.S. Senate race. In the rest of the state in 1988, fewer than one out of one hundred voters for president were recorded as not voting in the U.S. Senate race. I carried the "big four" counties by margins totaling 121,000 votes, but a total of 210,000 votes had *disappeared* in those four counties—being recorded as not voting in the Senate race after having voted for president. If my margin of 55 percent in those four counties had held for 210,000 voters who "disappeared," my statewide margin of defeat would have dropped to about three-tenths of 1 percent, which would have required a mandatory statewide recount. An investigation of the Dade County precinct returns established that the drop-off in Senate voting was more than twice as likely to occur in heavily Democratic areas where blacks and retirees lived. If that was true, the big four drop-off, by itself, could well have resulted in my victory being recorded as a defeat. Sandy D'Alemberte, one of Florida's most respected experts on constitutional law, urged that I file suit in federal court. If I had followed Sandy's advice, I might have been a U.S. senator, and Al Gore might have been spared the same fiasco twelve years later. However, I was exhausted, out of money, and sick at heart, and after a partial manual recount in Palm Beach County, I conceded. My 1988 experience with Florida's bizarre voting machines was spelled out six years later in a feature article in *Campaigns and Elections*, a national magazine. The conclusion of the article was that I had been cheated, but no one could prove it.

Looking back, I have no complaints about the 1988 Senate race. Dukakis, whose name was on the top line of the Democratic ticket, lost Florida by an unprecedented 24 percent margin. Nevertheless, I had almost won. The number of Republicans crossing over to vote for me was roughly equal to the number of Democrats voting for Mack. Politics is a rough business. In fairness, we gave as good as we got. The absentee ballot campaign among the overseas military personnel was perfectly legal. I could only wish the Democrats had been smart enough to compete for this vote. Even with the questionable independent ad campaign, I still would have won the race if all the votes had been counted. What still rankles me is the inaccurate voting machines and the realization that, even after the undercount of Democratic votes in my U.S. Senate race, nothing was done to correct this problem until after the 2000 election. The same undercount in the same Florida precincts cost Al Gore the presidency twelve years later. Worse yet, the same thing could happen again.

The Chiles-MacKay Campaign, 1990

Recruiting Lawton

At the start of 1990, Lawton Chiles was living in Tallahassee, teaching a graduate seminar at the University of Florida. It had been two years since he had retired from the U.S. Senate, where he had served three terms with distinction. I had also "retired" from politics in 1988, after losing the race for Lawton's Senate seat to Connie Mack. I was practicing law as a partner in the Miami law firm, Steel, Hector, and Davis. Bob Martinez, the incumbent governor, was running for reelection with Bill Nelson, a Democratic member of Congress from Melbourne, as his leading opponent.

Polls showed that Martinez was vulnerable because of the services tax fiasco. Politically, however, Martinez was formidable, having demonstrated the ability to raise unprecedented sums for his campaign. The press had written extensively about Martinez's fundraising tactics, which were cynically known as "Pay to Play." The thesis, which had originated with Martinez's campaign manager, Mac Stipanovich, was that anyone wanting to do business with the state of Florida was expected to make a substantial contribution. Instead of challenging the Pay to Play concept,

Nelson's campaign advisors had adopted the same approach. The result was that both Martinez and Nelson had amassed substantial campaign war chests well ahead of the time for active campaigning.

In early January, Bob Joffee, Florida director of the Mason-Dixon poll, acting on his own, included my name as part of the potential field of Democratic candidates for governor. I was projected a 48 percent to 38 percent favorite over Governor Martinez. In the primary, I was projected at 38 percent to 18 percent over Bill Nelson, with George Stuart and Alcee Hastings at 11 percent and 6 percent respectively. Somehow, this news didn't fire me up, after the disillusioning loss to Connie Mack. In addition my finances were still in shreds. Our family's citrus groves had been destroyed in the disastrous freezes of the 1980s, and I was scrambling to pay my creditors. Joffee and Jim Krog, ignoring my protests, leaked the Mason-Dixon poll results to the *Tampa Tribune*. Nelson was well liked, but many Democrats felt he couldn't win.

At the end of February, Krog and others started pushing the idea of a Chiles-MacKay ticket. They argued that Chiles and I felt passionately about the same issues, and that I could play a significant role as his running mate. They also argued that the risk to my fragile finances would be significantly reduced. On March 2, I made an unpublicized trip to Tallahassee to talk to Lawton and his wife, Rhea. Both of them had already reached the conclusion that the corrupting influence of big-money campaigns and the Pay to Play schemes needed to be made the central issue in Florida politics. If we could win on this issue, we might be able to achieve public financing reform of campaigns in Florida. Lawton and Rhea had some personal concerns, but we all agreed we should at least think it through. A week later, Lawton called and cancelled a second meeting. He said he was afraid he had been too high emotionally, and he didn't trust himself. He had been battling depression and feared he wouldn't be able to handle the stress of a statewide campaign.

Near the end of the month I met in Washington with Tom Foley, the newly elected Speaker, and Dick Gephardt, the new majority leader, who assured me a seat on the Ways and Means Committee if I would campaign for my old congressional seat. This had been an impossible dream during the speakership of Jim Wright, where I had been treated as an outsider and a troublemaker.

Early in April, Sandy D'Alemberte and I went to Bradenton and met with Lawton and his close friend, Wilbur Boyd. Lawton said he had decided we should run as a team. In order to make campaign finance reform the central issue, he wanted to limit our contributions to the same limit he had imposed in his original statewide race—$100 per person. I agreed, although this would greatly increase our risk of defeat. We would enter the governor's race with less than five months remaining before the primary and only seven months before the general election. Both Bill Nelson and the incumbent, Bob Martinez, had already raised several million dollars. We were starting from zero, and would be limiting our contributions to $100 or less. The Tallahassee Democrat called us Butch Cassidy and Sundance Kid because of Lawton's audacious fundraising plan. Most readers thought the label was a reference to our willingness to take big risks. At least one person opined, however, that the label should stick because we were a couple of bandits. We announced on April 12th at noon, after having been endorsed—before announcing—by the *Tallahassee Democrat* and the *Palm Beach Post*. I had the feeling nothing would ever be normal again.

The 1990 Campaign Begins

Lawton's most recent campaign had been his 1982 Senate reelection effort eight years earlier. As a consequence, his campaign lists were badly out of date and would have to be rebuilt from the ground up. I had run a U.S. Senate race only eighteen months earlier. My phone lists were current, I still had all my campaign computers, my software programs complied with current law, and my campaign staff was ready to go.

What we had not anticipated was the immediate need to state Lawton's positions on abortion and other hot-button issues of 1990. Lawton had not been in a close political race since abortion had become such a dominant issue, and he found himself torn between family and church, on the one hand, and the pro-choice position of the Democratic Party on the other. I had always been pro-choice, and argued strenuously that the best position was simply to say: "I'm pro-choice." I felt that was the right position, from a philosophical, moral, and political point of view. We agreed that I would put together a pro-choice position paper, and we would revisit the issue the next day. To my surprise, the next morning Lawton still hesitated. It turned out that Lawton's friend, Dr. James Dobson, had sent his top preacher on Dobson's private jet to counsel with Lawton overnight. After more intense debate, Rhea proposed, as a compromise, that our position include the requirement that parental consent would be required in the case of abortions for minors. Lawton was still uncomfortable with the issue, and his sincere concern was apparent throughout the campaign.

As soon as it became public knowledge that I had agreed to be Lawton Chiles's lieutenant, I began to receive cryptic messages from longtime Chiles people. Tom Staed, a respected hotel owner from Daytona Beach who had been the Chiles finance chair in every campaign back to 1970, was typical. His first words were: "Welcome to the gang that can't shoot straight"—a reference to a humorous movie about a fictitious gang of bumblers.

Chaos at Bill Thomas Chevrolet

Every campaign has a couple of war stories, but this campaign was different from the very first day. Word had leaked that, after two years in retirement, Lawton Chiles was thinking about entering the governor's race. Contributions started pouring in, even before we formally announced. This presented a unique problem, because the law required checks to be deposited within twenty-four hours of receipt, and we had no headquarters, no campaign, no campaign manager, and no phones, not even a mailbox! The campaign headquarters problem seemed to miraculously solve itself. Bill Thomas, a Republican Chevrolet dealer, called and offered his almost-vacant dealership facility as our headquarters. It was a modern, well-located facility with lots of phones and plenty of parking. All we had to do was move in.

Next we met to decide on a campaign manager. When we could not agree on who that should be, Lawton said, "That's no problem. Campaign managers don't matter that much. Let's rely totally on volunteers. I've always wanted to see how that would work." I remember thinking: "This is going to be interesting to watch." The third challenge emerged when we moved into the new campaign headquarters. Bill Thomas had neglected to mention that while his new car business had moved, his used car business would remain in place until his new facilities for used cars were completed. It was too late to turn back. Checks were coming in by the bushel—from as little as $1, up to Lawton's limit of $100. Our opponents sought to embarrass us by sending in $10 checks from Fido Smith (occupation: dog), Tweetie Jones (occupation: canary), and Buster Brown (occupation: kindergarten). Our volunteer committee ignored the identity of the contributors, recorded the data, and deposited the checks. Needless to say, the press had a field day at our expense. We then set up a separate Volunteer Committee on Sending Money Back. I was told that a form letter was developed: "Dear Fido: Thank you for your help, but we regret we must refund your contribution. It appears you are a dog. If you are not a dog, please send the money again along with a photo or other ID."

Then there was the issue of the phones. The car dealership was essentially like all car dealerships—one huge room with cubicles, or closing rooms, strategically scattered about. Phones were constantly ringing as people and press called about everything from our position on the death penalty to banning thong bathing suits. On top of everything else, there was the constant, loud interruption of the dealership intercom: "Bill, pick up line six!" Depending on how many volunteers we had named Bill, line six would either be answered "Chiles MacKay," or "Thomas Chevrolet." Lawton opined that this shouldn't be a problem. Used car salesmen, he said, were probably better able to handle political questions than political volunteers were at selling used Chevys. I took one prominent political editor on a tour of our operation, and he said, "This is sheer genius. You've thrown everybody completely off the track. What I want to know is, where is the real headquarters?"

Garbage Out

I was at our "dealership" headquarters every day for several weeks, alternately laughing or totally stressing out. A volunteer came in each day and gave foot massages to relieve stress. Nobody was focusing on raising money or scheduling the candidates, which is what I had always thought campaigns were all about. On the other hand, the Florida press was intrigued. Every day, we were in the newspapers and on nightly news. Checks were pouring in because Lawton's denunciation of "Pay to Play" campaign financing resonated with the people. We adopted the slogan: "This time the people win!" Each new poll showed we were gaining strength. My close friend, former campaign manager and chief of staff, Greg Farmer, called and said: "I don't know what you're doing, but it's working. For goodness sake, don't start campaigning, or you'll screw everything up!"

After several weeks' delay, our computer experts were ready to send out our first fundraising letter. To do this, they had had to merge the Chiles database with the MacKay database. Both were sophisticated lists set up to allow each potential contributor to be addressed by his first name, or even a nickname. Lawton's list was eight years out-of-date, so it had to be purged of names of people who had died or moved away. What made it particularly complicated was that one list was part of an Apple system, while the other was IBM, and the two were incompatible. Two hurried and frustrating weeks went by with nothing happening. Finally, with much jubilation, the merged lists were sent to a contract mailing house. Bentley Lipscomb, our computer expert, called me late the next night. To calm his nerves, he had gone over to the mailing house for one last look. What he found was 250,000 personal letters signed by Lawton and me, already printed, folded, stuffed, and stamped. All that remained was sealing and mailing. The first letter Bentley pulled and checked began: "Dear 32671:" Bentley looked further and found this same salutation on one in every hundred letters. Bentley and I decided if we waited and took two more weeks to straighten this out, the fundraising letters would arrive after the primary, so we went ahead. The solicitation was a big success, although a number of the checks we received were signed

"32671." When I related this story to Tom Staed, he said: "I told you it would be like this. Welcome to the gang that can't shoot straight."

Lawton: Root-Canal Politics

From a substantive side, being Lawton's lieutenant was not a new experience. On budget issues, I had effectively been his lieutenant for six years in the Congress. When I arrived in the Congress in 1982, Lawton had already been in the Senate since 1970. He was highly respected by his colleagues in both parties, having launched the effort to reform the budget process in his role as chair of the Senate Budget Committee. As a member of the House Budget Committee, I often played the role of emissary when the proceedings became adversarial between the House and Senate. Not only had Lawton and I become friends, but we had similar political views regarding the budget mess and our responsibilities to taxpayers. Working with Lawton on federal budget issues, I learned quickly that trying to balance the budget was neither sexy nor popular. Many people referred to the effort as root-canal politics.

There have been a few superficial observers who have argued that Lawton Chiles wasn't a very effective U.S. senator because he received little attention or credit for the work he did in the U.S. Senate. The truth is, from 1970 to 1988, he led the efforts to pass the Congressional Budget Act, reduce deficit spending, and implement campaign finance reform—three of the most far-reaching congressional reform initiatives of the latter part of the twentieth century. I admired him, both as a person and a political leader. In many ways, he was my role model.

Dueling Fundraisers

After trying for several days to make sense out of the campaign headquarters, Wilbur Boyd, Lawton's closest friend, decided to concentrate his energies on fundraising, the area where we faced major problems. Without telling any of us, Wilbur hired a person to help him, locked himself in a room away from the chaos, and started a full-time telephone campaign: "I get them on the phone, and it takes me half an hour to work them up to a peak. Then I ask them to take four weeks off and do nothing but call people for money. I tell them I'm going to check on them, and they must send the money directly to me, to make sure they get credit toward their membership in the 'Fifty-Five Club.'"(No one knew what the Fifty-Five Club was, and Wilbur was too busy to take time out to explain.)

At the same time Wilbur was launching the Fifty-Five Club, Dean Saunders, a longtime Chiles staffer with extensive contacts in all parts of the state, was hired to do fundraising "the way Charlie Canady always did it" (Charlie Canady had been Lawton's longtime chief of staff, as well as his campaign manager). Canady's method consisted of having books of ten tickets printed up, and delivering these books to each county's "Chiles People." Each county was given a fundraising quota, and a date was set for the county rally. This made a lot of sense, particularly in small rural counties. It set deadlines, got a handle on accountability, and generated a campaign schedule. Once this system was set up, Dean simply got on the phone, called his county contacts, and asked, "How many tickets have you sold?" Dean was not aware of Wilbur's parallel effort. As a matter of fact, neither were we.

From my point of view, a campaign should focus on the places where the voters are. As a result, I had always campaigned primarily in Florida's heavily populated urban counties. If there was time, I traveled to the rural counties, but if not, I relied on surrogate speakers and media in the small counties. I assumed everyone did it this way. By the time I found out about Dean's ticket book method of fundraising, we were locked into a system which allocated time equally between counties, regardless of population. As an example of what this meant to our campaign schedule, Florida is a very elongated state with a total of sixty-seven counties. In 1990, the smallest thirty-four of these had a combined population of somewhere around 4 percent of the state's total population; but we were locked into a system that assured at least one day of our time in each county. In a "normal" campaign of two or three years' duration, this might make sense. But we had less than five months before the primary!

Wilbur was calling from a list that included every person who ever gave Lawton a contribution. One of the first people he contacted was Bob Fletcher, a union retiree in Lake County who told Wilbur he had never made a fundraising call in his whole life. At the end of Wilbur's half hour, Bob enthusiastically agreed to raise $30,000. Naturally, the first people he called were the Chiles regulars in Lake County, all of whom were waiting for their ticket books to come in the mail. Wilbur was too busy to waste time talking to us, so Dean and I were left wondering how many other people Wilbur had called and what commitments had been made regarding the Fifty-Five Club. In the absence of a campaign manager, Dean and I took the problem to Lawton, who said in his usual phlegmatic way, "I guess you'll just have to straighten it out."

Inner Voices

During the chaotic early weeks of the campaign, Lawton was relaxed and almost mystically confident. He delighted in telling the press that he took long walks in the woods, because that is where he heard his "inner voices." I tried to finesse this entire issue by saying what Lawton really meant was that he liked to commune with nature. The issue would almost go away, when Lawton would once again tell reporters about his inner voices, after which another round of humorous articles would appear. Early interviews and questions by editorial boards went as well as could be expected, until our opponents began asking questions about Lawton's health. There were rumors that his retirement from the U.S. Senate had been related to recurring bouts of depression, and he was repeatedly asked about his health. I had not given this much thought, having worked with several congressmen and senators who occasionally used antidepressants. The pressure and chaotic demands of a congressional career made the periodic use of antidepressants a reasonable precaution.

As luck would have it, 1990 was the year that America's perennial drug-related hysteria focused on Prozac, the widely prescribed antidepressant. Lawsuits were popping up across the country based on allegations that the use of Prozac had resulted in several suicides. Lawton was using Prozac, a fact that would have been revealed if his medical records were released. The first major crisis of the campaign occurred when Lawton refused to release his medical records. The matter seemed to be resolved when Lawton authorized the press to look at his records in the presence of his physician. Lawton's physician, low-key, articulate, and thoroughly professional, did a stellar job of explaining the Prozac issue so that common folks could understand. Without giving a lecture, he explained what periodic clinical depression is, and how antidepressants work. What the physician did not say and what we did not know was that midway through the primary, without telling anyone, Lawton had started feeling upbeat, and had decided to stop taking Prozac.

What we subsequently learned is that with Prozac, any change in dosage takes weeks to become effective. In our case, there weren't many weeks before the primary, and half of them were gone before we realized we had a problem. The occasion was the day of the last debate before the primary. Lawton wasn't interested in the issue briefing and seemed almost totally disengaged. Rhea's advice to us was to leave him alone. "He'll be all right," she assured us. So Lawton's debate prep that day was a long walk in the woods, listening to his voices. He got through the debate reasonably well. His answers were occasionally rambling and vague, but no worse than those of his opponents. In the days following the debate, however, he suddenly lost energy and became withdrawn. The campaign adjusted, reducing Lawton's schedule and keeping him away from the press.

Everyone in the leadership of the campaign was concerned. After some prodding, Lawton visited his physician and the truth came out. At his doctor's insistence, Lawton resumed taking Prozac. That was the good news. The bad news was nobody could predict how long it would be before the antidepressant took hold, and then there was the matter of getting the dosage right.

Misadventures abounded in this early phase of the campaign, but fortunately the momentum was on our side. Lawton was better known and more trusted statewide than his principal rival, Bill Nelson. Chiles-MacKay swept to victory in the primary.

Starting Over

The following week was like starting all over. Lawton was not persuaded that we needed to be in a hurry to do anything. We had endless strategy sessions, with up to sixteen volunteers participating. The *Miami Herald* had a helpful editorial that opined that if Lawton and I managed to lose this race, it would be because of our failure to act decisively and lay out a platform before Martinez's ad people started the heavy artillery.

But Lawton was unmoved. Here is an example of one of his press interviews:

Q: "What are your main criticisms of Governor Martinez?"
A: "That will all come out in the next few weeks."
Q: "Don't you think it's time to start the attack?"
A: "There's plenty of time. You worry too much."
Q: "I'm not worried, but shouldn't you worry, with polls showing the governor pulling even with you?"
A: "We expected that, with all the money he's spending on TV."
Q: "But that's the point. He can outspend you, three to one. Don't you have to be more aggressive in getting your message out?"
A: "We trust the people. It worked out OK in the primary."
Q: "What about abortion?"
A: "I don't intend to make an issue out of it."
Q: "But it is an issue. It has been an issue for ten years."
A: "I'm not comfortable bringing it up."
Q: "Well, what is your position on abortion? Polls show many women don't know."
A: "They know. You worry too much."

The only person more frustrated than the reporter was me. The week of September 21, reality crashed the party. A Mason-Dixon poll reported that the race was tied, at 45 percent to 45 percent, a significant improvement for Governor Martinez. This was followed by the onset of Martinez's first negative television barrage. It pounded away at the votes Lawton and I had cast to restrain the escalating costs of Social Security and Medicare. The ad was very effective in retirement communities across the state. As usual, Florida's press reinforced the impact of the paid ads by reporting at length on the "strength of the buy" (unprecedented), the strategy and effectiveness of the ads (clever), and our probable tactics in response (no clue). The part about our response was totally accurate. We had no clue what we were going to do next. The campaign had not hired a media consultant because Lawton didn't trust consultants. Frank Greer, my friend who had been the media consultant in my 1988 campaign, had one theory, and various volunteer experts had others. As Tom Staed pointed out, it really didn't matter. We didn't have enough money to run television ads, even if we were able to agree on what to say. One good thing came out of it: The sense of complacency vanished like the morning fog.

That Thursday, Lawton was scheduled to give the keynote speech to the annual conference of the Florida Association of County Commissioners. Close to 1,000 people, most of whom were our friends, planned to be there. Wednesday night was set aside for speech preparation. Only those persons actually involved in campaign strategy were to be included. In my mind, this should have been limited to Lawton, Rhea, Jim Krog (now officially designated as campaign manager), Ron Sachs (hired as speechwriter), and me. But Lawton decided to invite everyone who had suggested a particular theme for Tuesday's speech. At the meeting at 9 p.m., Wednesday, before his Thursday morning speech, we had more than a dozen people, each with his or her own "great idea for a speech," and five different drafts of speeches. When I expressed my frustration with this process, Lawton opined that we'd just have to "mix and match." The meeting adjourned. I decided it was time for at least one double scotch, and found myself philosophizing with Bentley Lipscomb, a longtime staff director for Lawton. Bentley's advice was not to worry. He said, "I've been here before. When he's ready, he'll make the speech he wants to make. He trusts his own instincts, and doesn't like to rely on strategists, consultants, and speechwriters."

Sequel: Lawton was at the top of his game that Thursday morning. He mixed, matched, joked, and ad-libbed one of the best speeches of the campaign. He began by outlining our basic indictment of the corrupting impact of "Pay to Play" fundraising, and then laid out the basic thesis of David Osborne's book, *Reinventing Government*: Florida's options were not simply liberal or conservative. There was a third way which involved decentralizing, downsizing Florida's centralized bureaucracies, and adapting many of the ideas being used successfully by America's new, more entrepreneurial businesses. These same ideas and techniques were already being utilized at the local government level, and many of Florida's new innovators were in the audience. This was the perfect theme for the occasion, and the speech was a major success. As Bentley had said, Lawton's poker-faced demeanor and appearance of unconcern during the speech preparation was all part of the game. Lawton had enough self-confidence to disregard campaign advisors and rely on his inner voices, just like he said.

Listening, Then Going Silent

During the week of September 28th, we devoted much of our time trying to express the details of the *Reinventing Government* theme in a way that would appeal to ordinary citizens. It was easy to capture the negative. Everybody had a horror story about bureaucratic inertia and waste. Making the case for change was more difficult. Even Lawton had trouble talking about reinventing government without sounding academic. After numerous false starts, I proposed that we find the best new ideas in local government, the volunteer community, and the private sector, and hold campaign events with Lawton, Rhea, and me visiting those programs and discussing their potential for state government. We called this idea "listening to the people." It was the most unorthodox—and many thought the dumbest—campaign plan of modern times.

The typical political event is designed to attract television reporters at no cost to the campaign, reveal the candidates interacting with the public, and be sufficiently interesting to make the evening news. The theory is simple: "If it ain't on television, it didn't happen." Our first "listening to the people" session was half a day at the Tampa Housing Authority. Three television crews showed up, stayed half an hour, and left noisily. We didn't make the evening news. Our second session involved another half day in West Palm Beach listening to an explanation of a dropout prevention program called Cities in Schools. No television crews showed up, and even the print reporters assigned to travel with our campaign boycotted the event. One reporter confided to our press aide, "This campaign is as boring as a two horse apocalypse. If you want any press coverage at all, you'll have to come up with a totally different plan."

Meanwhile, the Martinez campaign rolled out its second barrage of negative ads: "No matter what they try to tell you now, both Lawton Chiles and Buddy MacKay voted to cut Social Security." I told Lawton I was really nervous. Somehow, we had to set the record straight on Social Security before the opposition defined our position with senior voters. Lawton smiled and said there was no need to worry. He could feel the momentum of the campaign shifting in our direction. Despite Lawton's reassurance, I worried enough for both of us. We had enough money to pay for four weeks of statewide television advertising. The problem was that six and one-half weeks remained before election day. This meant we would have two and one-half weeks without paid television. Free media became more important than ever.

A Birthday Party on NPR

Midweek, I was told we had made it big time: National Public Radio was doing a major segment on our unorthodox campaign on All Things Considered. I was momentarily ecstatic until I discovered that NPR, without informing us, had sent a reporter to a birthday party for a couple named Mildner, where I was scheduled to represent Lawton.

Harry and Pauline Mildner lived in a high rise condo on North Miami Beach. They were Democratic leaders in the land of the condo commandos. A condo development like theirs was nearly large enough to have its own state representative. Earlier in the year, when it had appeared Governor Martinez was going to coast to a second term, Al

Gutman, the local incumbent member of the Florida House of Representatives, had switched to the Republican Party. Now that Lawton was leading, Gutman knew he had to do something special to make it right, so he sent a band to provide live music to the Mildners' birthday party rally. There was only one catch: The band refused to perform unless Harry and Pauline played Gutman's campaign video first.

An argument broke out. Since everyone in attendance was a Democrat, they resented Gutman's people trying to show his Republican video, especially since he had failed to come in person. The bandleader was adamant. The band wouldn't play unless the Gutman video was shown first. Pauline attempted to bring peace by suggesting the birthday cake be served while Gutman's video was being shown. The entire crowd made a break for the cake, so there was a riot (or as near as you can get to a riot when a majority of the participants are over eighty).

Not to be outdone, the bandleader said, "Watch the video," and turned the video sound track up wide open to try to out-compete the cake fight. I had to leave then, and Harry banged on a glass and wished Chiles-MacKay good luck with the campaign. Someone shouted, "Who is Charles MacKay?" NPR ran their piece, and deadpanned that America should watch this race. It could be the politics of the future. That was our free NPR media for the week!

An Up—and More Downs

Polls during this campaign were all over the map, and gave no one confidence in the outcome. More encouraging for our sake were the numerous campaign contributions that came from working class Floridians. Contributions first came in a trickle, then in a torrent. There were batches of $100 checks from average folks, anxious about the future of their state. As news of our increasing momentum appeared in press reports, people we hardly knew were calling, saying things like: "I have $30,000 in checks, all delivered by the lobbyist for X, who controls healthcare in X county. He wants to 'come to the foot of the cross' (i.e., repent). What shall I tell him?" Lawton's response was that we didn't want his money. What a great feeling of freedom! After it became clear we were not going to empower patronage bosses in each urban area, many of those whose "bundled" checks had been sent back now sent their own separate contributions, often with personal notes saying they appreciated not being coerced to contribute to a campaign for the first time in their memory.

I attended a fundraising event in Punta Gorda during the week of October 3rd, where I was introduced by Vernon Peeples, a member of the House from Charlotte County. Vernon, a longtime friend, is the kind of plainspoken person not often found in politics. The following is my recollection of Vernon's introductory remarks: "The Florida Constitution didn't provide for a lieutenant governor from 1868 to 1968. During those one hundred years, nothing happened which would lead a normally intelligent person to believe we needed a lieutenant governor. Since the constitutional revision of 1968, we've had a lieutenant governor, but still nothing has happened to make people think it's something we've always needed." At that point, I started laughing, along with most of the audience. Realizing he had painted himself into a corner, Vernon reversed direction, ending up opining that if anyone could make the office of lieutenant governor amount to anything, it would be his friend, Buddy MacKay.

October 7th was my blackest day during the campaign. That morning, a reporter asked our views on teaching creationism in the public schools. Lawton ducked the question, saying that the decision was up to the local school boards. I said I was opposed to teaching creationism in the schools, although people I respected strongly supported it. Matters of faith should be taught in the home and the church. The reporter, sensing I was willing to step into his trap, said, "What if a majority of the school board believes in creationism?" I responded: "A lot of people believe the world is flat, but that doesn't mean we should teach that in school." Lawton said: "You're on your own. Good luck." I didn't give it much thought until I got a call from the press later in the day. Seven fundamentalist preachers had held a press conference demanding an apology for my remarks linking creationism to flat world thinking. My comments, they declared, "showed disrespect and a lack of sensitivity for the religious beliefs of others." I wanted to fight, but my advisors said this is a political campaign—cut your losses. I apologized for my lack of sensitivity, and then faced two days as the straight man in phone call discussions with Christian radio stations. As Lawton had promised, I was on my own.

The week of October 18th, the Florida Council of Churches published a letter saying I should not have apologized to Pat Robertson's group for my creationism/flat world remarks. The letter, signed by clergy from several mainstream Protestant denominations, said the real issue is that religious beliefs should not be taught as science in the schools. Of course, the press did not pick up on this letter. My troops had taken the field a week after the battle had ended.

Rallying to a Victory

We celebrated Panhandle Day with Senator Sam Nunn of Georgia and an entourage of twenty-eight people later that month. This event had been a dream of Lawton's from the beginning of the campaign. The day included a total of eight stops across North Florida's sparsely populated "Panhandle," with a bluegrass band in the lead, followed by a sound truck and a flatbed semitrailer. The sound truck drove through each downtown half an hour ahead to drum up a crowd. Small crowds, small towns, and lots of fun! No television.

That Sunday, Anne and I went to Miami for a major breakfast of bagels and lox for a thousand Jewish condo dwellers. Janet Reno—then the state attorney for Miami—was the headline speaker, and we were endorsed by the legendary Annie Ackerman, the original condo commando. Then I met with black leaders, then Cuban-American Democrats, and finally with the leadership of Florida's significant Hindu community. I found myself contrasting Miami politics with the politics of the Panhandle. Miami's ethnic politics is more like the politics of Boston or Chicago, while the Panhandle counties still reflect the traditions of the Old South. Most political experts now assumed that we were we going to win, and many thought Lawton's coattails would bring a Democratic sweep. The day ended in West Palm Beach, with Merril Stumberger and her condo troops. One of them, Joe, dragged Anne and me from table to table: "Meet Buddy MacKay, Florida's next lieutenant governor, and Anne, his next wife!"

Back at Bill Thomas Chevrolet the next day, the disorganization was so bad that Anne had to get me out to keep me from losing my cool. Nothing had changed: it had only become noisier and more crowded. The next day was to have been spent in preparation for the debate, but as usual, there were sixteen advisors and Lawton decided to go listen to his voices in the woods. This time the voices must have been as confusing as the advisors. Lawton didn't do particularly well in the debate. Unrelated to the debate, but still troubling, our nightly tracking poll showed a precipitous drop in our numbers. Our pollster, Geoff Garin, was one of the few political consultants whom Lawton trusted. Geoff had done the polling in my 1988 race against Connie Mack, and had continued working even when my earlier campaign had run out of money to pay him. His advice was straightforward, and he had an unusual understanding of Florida politics. In this case, Geoff felt that our declining support was a direct result of the cumulative impact of Martinez's negative attack ads. Lawton's instinct was that our issues would ultimately prevail, and we decided to stay with our plan despite the effectiveness of Martinez's negative attacks.

On November 1, we held a half-day roundtable meeting to summarize the lessons learned while listening to voters. I remember thinking: "Here we are, five days from election day. The participants lack a clear understanding of what we're doing. The press continues to be bemused." The first of November was also the fundraising deadline. Believe it or not, we had raised a total of $5 million, and could be competitive with Martinez in communicating our message on television. After a long and passionate discussion, we thought we had convinced Lawton that negative attack ads were not immoral as long as (a) they were responding to an ad attacking us, and (b) they were factually accurate. Based on this understanding, I authorized the immediate release of a series of hard-hitting attack ads, which ran that night. The next day's tracking polls showed us in much better shape (10 percent lead and gaining momentum). Obviously, we had misunderstood Lawton's position. He was upset that we had run negative attack ads, and insisted on producing his own ad. A big flurry of phone calls followed, with my friend and media consultant, Frank Greer, saying he would do everything possible to get Lawton's ad on the air. (He later said that Lawton relaxed when it became apparent we were not trying to manipulate him.)

Lawton and I separated at noon the Saturday before the election. He went to Miami for a Cuban rally, followed by a "father/son" rally at Ft. Myers. For my part, I spoke to a large crowd at a men's breakfast in a North Broward County synagogue, campaigned at a Miami Dolphins game, and finally went to the Sanford airport for a one-minute live shot on the statewide evening news. Election day was quiet until the big party at the Orlando Marriott World Center, where the evening was over almost as soon as it began. The networks projected Lawton as the winner five minutes after the polls closed, and Martinez conceded at 9 p.m. Lawton's victory speech mixed and matched, ending with: "If we all work together, we might bring back Camelot."

The Chiles-MacKay Administration

The First Term

Lawton's inauguration speech was one of his best, summarizing the themes of the campaign. The crowd, most of whom had been actively involved in the campaign, was large and enthusiastic. The inauguration ceremony was uneventful, with one major exception: unbeknown to us, the National Guard, in planning the ceremonial nineteen-gun cannon salute, had been denied the traditional placement site for their cannons by some obscure capitol bureaucrat. The closest bureaucratically acceptable site was almost a quarter-mile distant. Miffed at this indignity, and worried that their cannons would appear less than majestic, the Guard's ceremonial cannon detachment had unilaterally decided to aim their guns directly toward the capitol. What they had not taken into account was the dramatic impact of the muzzle blast from large-bore cannons at little more than point-blank range. As the barrage began, combat veterans in the crowd scrambled, as if to get under chairs. On the podium, dignitaries flinched. National Guard generals had facial expressions that plainly said, "Oh . . . . . . !" The comment was made: "I don't know how the remainder of the Chiles-MacKay term will go, but it certainly started out with a bang!"

The bureaucratic cannon fiasco served admirably as a symbol of our first year. The situation in the governor's office was just like that at our campaign headquarters at Bill Thomas Chevrolet. Former Chiles staffers moved from Washington to Tallahassee, found a chair and a desk, and resumed the roles they had played in Washington. Within the governor's office itself were numerous workers—mostly appointed by Governor Martinez—who were doing many of the jobs necessary to keep the office functioning smoothly. Each of these people had good reasons why he or she should be continued. Making vigorous counterarguments were our own staffs and campaign workers.

I tried to stay out of the chaos in the governor's office. My initial challenge was to make sense out of the agencies of the executive branch. Some agencies, under the Martinez administration, had become accustomed to working directly with their own patrons in the Democrat-controlled legislature. The Department of Environmental Regulation, for example, had become accustomed to working out its own program with Senator George Kirkpatrick, from Gainesville. One of my early challenges was to convince Kirkpatrick, a friend and influential leader in the state Senate, that the DER would actually function more efficiently if we managed it as part of the executive branch. It was not easy. We had to pretend not to notice that a couple of the smaller programs continued to report to Kirkpatrick instead of us.

Our entire first year in office was spent trying to stay off the rocks of fiscal insolvency. Florida's fiscal year begins the first of July, and a new governor "inherits" the last six months of his predecessor's final budget. Three days after Governor Chiles took office, he presided over a cabinet meeting where he had to cut the general revenue budget by 5 percent. The problem was, we were already six months through the fiscal year, so it took a proportionately larger reduction for the last half of the fiscal year to achieve an annualized 5 percent cut. Because of a worsening economy, that situation occurred three more times before we got through Bob Martinez's final budget year. All told, Lawton made four budget cuts in our predecessor's last budget before we got to July first of our first calendar year. In six months, $1 billion had been cut out of a $30 billion budget. Our programs were in a state of uncertainty, and our state employees were demoralized. At the end of six months in office, we introduced our first budget, which started a billion dollars lower than the final Martinez budget. Ninety days after we adopted this new budget, it had to be cut by an additional $600 million. Mind you, we had still only been in office a total of nine months, and we had already cut Florida's budget more than any governor in Florida's history up to that time.

To make matters worse, during the same period we cut $1.6 billion from the state budget, 250,000 more people (including 100,000 children) had moved to Florida, and more than 200,000 new Medicaid applications were filed. So we were dealing with 250,000 new people and the problems that they brought with them, at a time when our revenues were in a nosedive. At the end of our first twelve months, we had a total of 1,345 fewer employees on the payroll than when we took office.

Tax Reform Runs Aground

The revenue crisis Florida faced in our first year was, in part, the result of the failure of the services tax, which had passed and then been repealed during the Martinez years. We were in a double bind. Florida desperately needed new revenues to meet the needs of its citizens, but the legislature was shell-shocked from the services tax fiasco.

Shakespeare's line about the tide in the affairs of man proved to be directly on point. Taken at the flood it leads to greatness. Neglected, one spends one's life in the shallows. For us, the "shallows" were represented by the Florida Chamber of Commerce Foundation's recently completed study of Florida's revenue structure, called the Cornerstone Study. This study, a major effort paid for and endorsed by the board of directors of the Chamber, proposed replacing Florida's existing tax on retail sales with a Value Added Tax on sales at the wholesale level. Believing we had the support of the Florida Chamber of Commerce, Lawton and I endorsed this and set about trying to explain it. Basically, the proposed Value Added Tax produced much more revenue at a lower rate than the existing sales tax. This tax proposal would have enabled the legislature to reduce the tax rate significantly and still produce the same amount of revenue. Thereafter, because the tax base would no longer be riddled with loopholes, the amount of annual revenue would grow as the economy grew, without having to raise the tax rate. The Value Added Tax had recently been adopted by the Michigan legislature, and seemed to be well accepted by Michigan taxpayers. There was a major problem, however: without realizing it, the Florida Chamber had proposed resurrecting the ill-fated services tax, with the added wrinkle that the tax would be collected at the wholesale level. Once they understood that their VAT proposal meant the repeal of their cherished exemptions, the Florida Chamber abruptly and without shame changed sides in the struggle and led the fight to defeat "Chiles and MacKay's Value Added Tax." The proposal vanished without a trace, and with it, Lawton's enthusiasm for tax reform.

A Penny for Your Thoughts

Watching with dismay the impact of across-the-board budget cuts at a time when Florida's need for services was increasing, I became convinced that without a dedicated source of new revenue, Florida's schools and universities (the state's future) were locked into a downward spiral of mediocrity. As a center for retirement, Florida had America's oldest population, and our de facto commitment to becoming rich by promising a carefree retirement meant our demographic challenge would only intensify. Without a dedicated revenue source for schools, there would never be enough money to meet the exploding costs of Medicaid for Florida's seniors, without cutting back on the per-student funds for educating Florida's children. These were unacceptable choices. Unwilling to raise taxes, and unable to cut Medicaid, the legislature proposed to do little. Because of their inaction, we would have to underfund education, ignoring that we were already ranked forty-ninth or fiftieth in per-student public funding. Some legislators asserted that we must "run schools like a business" or "make them stop squandering the lottery money." You don't even have to cut school funding; just pass a nominal annual increase and talk about how the lottery dollars should make up the difference, if only educators would stop wasting money.

After the fiasco with the proposed Value Added Tax, I concluded that Lawton and I should bypass both the legislature and the business community by taking the proposal for dedicated school funding directly to the people of Florida. Governor Richard Riley of South Carolina, a friend from my days with the Southern Regional Education Board (SREB), had recently done this, leading a year-long grassroots initiative which ended up convincing South Carolina's business leadership and its ordinary taxpayers of the necessity of added investment in public education. Riley's "Penny For Your Thoughts" initiative increased South Carolina's sales tax by a penny, and dedicated the additional revenue exclusively to South Carolina's schools and technical colleges. The result was just as Governor Riley had envisioned: BMW and other global companies flocked to the Greenville-Spartanburg corridor, primarily because of the availability of a highly trained and educated work force.

At my request, Dr. Charlie Reed—then serving as chancellor of Florida's university system—brought Dick Riley's former chief of staff to Tallahassee. Together, Dr. Reed, Dick Riley's expert, and I presented the proposal for a grassroots Penny for Your Thoughts initiative directly to Lawton. After hearing us out, Lawton turned the proposal down. His judgment was that we lacked credibility because of our failed effort with the Value Added Tax. He felt we could only regain our credibility by operating more efficiently and making do with the revenues we had. This was doubly frustrating because the revenues we had were eroding like sand in an outgoing tide while the state's student population continued to increase dramatically. During the remainder of our time in office, the result was a poorly performing school system with too many students per teacher—particularly in kindergarten and elementary schools—and overcrowding at every level. Later, in a ballot initiative led by Kendrick Meek, Florida voters approved a constitutional amendment limiting class size in public schools. As of this writing, the results are mixed. Classes are smaller, but chronic underfunding has resulted in continuing stresses throughout Florida's public education system.

The Elephant in the Living Room

Florida's revenue dilemma was like an elephant in the living room. Nobody wanted to talk about how it got there. At first it had been a cute infant. Now it was so large that moving it was impossible without wrecking the infrastructure. The dilemma resulted from two conditions, both of which continue to exist today. The first was a tax base so riddled with giveaways that Florida's revenues couldn't possibly keep up with the costs of growth. The second was an explosion of unavoidable costs resulting from Medicaid (a federal entitlement program in which the states are required to pick up half the cost) and other decisions made someplace else. Except for Claude Kirk, Jeb Bush, and Charlie Crist, every modern Florida governor has tried to remove the elephant from the living room without destroying the building. Reubin Askew and Bob Graham each met with limited success. The services tax fiasco destroyed the Martinez administration. Lawton and I avoided being stepped on, but only by making the most drastic spending cuts by any governor in Florida's history until Charlie Crist. As of this writing, with the subprime mortgage disaster having triggered a global recession, Florida's revenue base has literally imploded. The elephant is still there and still wreaking havoc.

The Reality of Reinventing Government

In 1991, while Lawton Chiles was cutting the budget more than any governor in Florida's history, I had the responsibility of turning our campaign theme—"Reinventing Government"—from rhetoric to reality.

Our main campaign promise had been to dismantle Tallahassee's centralized, command-and-control management structure, and replace it with a community-based decentralized system which would be locally controlled and accountable in terms local citizens could understand. Simply put, we set out to make Florida's management look less like General Motors and more like Apple Computer. To lead the effort to turn this rhetoric into political reality, we appointed a top-level citizens commission. Bill Frederick, my former classmate whose innovations as mayor of Orlando had been featured in David Osborne's book, *Reinventing Government,* agreed to chair the commission, and David Osborne was retained as a consultant. The Frederick Commission, following a series of public forums, issued a report which became our blueprint for reforming Florida's government. Combining the experience of Bill Frederick and the political clout of other commission members from the public and private sectors, the Frederick Commission report had real credibility.

One of the first major legislative initiatives to come out of the Frederick Commission was the effort to authorize charter schools. Now, almost two decades later, with charter schools operating across Florida and all of America, it is hard to fathom why the initiative generated so much controversy. But our proposed charter schools bill was among the very first in America. With Democratic majorities in both houses, we expected cooperation and easy passage. To our surprise, we were attacked from all sides. On one side, teachers' unions predictably saw the bill as a cleverly disguised effort to undercut their hard-won collective bargaining rights, and minorities were convinced charter schools would be discriminatory. From the other side, advocates of private schools and vouchers argued that it was nothing more than a way to avoid introducing real competition and real choice into public education. The first year's effort resulted in much fulmination and gnashing of teeth, but no legislation. After applying continuing pressure and advocacy during the interim, we finally persuaded legislators in our second legislative session that this proposal was in the best interest of Florida's families.

The other recommendations of the Frederick Commission also ran into far more political resistance than we had anticipated. From the standpoint of Democratic legislators—then a majority in both the House and Senate—our first year had been traumatic. The brunt of the budget cuts had been borne by public employees. Despite the draconian budget cuts necessitated by the 1990 recession, Florida had grown by another 175,000 new residents. The result had been a work force with 1,300 fewer workers handling dramatically increased workloads. Everyone was demoralized—from schoolteachers, with more students crowded into their classrooms, and on double sessions in many cases, to mental health and welfare caseworkers. Our 1992 budget was still lower than the final Martinez budget, and yet we were now proposing untried new ideas about reinventing government! The police unions had not forgotten my earlier effort to reinvent government by reforming law enforcement pensions. They pointedly reminded Lawton that they had warned him against teaming up with that troublemaker, MacKay.

Over the next six years, we pushed through most of the recommendations of the Frederick Commission. Beginning with reform of civil service, we eliminated entire agencies through privatization, combined agencies with duplicating functions, and systematically eliminated state regulations (cutting the state's twenty volumes of administrative rules in half). We began the process of decentralizing the Department of Health and Rehabilitative Services, then the largest state agency in America. One of our most significant reforms was establishing an Innovation Fund that functioned like an internal working capital fund to finance innovations and productivity-increasing ideas. The return on the first year's investment of $8 million exceeded $50 million. These savings went to reimburse the Innovation Fund, with the remaining savings being divided between the general revenue fund and the agency which had come up with the idea.

From the standpoint of public policy, Reinventing Government was one of the most significant but least understood accomplishments of the Chiles-MacKay years. From the standpoint of my political future, it was a disaster. Because Reinventing Government began in Florida and was perceived by some as a threat to government employees, many state government organizations, including AFSCME, the union that represented most of Florida's public employees, openly opposed our efforts. In 1998, Florida's teachers supported me, but unions representing police, firefighters, and corrections officers joined AFSCME in endorsing Jeb Bush. Ironically, his policies toward public employees made Lawton and me look like the moderates we were.

Bill Clinton and Al Gore were also familiar with David Osborne's book, *Reinventing Government*. After their election in 1992, they began efforts similar to those we were making. The Clinton-Gore efforts were led by Vice President Al Gore. Much like our efforts, the Clinton-Gore reforms—although not well understood by the public—helped government operate more efficiently. Like me, Al Gore subsequently found these successful reforms to be more of a liability than an asset, from a political standpoint.

Education Accountability—Unraveling the Backlash

Every fisherman who has ever cast a line has experienced a backlash. Instead of flowing smoothly off the reel, the line occasionally becomes tangled. The momentum of the cast causes the reel to continue to run although the line is snarled at the point where the tangle occurred. The result is a spaghettilike mass of fishing line resembling a bird's nest wrapped around the reel. Fishing partners can be relied upon for a steady stream of jokes and uncharitable remarks when this occurs. The temptation is to pick out a string and pull with great vigor, hoping to unravel the knot at the center of the bird's nest. Every fisherman who has experienced a backlash knows that pulling on a string before finding the original snarl only compounds the problem.

By 1991, Lawton Chiles had served in three separate legislative bodies and had thirty years of experience. I was the junior partner, with eighteen years of legislative experience. Both of us knew that complicated issues like education, health care, or juvenile justice are, in fact, not single issues at all, but rather a complex web of issues. In all these instances, the temptation is to grab a string and pull relentlessly—which is exactly why single-issue politics is so frustrating and unsuccessful. While the interest groups struggle over which policy string to pull, the backlash gets more tightly snarled than before. Public school education is Florida's greatest challenge. Every interested party, from the teachers' union through the superintendent, school board, PTA, and even the legislature wants to grab a separate string and jerk it with all their might. The result, predictably, is a snarl that has only gotten tighter and more unworkable.

The long-running radio show, *Prairie Home Companion*, concludes each week with the host, Garrison Keillor, describing the mythical town of Lake Wobegon as a place where "all the women are strong, all the men are good looking, and all the children are above average." In 1991, the "Lake Wobegon Effect" had become common in Florida education circles, as parents and employers, having been flooded with mind-numbing statistics, felt that although schools in general were failing, their individual schools were "above average." Lawton and I felt Florida needed a mechanism to allow all of us to step back from the fray and try to construct a consensus on ways to unravel the snarl in the line that hampered education reform. We opted for a bipartisan citizens' commission on which the legislature and various education interest groups were represented, along with leaders of Florida's private sector who were employing our graduates. I co-chaired this commission with Betty Castor, my longtime friend from Tampa who was then serving as Florida's elected commissioner of education. Betty was one of Florida's earliest and most effective female elected officials, having served as a county commissioner, state senator, and now an elected member of the cabinet.

Established by a statute named Blueprint 2000, the commission was funded and staffed independently by the Florida Department of Education. The goal behind Blueprint 2000 was to untangle all the other knots that impaired our ability to reform education and establish accountability. Over the years, the state bureaucracy, through regulation to centralize public school education, has attempted to make local educators accountable to Tallahassee. Florida's constitution, however, mandated the exact opposite by establishing a decentralized system governed by sixty-seven locally elected school boards. To make this decentralized system function effectively, accountability had to involve local parents, community leaders, and employers, and had to be expressed in language they could understand. If a school principal was ineffective, there had to be some kind of report card which alerted local school boards and parents. In other words, local people with the power to demand changes had to have the information which would enable them to make the appropriate changes. Under our program, School Advisory Councils were mandated for each school. Accountability was to be based on a "plain language" report card evaluating each local school. It was to be augmented by a program of statewide testing. The commission adopted the concept of outcome-based accountability. In short, this meant statewide testing, with each school receiving a grade based on its students' test scores. The test—which was controversial from its inception—was named the Florida Comprehensive Assessment Test, or FCAT. The report card, called the Annual Report of School Progress, was developed and sent home to each parent.

As the work progressed, tension on the commission between the Department of Education and the business leaders heightened. Our able and effective staff director, Dr. Michael Biance, found himself in an increasing struggle to maintain his independence as the Department of Education constantly attempted to mitigate the findings of the commission. Socioeconomic data on individual schools revealed that failing schools had a great deal in common: they typically had students from poor, broken, and transient families. Clearly, these schools faced a greater challenge than schools with students who came from predominately English-speaking, educated, middle-class families. I felt strongly that the grading of schools should take into account the additional difficulties faced by rural and inner city schools that had a disproportionate population of immigrant and minority students. This did not mean such schools would not be held accountable. Like other substandard schools, they would be put on probation and given a specified period of time to improve or face being put into academic receivership. In receivership, new management would be brought in, with authority to replace underperforming faculty. During both the probation and the receivership, additional resources would be invested, without which intensive remediation would be impossible.

As of this writing, the controversy over accountability remains at the center of the debate over public schools. Under Jeb Bush, public school accountability was based solely on the FCAT, the standardized statewide test. Failing schools receive *less* funding, while schools making "As" are rewarded with *additional* funds. My belief is that this mindless application of free market theory, plus the unwillingness to pay competitive salaries to Florida teachers, has greatly reduced the potential rate of improvement in Florida's schools. As of this writing, the FCAT

remains Florida's simplistic answer to the complex issue of accountability in public schools. Short term, test scores are showing modest
improvement. Long term, I predict that some future governor will appoint another Education Accountability Commission to untangle the
same mess.

The Education Reform Commission

By the conclusion of our first term, two years of budget cuts, coupled
with continuing population growth, had caught up with us. Our schools
had fewer dollars per student than when we had started, but more than
100,000 additional students. This meant more students per teacher,
crammed into overcrowded classrooms. Budget constraints had precluded going forward with mandatory kindergarten, and early child-
hood education or Pre-K was not even under serious consideration.
Lawton built much of his travel schedule around visits to schools. This
assured that the nightly news regularly showed overcrowded classrooms, and set the stage to make school overcrowding a central issue
in the 1994 reelection campaign. Despite this, after our election, the
legislature—now controlled by Republican majorities in both houses—
refused to consider more capital outlay for schools. This impasse led Dr.
Charlie Reed and me to once again press Lawton to appoint a citizens'
commission. This time, the issue was not so much our inability to define
the problem. What we needed was the political muscle to force the legislature to act. Knowing that getting legislative funding or authority for
a study of classroom overcrowding would not be possible, Charlie Reed
and I obtained independent funding from three foundations: Knight,
MacArthur, and Bell South. We also urged Florida's Council of 100, a
business leadership group interested in economic development, to take
on this issue as their top priority. This culminated in the Governor's
Commission on Education Reform, which I co-chaired with Dr. Jack
Critchfield, CEO of Florida Progress.

The private sector membership of the commission consisted mainly
of members of the Council of 100. Lawton, Charlie Reed, and I chose
public sector membership. Lawton insisted on appointing Senator

George Kirkpatrick. When Charlie and I pointed out Senator Kirkpatrick's well-earned reputation as the proverbial "Bull in the China Shop," Lawton responded by quoting Lyndon Johnson's famous proverb: "It's better to have him inside the tent peeing out, than outside the tent, peeing in." As staff directors, we recruited Rick Edmonds, a former editor of *Florida Trend* magazine who often worked with the Council of 100, and Alan Stonecipher, who was on loan from Charlie Reed's staff. The work of the commission focused primarily on classroom overcrowding and readiness for school. As the organization of the commission was coming to completion, I was increasingly concerned that my beginning political campaign to succeed Lawton as governor would conflict with my role in leading the commission, and Governor Chiles took my place as co-chair.

Two major initiatives resulted from the Governor's Commission: an appropriation of $2 billion for new classrooms, and legislative support for a constitutional amendment mandating statewide kindergarten. Neither of these would have been possible without the strong support of Florida's Council of 100. Lawton's intuition about George Kirkpatrick was correct: Once he became convinced of the importance of the issue, he played an important role in persuading his legislative colleagues, many of whom had been elected on a platform of no new public spending.

Dinner at the Mansion

The grand scheme to fund the Frederick Commission, concocted by Jack Peeples, a close friend of Lawton's and one of Tallahassee's most experienced lobbyists, was to invite wealthy people to the governor's mansion for cocktails, an elegant dinner with wine, then after-dinner drinks and coffee, and finally a leisurely discussion leading to offers of financial support for the Frederick Commission. In practice, this approach worked less effectively than we thought. One of the ten potential donors enjoyed a bit too much alcohol. Our agenda became entangled with his desire to share personal history.

As he drank more, he revealed substantial aspects of his youth as a learning disadvantaged child who had access to great wealth. To my dismay, he seated himself next to the wife of one of the potential donors who happened to be a teacher at a private school for gifted students. Learning this, he advanced the thesis that if only dumb kids could be recognized as gifted but learning disadvantaged, schools would be much better. The teacher tried politely to make the argument that all the research findings were contrary to his conclusion. He responded that he was funding an experiment in a private school that specialized in dumb but gifted rich kids. Based on the progress his son was making, he was sure he would be able to change the world's thinking on this topic.

After much delay, four of us made our pitch at 10:30 p.m. To my horror, I discovered for the first time while listening to my co-conspirators' proposals that we were not in agreement as to what we were trying to accomplish. Bill Frederick and I were emphasizing reinventing government, while Jack Peeples sounded more interested in zero-based budgeting. Fortunately, the guests' sobriety was insufficient for them to realize that we were not in agreement. That was the good news. The bad news was that they did not seem to realize that we were soliciting their financial support. So when we asked for their advice and help at 10:50 p.m., our request triggered a soggy but spirited discussion which centered around the following themes:

1. Federal tax reform has made things tough for foundations, i.e., less taxes = less charity.
2. You have to watch out for consultants (obviously aimed at our budget, which included many consultants' fees).
3. It is not unusual for a child to be dumb and also gifted. One of the interesting things other foundations might want to do is help fund a school for dumb, rich, gifted kids. This turned out to be the most spirited part of the evening, because the gifted teacher finally came straight out and opined that "dumb" and "gifted" were mutually exclusive categories.

By 11:10 p.m., we were rapidly losing control of the discussion. Peeples told a funny story and took control of the agenda. What we were talking about was funding for the Frederick Commission. Our problem was still not resolved. The head of one of Florida's top foundations said the problem was that our Reinventing Government proposal wasn't an issue and that their foundation preferred to fund issues. Another followed by saying our proposal was a commission, and her foundation didn't "do" commissions. The others nodded in agreement, although the whole point of the proposed commission was to remedy dysfunctions of government. And that *was* an issue, if not *the* issue of our time.

One potential donor, painfully shy, had remained quiet and sober throughout the entire evening. Finally, around 11:30 p.m., he excused himself. He said that although he didn't fully understand the project, his family trust would be willing to provide a gift of $25,000. The soggy donor who had the dumb but gifted child promised to send all of us a written proposal to fund his research into gifted stupidity. The clear lesson is that if you only ask for $25,000, and you are prepared to sit long enough, you can get foundation support, even for an idea that you explain poorly!

The Green Swamp

The Green Swamp, lying west of Disney World, functions as a water recharge area for a major part of the Floridan Aquifer. Because of its proximity to the fast-growing I-4 corridor, it is also potentially prime development land. Our Growth Management Group, which I chaired, had held the line on stringent land use regulations that minimized drainage and development in the Green Swamp region. This had caused a major outcry. One of the areas most affected was immediately north of Lakeland, Lawton Chiles's hometown. Lawton had taken the heat, often from people who had been his lifelong friends and neighbors. The only thing he asked was that I chair a joint town meeting of our Growth Management agency heads in Lakeland. I agreed, and arranged to be accompanied by the secretaries of the departments of Environmental Protection, Community Affairs, Transportation, and Commerce. When we arrived, the room was packed and the atmosphere totally hostile. The local sheriff had sent extra deputies, but as Ben Watts pointed out, they clearly agreed with the crowd. As the first speakers made clear, the issue was simple: Big government, through its heavy-handed regulations, was effectively taking away their right to use their land, but was not willing to compensate them. Because of the large number of people wanting to be heard, I limited speakers to two minutes. This only made things worse.

After four or five speakers had raked us over the coals, the next speaker, a gaunt old man with white hair and a wild-eyed look, stood up and started reading a prepared statement. To my delight, the topic was not the Green Swamp. The situation was tense as the old man hurled accusation after accusation. His complaint arose from a decision by the County Commission to put a sewage treatment plant in his neighborhood, adjoining his property. His diatribe went something like this: Our County Commission continues its tradition of helping the big developers and ignoring the common taxpayer (murmurs). In this case they have an incestuous relationship with John Smith. He paid them off and everybody knows it (applause). Their reason for locating the sewage plant next to us is so their puppeteer can have sewage for his next golf course and development (applause).

The old man was talking a mile a minute and in all the commotion, it suddenly became apparent that somebody was shouting, "Stop! Stop!" Charlie Creel, my security guard, was uptight. The highly emotional outbursts by the crowd had the sound of an old-fashioned lynching, or at the least a tarring-and-feathering. When the shouting started, I saw Charlie pushing his way toward me, expecting some kind of altercation. Just as he got to the front of the room, along with a couple of worried looking deputies, it became apparent the shouting was coming not from an aggrieved taxpayer, but from the overweight, perspiring Baptist preacher who was "signing" for the hearing impaired: "I can't keep up. My hands won't work as fast as you're talking. You've got to slow down." The old man replied, "I'm determined to read my whole statement, and the only way I can do it in two minutes is to read as fast as I can." Not wanting to be associated with the local officials oppressing the ordinary folks, I waived the two-minute rule and the old man proceeded at a leisurely pace, slandering everyone in power in Polk County.

Realizing that as soon as the old fellow finished, the rest of the speakers were going to resume attacking us for taking their property without compensation, we panelists enjoyed the old man's eloquence as much as anyone in the crowd—and almost as much as the deputies. When I saw Lawton again, he said he had received several reports on our meeting. People were still upset about the regulation, but respected us for meeting with our critics and not trying to put the blame on someone else.

Saving the River of Grass

In 1990, when Lawton Chiles and I took office, we inherited a number of lawsuits, two of which involved rivers. The first of these was a suit by the federal government against the State of Florida, alleging that the South Florida Water Management District had failed to require sugar growers in the Everglades Agricultural Area to comply with the state's water quality standards. The alleged result was the pollution of Everglades water. The South Florida Water Management District had paid over $6 million in legal fees, seeking to prove that (A) the Everglades waters were not polluted, and (B) even if the Everglades were polluted, it was not the state's fault.

Shortly after taking office, Governor Chiles and I appeared in person in the federal courtroom. Lawton astounded the lawyers representing the state of Florida, and everyone else present, by taking the stand as a witness and agreeing that the Everglades waters were polluted. Lawton then offered to settle the lawsuit, with the State of Florida assuming part of the responsibility for the cost of restoring the Everglades. This courageous act led to the settlement of the litigation, and ultimately to legislation spelling out shared responsibility for cleanup costs, with the sugar industry paying approximately one-third of the costs. This legislation was named the Marjory Stoneman Douglas Act. Instead of being complimented, however, Marjory denounced the legislation as a sellout to Big Sugar. Her position was that the entire Everglades Agriculture Area should be restored to its natural state, as the "kidneys" of the Everglades. She demanded that the act be renamed so that her name would not be associated with it. The legislation thus became the Everglades Forever Act.

Despite periodic disagreements between Congress and the State of Florida, the South Florida Water Management District and various federal agencies initially made steady progress. Land was being purchased in and around the Everglades to restore sheet flow and reduce further encroachment. Modified farming techniques soon reduced pollution by more than 30 percent. Construction of the giant system of filter marshes and water storage areas mandated by the Everglades Forever Act was well under way. Unfortunately, after Lawton Chiles and I left office, this progress stalled, with Congress bearing most of the blame. As of this writing, Governor Crist has committed to purchase much of the land of U.S. Sugar, which lies between Lake Okeechobee and the Everglades. This is an important step, but with urban growth continuing in the areas surrounding it, the future of the Everglades becomes more complicated as each year passes. At some point in the near future, the diversion of water from the Everglades will be so great that this fragile ecosystem will not receive the water it needs in order to survive. At that point, unless the federal court again intervenes or the legislature mandates that future developers must assure adequate water for their proposed developments, the Everglades will be doomed. This time, we won't be able to blame our failure on Congress. Without additional water from alternate sources, such as desalinization, South Florida's growth is simply unsustainable.

Slow Talking: The Apalachicola

Another of the unresolved lawsuits we inherited from the Martinez administration was the dispute over the Apalachicola-Flint-Chattahoochee River. Carol Browner, then our secretary of environmental protection, was our team leader. This unfortunate dispute continues to drag on almost three decades later. In fact, it will probably have to be resolved by the U.S. Supreme Court at some point. But we almost settled it in 1991.

The basic problem is that the City of Atlanta has no underground source of water, and has to rely on the Chattahoochee River for all of its water. Under federal law, if Atlanta performed the necessary technical work to demonstrate its future needs, it could then file a Notice of Intent to Withdraw and the proportionate part of Lake Lanier, the man-made reservoir created by damming the Chattahoochee, would be set aside for Atlanta. When we took office in the early 1990s, the City of Atlanta had done a sophisticated growth plan that covered the period of time out to 2050. The city then filed a Notice of Intent to Withdraw, which would ultimately give Atlanta and its developers a prior legal right to all the water in the Chattahoochee River. Needless to say, Alabama and Florida filed suit. Preemption by Atlanta, if allowed, would ruin areas downstream in Georgia and Alabama as well as the livelihood of Apalachicola oystermen, all of whom depended on adequate and non-polluted water from the Flint and Apalachicola Rivers—which were in reality the Chattahoochee River with different names in each state.

The negotiation was taking place in Tallahassee the second week of June, in Carol Browner's conference room. On the second day, Carol called and reported the negotiations were at an impasse, and asked me to come over. When I arrived, the problem became apparent as soon as I was introduced. The negotiators from Georgia and Alabama were Skeeter, Buddy, and Joe, straight out of a novel by William Faulkner. Florida's team, led by Carol, included an environmental expert and a hydrologist. Both wore earrings; one had a pigtail. Alabama's interests were closely aligned with those of Florida, but somehow, Skeeter had found himself uncomfortable in agreeing with Carol and her pigtailed flower children. As soon as I was introduced as Buddy and started "speaking Southern," you could feel the tension go out of the room. Over the next two hours, Skeeter began to warm to our side of the debate. This was fortunate, since Alabama and Florida were co-plaintiffs. Skeeter and Joe got into a slow-talking contest, which is the Southern version of a highly emotional debate. Carol Browner told me later that this had been her first opportunity to appreciate slow talking as a negotiating technique. Slow talking works like this: The opposition anticipates the point and has time to go through the complete cycle of rejection, anger, cooldown, and preparing alternate responses. The slow talker, knowing this is taking place, plods earnestly along, just fast enough not to lose his train of thought. By noon, Skeeter was even more firmly on our side, and we were slowly presenting our joint demands. Joe was not giving in, but at least everyone was smiling. Carol opined that she and the flower children could take it from there, but she asked that I remain on call in a consulting capacity.

In contrast to the historic Everglades settlement, the state and federal entities involved in the Apalachicola dispute have been unwilling or unable to rein in the water demands of their respective interest groups, and this litigation is now nearing the end of its third decade. The Apalachicola River, which has America's richest, most productive estuary, is in the same position as the Rio Grande and Colorado Rivers. It is being slow talked and litigated to death.

The Clinton Connection

By the end of September 1991, after nine months in office, the Chiles-MacKay administration was in deep water. Instead of reinventing government, we had been in a constant crisis mode: cutting budgets, laying off workers, and arguing among ourselves about tax reform/revenue enhancement. Instead of Butch Cassidy and the Sundance Kid, the press had begun referring to Lawton as Don Quixote. I was referred to as Sancho Panza, the comic sidekick who thought Quixote was sane, despite evidence to the contrary. We had enough problems of our own, and did not need any outside distractions. The Democratic primary for the 1992 presidential election had begun, however, and the Florida Democratic Party made sure Lawton and I were involved, whether we liked it or not.

Nineteen ninety-one was an off year as far as Florida Democrats were concerned. There were no elections, and thus there was no real reason for a political convention. The Florida Democratic Party saw an opportunity to use a convention as a means of fundraising, however, and thus moved forward with enthusiasm. The key was a potential presidential straw ballot, which would be billed as the first head-to-head contest among the Democratic contenders, a full year ahead of the Iowa primary. There would be no limit to the number of delegates. Each delegate who paid the admission fee to the Florida convention would be entitled to vote. National media would focus on the outcome of the vote. This meant no presidential candidate could afford to forego Orlando. There were six announced Democratic candidates, five of whom were friends of Lawton's from his time in the U.S. Senate. The sixth was the little-known governor of Arkansas, Bill Clinton. Because of his friendships in the Senate, Lawton made it clear from the outset that he would remain neutral. In my prior career as a state senator from Florida, I had worked with Governor Bill Clinton on the Southern Regional Education Board and admired his efforts to improve public schools in Arkansas. More recently, I had worked with him in the Democratic Leadership Council. He was the national chair of the DLC in 1991, and I had been active in organizing DLC chapters in Florida. When Clinton asked me to chair his campaign in Florida, I enthusiastically agreed.

The strategy was simple. While better-known candidates made frequent Florida trips and chased television cameras, the Clinton campaign quietly hired a professional grassroots organizer to work exclusively on the Florida straw poll. I started calling my precinct captains in the "vertical counties" of South Florida. Having been my supporters in 1988, and again in the 2000 campaign, these people were enthusiastic and reliable campaigners. All they needed was a call to action. Their initial reaction was: "Arkansas? Where the hell is Arkansas?" What I said in response was: "He's not a redneck. He's one of us." After that, they were ready to go, and they came to the Democratic convention by the busload. Bill and Hillary Clinton were tireless, enthusiastic campaigners. At that early point in the primary race, having local Democratic leaders vouch for them was more important than specific positions on issues. Instead of spending their time being interviewed by the national press, Bill and Hillary Clinton were shaking every delegate's hand and posing for pictures with the condo commandos enthusiastically crowded around "their boy, Bill." The result was that Bill Clinton swept the 1991 Florida Democratic convention, and national pundits proclaimed him the surprise Democratic frontrunner for president. Right on the heels of this development, however, Gennifer Flowers appeared on television to discuss her alleged long-term affair with Bill Clinton. Only when Hillary decided to bail Bill out in a joint television appearance did the

Flowers issue disappear. Then came a close showing in the New Hampshire primary and Clinton's proclamation that he was the "Comeback Kid." He won the Democratic nomination, buoyed by carrying Florida and other southern "Super Tuesday" states. We were especially proud of the victory in the primary, where Clinton received 50.77 percent of the total vote in a field of five candidates. Paul Tsongas was in second place, with 34.54 percent, with Brown, Harkin, and Kerry receiving a combined total of 14.70 percent of the vote. Clinton's political skills—though more orthodox than Lawton's—were extraordinary. With a little help from Ross Perot, he went on to defeat the incumbent president, George H. W. Bush. In Florida, Clinton's vote in the general election was 39 percent of the total, with Bush receiving 40.9 percent, and the remainder going to Perot.

Over the remainder of the '90s, I had the incredible experience of speaking for Florida in the Clinton administration, while also speaking for the Clinton administration in Florida. At times it was gratifying, at times bizarre, but at no time was it boring.

For Sale—Half Off: Hurricane Andrew

Ask anyone about hurricanes who has lived more than one summer in Florida and you will get a tall tale. Here is mine:

Lawton had been governor for seven and a half months. We were "reinventing government" agency by agency. There were plenty of challenges. Those at the top of the reinvention list were agencies singled out by the legislature for reform or abolishment. Quiet, boring agencies with patriotic sounding names were at the bottom. We would reinvent them only if there was extra time available in our four-year term. When we took over, Emergency Management wasn't even an agency. It was either a bureau or maybe a division of the Department of Community Affairs. Actually, the division (or bureau) had been organized in the 1960s as part of America's civil defense effort to respond to a possible Soviet nuclear attack. Every county in America had a director of civil defense. This person was usually a county employee with other duties. Civil defense was typically housed in a World War II Quonset hut equipped with a two-way radio capable of communicating with lo-cal law enforcement, firefighters, and hospital emergency rooms. Local civil defense people could also talk to the state director of civil defense, who was based in his own Quonset hut in Tallahassee. The state direc-tor, in turn, could communicate with the Florida National Guard and the secretary of the Florida Department of Community Affairs. No one thought he was relevant, however, and there was no provision for him to communicate directly with the governor's office.

The system in the 1960s was originally intended to protect Floridians from the imminent threat of nuclear attack by Fidel Castro. In 1991, civil defense conducted hundreds of fire drills and was federally funded. It was good at fire drills, but not much else. Lawton and I had troubles enough keeping Castro at bay. So we left it alone. Failing to give prior-ity to Florida's antiquated emergency management agency proved to be an unwise decision when Hurricane Andrew struck. The hurricane came ashore about thirty miles south of Miami in the wee hours of the morning on August 24, 1992. By daylight, it had moved into the Gulf of Mexico, leaving the southern part of Miami, plus the cities of Home-stead, Florida City, and Perrine in shambles. Homestead Air Force Base was flattened. Big yachts and even small freighters were stranded in residential and business areas, hundreds of feet from the nearest wa-ter. Trees were toppled, broken off, or denuded. There was no electric power, no traffic lights—not even street signs. Trees, power poles, and debris were everywhere. Nobody had water, food, or air conditioning—not even any shade. Knowing that we faced a major crisis, Lawton and I left Tallahassee at daybreak and landed at Hialeah airport by early morning. He went by auto to survey the damage, while I caught a ride in a helicopter operated by a local television station.

After viewing the devastated area from a helicopter, I went to the Miami-Dade Emergency Management command center to evaluate the response capability for the south half of Dade County. The command center was functioning because some resourceful person had comman-deered a crane truck and picked up the communications antenna, which had been blown down. It was swinging at a crazy forty-five-degree angle from the end of the crane, but at least it was functioning. It remained dangling like that for weeks as everyone focused on more immediate crises. That morning set the pattern for the next three months. Lawton was the public face of the state of Florida, walking in the ninety-degree heat, going to places where tempers were flaring, and reassuring residents that we were responding to the best of our abilities. The fact that he was there in the heat, and not sitting in an air-conditioned office, made a difference, even though we were often unable to deal with specific issues.

I was the "inside man." My challenge was to make sure our state agencies were on the job and that no state officials were holding things up by arguing about irrelevant bureaucratic issues like whose agency had jurisdiction. I spent the first day mostly bludgeoning hospital officials, all of whom were trying to redirect ambulances to other emergency rooms. They all seemed to be reading from the same script—lack of funding, fear of liability, and certainty that they were being called upon to do more than their share. My script included a reminder that the licensing board for hospitals reported to the governor, and that I was writing down the names of any hospitals that refused to accept emergency patients. There was shouting and cursing. I even attracted a small crowd of well-wishers at the Emergency Response command center, who gathered around the phone to cheer me on. Backed by the National Guard and local police, my script prevailed.

Lawton was focused on the federal dimension of the same problem—trying to embarrass or browbeat federal agencies and the Pentagon into setting aside budgetary and bureaucratic concerns and working with our state and local agencies. At one point during the second week, Lawton got into a shouting match with President Bush in front of a bank of television cameras as the president exited the door of Air Force One. Bush had just landed at Miami International Airport to show his concern, and Lawton decided to ambush him. Lawton's written request for military assistance had gone unanswered for the better part of a week, and he was outraged. President Bush's response (that Lawton's letter had been improperly addressed to the commandant of the Corps of Engineers instead of the secretary of the Army) only made Lawton angrier.

It made a great six o' clock television live shot—the president and the governor about to duke it out!

The secretary of the Federal Emergency Management Agency, or FEMA, arrived toward the end of the first week, and the chaos only got worse. This poor soul couldn't find anyone at the federal, state, or local level who would obey his orders or even stop to listen to him. I solved that problem by commandeering a Florida Highway Patrol vehicle, loading the FEMA director in, and ordering the trooper to drive him around to inspect the damage. Unfortunately there was incredible damage to inspect. There were several well-organized gangs in the South Dade area, and the devastation was made to order for them. Looting was out of control until several units from the 82nd Airborne Division were dispatched to Miami. In a burst of creativity, President Bush finally gave up on FEMA and asked Marilyn Quayle, wife of the vice president, to assume overall responsibility for coordination of federal relief efforts. She moved to Miami, took charge, and immediately began making sense out of the federal efforts. I couldn't help thinking how much better off America would have been if Marilyn Quayle had run the whole country. In the midst of all the confusion, people still had a sense of humor. One house situated on a major thoroughfare had been half blown away. On the remaining half was a large sign: "For Sale: Half Off."

Miami's private sector was a source of strength. Under the leadership of Alvah Chapman, publisher of the *Miami Herald*, and Ray Goode, vice president of Ryder Systems, a unique organization named "We Will Rebuild" came into existence and began coordinating a national effort at fundraising and relief. I continued meeting every week with this group, the Dade League of Cities, our state agencies, and the federal agencies. It was a full-time job for several months. At the next legislative session, an unusual law was passed, establishing a trust fund for the "windfall" sales tax revenues which resulted from the massive rebuilding effort in Dade County. These revenues were not distributed statewide, but sent back to Miami-Dade County to help fund its hurricane recovery efforts. Later, under President Clinton, FEMA became an independent agency.

Its director, James Lee Witt, was an experienced former county manager who had the respect of state and local officials and who reported directly to the president. FEMA quickly became known for its effectiveness. In Florida, following the recommendations of a citizens' commission chaired by Senator Phil Lewis, legislation was passed levying a fee on each policy of casualty insurance sold in Florida. The proceeds went to fund emergency management. We now have the most effective Division of Emergency Management in America.

A decade later, apparently nostalgic for the good old days of Quonset huts and civil defense, President George W. Bush buried FEMA somewhere down in the bowels of the new Department of Homeland Security. He refocused FEMA on civil defense and Fidel Castro, putting a vanity appointee (code named "Brownie") who had no clue about emergency management in charge. New Orleans, after Hurricane Katrina, was even more chaotic than Miami after Hurricane Andrew. Brownie, like our FEMA director years earlier after Hurricane Andrew, was nowhere to be found during the day, but constantly on the nightly news explaining why the confusion couldn't possibly be the fault of the federal agencies. Local and state officials were also on the nightly news, arguing that Brownie and his confused, ineffective bureaucrats were a major part of the problem. Unlike his father, President George W. Bush didn't land at the airport to express concern, but flew over New Orleans and surveyed the damage out of the window of Air Force One. The public properly concluded that FEMA was a worse disaster than Katrina! I received several calls from New Orleans immediately after Katrina, asking how to make sense out of the federal bureaucracy. I advised them to get President George W. Bush to do like his daddy had done: get FEMA out of New Orleans and put Marilyn Quayle in charge!

Florida's Foreign Policy

Campaigning with Bill Clinton was an exhilarating experience. With boundless energy and an extrovert's love of people, he became more energized as the crowds got more enthusiastic. Unlike most candidates, he had no need to rest between events, and preferred to spend this time discussing public policy. It was as if he had already been elected, and wanted to be sure he had heard and discussed every possible idea or issue he might confront. One of the ideas I proposed to him during his first campaign was making Miami the trade capital of the Americas. When I had first proposed this idea months earlier, the press had responded cynically that Florida would be the only state with its own foreign policy. Clinton, however, reacted positively. He saw the potential of the idea as clearly as I did. Miami was a microcosm of what the nation was fast becoming, with a mix of whites, Hispanics, and blacks, where the whites were no longer the majority. If there is a single thread that runs through Miami's tumultuous history, it is that Miami's leadership and residents have shown how to make diversity an asset rather than a liability. Many Hispanics who could not live together peaceably in their native country somehow managed to do so in Miami. Instead of being Florida's (and America's) perennial problem, Miami could potentially become one of the nation's greatest assets as its hemispheric trade capital.

Early in his administration, President Clinton urged Congress to ratify the North American Free Trade Agreement, or NAFTA—the free trade agreement with Canada and Mexico that had been negotiated by his predecessor, President Bush. In 1993, as part of the effort to ratify NAFTA, Clinton had pledged to start a broader negotiation to achieve a hemispheric free trade agreement, the Free Trade Area of the Americas (the FTAA). He launched this initiative with an unprecedented Summit of the Americas. Lawton and I wanted Miami to be the host city for the Summit of the Americas, as the first step in an effort to make Miami the trade capital of the hemisphere. The competing cities ranged from Washington, D.C., to Atlanta, Houston, New Orleans, and Los Angeles. The White House staff was divided, but they unanimously opposed Miami. In their eyes, the risk was too great that Miami's expatriate Cuban freedom fighters would seize on the summit as an opportunity to stage anti-Castro protests. After seeking assurance from Miami's civic leadership that this would not happen, Lawton and I made that pledge to President Clinton and his staff. With that pledge, President Clinton selected Miami. I was subsequently the designated coordinator for both the president and the governor, charged with the responsibility of assuring that all federal, state, and local agencies, as well as Miami's business and civic leadership, worked together. Fortunately, I knew many of Miami's leaders from my prior experience with the Hurricane Andrew recovery effort.

1994—the He-Coon Walks

To make life even more complicated, while the preparations for the summit were ongoing, our reelection campaign began. By this time, Lawton had succeeded in passing campaign finance legislation which assured that public funds would be available for candidates who would abide by restrictions on private giving. The primary restriction was that if a candidate agreed to take public funds, no person or entity could contribute more than $1,000 to his campaign in any primary or general election cycle. In many ways, this was the capstone of Lawton's twenty-five-year effort, which began with his historic 1970 campaign. How fitting that Lawton—the first gubernatorial candidate to elect to abide by the restrictions of the new law—should be opposed by Jeb Bush, who refused public funding and thus was not bound by the new restrictions on fundraising. And yet, despite the 1994 Republican landslide, Lawton won this race. Outspent substantially, Lawton transformed the campaign into a contest where Jeb was cast in the role of Wile E. Coyote and Lawton was the Roadrunner. The humor of the situation captured the public's attention. Several seasoned observers commented that Jeb's slick television ads actually reinforced the case Lawton was making.

In their first debate, the stylistic differences between the candidates could not have been more pronounced. Jeb opened his remarks in Spanish, which played well to an enthusiastic Miami audience. That would have gone unnoticed, except that he turned to Lawton in a patronizing manner and said, "Governor, I thanked them for coming, and asked them to welcome you to Miami." As Jeb turned to take his seat, Lawton gave his response: "I don't speak Spanish, I speak Cracker!" This remark could have easily been misinterpreted, and it certainly was outside the bounds of political correctness. But native Floridians understood it to mean that Lawton, a lifelong Floridian, was not going to be patronized by a newcomer who knew Spanish but didn't know Florida.

Lawton's Roadrunner-inspired free media saved our campaign. We could not agree at the outset on a campaign manager, so we started out, as before, with an all-volunteer organization. There was little focus on fundraising, and Lawton was more interested in being a good governor than in campaigning. I was distracted by the necessity of being in Miami almost constantly to settle bureaucratic and personality disputes in preparation for the Summit of the Americas. In midsummer, a political earthquake occurred. Congressman Mike Synar, a highly respected Democrat from Oklahoma, was defeated in that state's Democratic primary. His opponent had been recruited by the AFL-CIO, in punishment for Synar's vote in favor of NAFTA. As other Democratic incumbents were challenged by labor-backed primary opponents, all of us realized for the first time that the foundations of the Democratic Party were in danger of collapsing. Our left flank, usually our strong point, was in a state of chaos. Organized labor, a major Democratic constituency, was actively opposing Democrats who had voted for NAFTA. At the same time, on our right flank, Democrats who had voted for Clinton's tax increase were being challenged. To add to our growing sense of urgency, running against Jeb Bush was not at all like running against Bob Martinez. Bush had a smooth, professional campaign with none of the controversy that Martinez had to contend with. As the saying goes: "When all else fails, read the directions." For us, reading the directions meant getting organized, bringing in a campaign manager, and raising as much money as possible. Jeb's ads were portraying Jeb as a young energetic leader who would run Florida like a business. Lawton and I were portrayed as tired oldsters, unable and unwilling to change with the times. The irony of Jeb running ads advocating reform, while refusing to be a part of our effort to reform campaign financing, seemed to escape Jeb's experts, but the people of Florida apparently got it.

The campaign climaxed with a televised debate moderated by Tim Russert. At that point, the polls were showing that the race could go either way. The final question to Lawton was something like this: "Governor, your opponent says you are out of ideas and energy, and need to be replaced. What is your response?" Lawton thought for a minute, and then said: "The old He-Coon walks just before the light of day." Russert turned to Jeb for a rebuttal. It was apparent that Jeb, a newcomer to state politics, had no idea what Lawton was talking about. The audience was intrigued, and the room literally buzzed as people whispered the inevitable question: "What in the hell does a 'he-coon' have to do with a governor's race?" Nothing else mattered that night. It was one of the most bizarre developments in the history of state political campaigning. Coon hunters knew what Lawton meant: the younger coons, driven by hunger pangs, left the den early and were at risk when the dogs caught their scent. The old He-Coon, however, waited until dawn, after the hunters had departed, before leaving the safety of the den. Translated, this meant that Lawton knew enough about Florida politics not to allow his campaign to peak too early. He was just getting started!

Political Tectonics

When the dust cleared in 1994, the election had, in fact, resulted in a major political earthquake. After holding political power in the U.S. House and Senate and in the governor's mansions and state legislatures, the Democrats had been thrown out of office at all levels. The leadership of the Democratic Party, increasingly self-satisfied and responding almost solely to special interests, had resisted changes that were taking place all around us, even within the party. While I was in Congress, I had been part of a moderate caucus within the Democratic Party. After being stonewalled by the party leadership for years, our group realized something more definitive had to be done. I joined with Senators Chiles and Nunn, Congressman Dick Gephardt, Governor Bill Clinton, Florida House Speaker Jon Mills and others to organize the Democratic Leadership Council, or DLC. We advocated coupling conservative ideas like a strong defense, pay as you go budgeting, and free trade with progressive ideas on education, health care, and social issues. This concept had originated years earlier with Senator Henry "Scoop" Jackson, and was much like the "Third Way" reforms that had already taken place in

Britain's labor party under Tony Blair. My DLC activities in Congress had led to a lack of enthusiasm for my candidacy by many of Florida's labor leaders in my 1988 Senate campaign. Believing that the national Democratic Party was too liberal, I had continued working with the DLC after I left Congress to organize local chapters in Florida's urban centers. Our plan was to "put a different face on Florida Democrats," by providing forums where young business and professional leaders could be introduced to national DLC leaders like Al Gore, Dick Gephardt, and Tim Wirth.

When Lawton Chiles and I entered the governor's race in 1990, we decided to adapt the DLC concept to issues faced by state governments. Our platform coupled fiscal discipline with reforms like charter schools, testing and accountability in education, and other ideas, many of which had been outlined by David Osborne in his book, *Reinventing Government*. In 1992, Bill Clinton ran on the DLC platform and became president. Even more surprising than Clinton's election was his determination to actually put the DLC platform into effect. He succeeded, but the result was chaos within the Democratic Party. Once in office, Clinton set about implementing many of the same ideas Lawton and I were putting into effect in Florida. Like us, he ran into opposition from liberals and conservatives alike. His tax increase—part of the effort to balance the federal budget—caused the defeat of several conservative Democrats who voted for it. This was paralleled by his push to ratify NAFTA, the North American Free Trade Agreement originally negotiated by President Bush. The NAFTA vote was bitterly resisted by organized labor. In 1994, labor made good on its threat and defeated liberal Democrats who had supported NAFTA. The whipsaw effect of this internal battle over the future direction of the Democratic Party was directly responsible for the Democrats' loss of majority control of the U.S. House in 1994. Rather than compromise, Democratic interest groups set out to defeat those Democratic candidates whose votes they could not control. This internal struggle also affected state political races. Of all of the governor's races in 1994, only two states elected Democrats—Georgia and Florida.

The Miami Summit of the Americas

Despite the stress and anxiety of preparing for the Miami Summit while also campaigning for reelection, 1994 ended on a triumphant note. In November, Lawton and I had gone against the tide and won an improbable reelection campaign. After teetering for weeks on the edge of disaster, the Miami Summit of the Americas, under the direction of a host committee chaired by David Lawrence, the publisher of the *Miami Herald*, finally came together without a hitch. Miami's homeless disappeared, its petty criminals were invited to take a week's vacation, and the FBI proudly reported that "all known Miami terrorists" had been rounded up. Six million dollars had been raised by the Miami host committee to ensure the success of the event. But we needed more funds to complete the beautification of the city and for local arrangements. After much gnashing of teeth, hand wringing, and begging, we had managed to raise another $3 million.

Maneuvering thirty-four presidential entourages through the city to the various meetings proved a logistical nightmare, as traffic had to be blocked off each time a presidential entourage passed. To minimize traffic snarls, all official travel was to be at high speed. Rehearsals commenced, to be sure none of the high-speed dignitaries ever met one another head-on. Hotel staff was encouraged to smile and be gracious—just for a week! Three thousand hospitality volunteers were trained. The U.S. State Department established a special embassy staffed by experienced retired ambassadors and career State Department personnel. Behind the scenes, an even more impossible feat was accomplished: After negotiations which had been quietly ongoing for several months, an agreement was reached at the last minute under which all thirty-four democratically elected presidents—everyone except Fidel Castro—committed to a detailed ten-year timetable for negotiating the Free Trade Area of the Americas—the FTAA.

It is difficult to understand the potential importance of the FTAA without first comparing the relative sizes of the economies of the Americas with those of our competitor, the European Union. At the time of the Miami Summit, the North American Free Trade Agreement had only recently gone into effect. Total trade between the three NAFTA countries—the United States, Canada, and Mexico—already exceeded the entire trade among the fifteen countries of the European Union. If completed, the FTAA would have greatly exceeded both NAFTA and the EU, becoming by far the world's largest free trade area. It was agreed that the framework of the new FTAA would be the same as the existing provisions of NAFTA, with modifications to correct the obvious deficiencies that had caused the controversy surrounding NAFTA. These deficiencies, known as "civil society concerns," were lack of enforceable protections for labor, human rights, rights of women and children, and environmental protection. Although these issues were ostensibly covered by NAFTA, it was already recognized that NAFTA's nontrade provisions were sketchy and unenforceable.

With the negotiations completed ahead of time, the high-speed travel working flawlessly, and the City of Miami spotless and smiling, the Miami Summit was a total success. Miami's Cuban Americans held an energetic and orderly parade which culminated in a patriotic celebration and added to the feeling of hemisphere-wide solidarity. The impact of the successful summit on my personal political situation came as a total surprise to me. During the pre-summit confusion, my main goal had been to avoid embarrassing Lawton Chiles and Bill Clinton. The end result, however, had been the opposite. Before all the summiteers had even left Miami, state and national Democratic activists were competing to be part of my campaign to succeed Lawton Chiles—four years later! Already, people I hardly knew were drawing up organizational charts and master plans for my 1998 campaign. My local supporters and condo commandos were not going to be elbowed aside without a fight. I couldn't imagine holding this unstable mob together for four years. As it turned out, I had nothing to worry about.

The Law of Unintended Consequences

Early in 1995, Lawton and I encountered our first bona fide political scandal. Allegations were made by senior citizens about receiving "scare" calls in the last days of our campaign against Jeb Bush. The message had been a warning that Bush, if elected, intended to cut their retirement benefits. The callers had allegedly identified themselves as part of an independent senior advocacy group. Having known nothing of this, Lawton and I denied that an organized campaign had been conducted. If it had, we denied any involvement. The drumbeat continued. Legislative investigations established that hundreds of thousands of calls had in fact been made and that the independent organization supposedly paying for the calls did not exist.

Finally, our own campaign staff confessed the truth. In the final days of the campaign, we had received over $1 million in public funds. Both the timing and the amount of the public funds were unanticipated. It was too late to spend the new money as part of our agreed campaign plan. Without informing us, campaign staff had authorized the phone campaign. Whether or not it changed the outcome of the campaign, it unquestionably skirted the law. For Lawton it was an embarrassment in his last election of a distinguished career, much of which had centered on the need for campaign finance reform and integrity in government. For me, it was not only embarrassing, but also curtailed early enthusiasm for my candidacy. Some voters and political writers surmised that perhaps Chiles and MacKay were not different, after all. Perhaps we were just like all the rest and the truth had finally come out. Political people dismissed this—the standard advice was simply to be tough enough to take the criticism and move on. To this day, however, I regret that this incident occurred.

Crazy Joe and the City of Miami

Lawton and I hadn't yet recovered from the Miami Summit when suddenly, out of a clear blue sky, we found ourselves once again in the middle of Miami politics. It started when we were notified that Miami's newly elected mayor, Joe (Crazy Joe) Carollo, and his equally new finance director were on a plane on the way to Tallahassee to talk to the governor about Miami's financial problems. By way of background, the FBI had just completed a two-year investigation dubbed "Operation Greenpalm," and had indicted Miami's city manager, finance director, two city councilmen, and numerous others on charges of corruption in office. Before it concluded, Operation Greenpalm obtained convictions throughout the ranks of the City of Miami and Metro-Dade County.

If we had understood Joe Carollo and his history in Miami politics, Lawton and I would have realized how much our world was about to change with Joe's visit. In the presence of his new finance officer as well as members of the *Miami Herald* and Associated Press, Joe Carollo demanded that we put the City of Miami into bankruptcy. He was prepared to do it on his own, but had been advised he couldn't do it without the permission of the governor. The first thought that came to my mind was "That's crazy!" With the statewide press sitting across the table, however, that was the one thing I couldn't say. Lawton, on the other hand, said two things: First, there would be no municipal bankruptcy because of the impact it would have on the state of Florida's credit rating in the bond market; and second, he would appoint an oversight board with authority to manage the City of Miami, to be chaired by the lieutenant governor. My friends immediately began referring to me as "Crazy Buddy!" In Miami, the State Oversight Board predictably became "MacKay's SOBs."

The good news was that Florida had a newly enacted statute on the books that contemplated this precise situation. It had been passed after New York, Detroit, Philadelphia, and other major cities had gotten into financial trouble, and their respective state governments had been forced to bail them out. The bad news was that the statute we were relying on was unconstitutional. Florida's constitution contains a unique Home Rule provision which clearly prohibits state takeover of a city. So the first thing I had to do was negotiate my way around this roadblock. We decided to accomplish this by having the City Commission sign an intergovernmental agreement under terms of which the State Oversight Board had the right to approve all hiring of top management, as well as all expenditures, contracts, personnel decisions, and budgets. Explaining this to Joe proved to be delicate, since his natural inclination was to suspect a plot by his enemies to use the situation to get to him personally. Secondly, he suspected I was using this situation to advance my candidacy for governor. The press did not understand the delicacy of the situation, although the bond rating agencies understood it very well indeed. The Sunshine Law prohibited my discussing the matter at a private meeting, although I could talk separately to the mayor, or any individual commissioner. Because of Joe's paranoia, it proved exceedingly difficult to accomplish anything by talking to individual commissioners. They took great pleasure in pulling Joe's chain by confiding that I had called them, but that the topic of the conversation had to be kept secret because of the Sunshine Law.

The solution came in the form of a parable that went like this: Pretend you are a small sovereign nation, and you are dealing with a large nation that wants you to do something very important but very unpopular. You may think you don't have to do it, because the large nation has no army. Don't overlook the fact that the large nation has a nuclear weapon. Translation: If you decide not to sign the oversight agreement, we're going to get into a war. While the constitution may not give Lawton the power to establish the Oversight Board, it does give him the power to remove the mayor and City Commission for misfeasance. So, while Miami might not have an Oversight Board, it also faced losing its existing mayor and City Commission! Needless to say, everybody signed the intergovernmental agreement. Seizing on Miami's turmoil, a group of well-placed citizens mounted a petition drive to abolish the City of Miami, turning its functions over to the county. The facts seemed to support the idea. Property taxes, for example, would be reduced by eliminating the duplication in local government. The idea, needless to say, had broad support. The proponents had overlooked one thing, however. Crazy Joe took this as a personal attack, and it drove him crazy. He mounted the now-famous "Fidel Castro Defense" ("You want to help Fidel Castro? Just do away with the City of Miami") and single-handedly blew the petition drive out of the water.

As if the Oversight Board and the drive to abolish the city weren't enough, Joe ran for reelection. He was narrowly defeated by Xavier Suarez, who had also been mayor and whose platform pledged to return Miami to normalcy, "like the old days." As soon as the election was over, Suarez, the winner, began acting as crazy as Carollo. He started out by firing all the key management people and publicly challenging the constitutionality of the Oversight Board. Suarez's antics included accosting an elderly woman at her home late at night after she criticized him on a radio talk show (she pulled a gun on him). He also cancelled all city advertising from the *Miami Herald* after it questioned his sanity. The *Herald* didn't use a pistol: they used a cannon and nicknamed him "Mayor Loco."

Meanwhile, Crazy Joe had taken his usual paranoid ideas to court, seeking to overturn the election on grounds of fraud, which included dead people voting and hundreds of absentee ballots in the same handwriting—just like Dixie County. Everybody laughed, and there was lots of talk about how Crazy Joe never changed. Then the court ruled that the fraud had been so pervasive in the absentee ballots that all absentee ballots would be disallowed. Carollo was declared the winner. Miami returned to normalcy, "just like the old days."

The Compassionate Computer

Given Lawton's passion for the health needs of children, he initially chose to oversee the Department of Health and Rehabilitative Services (HRS). HRS at that time was such a mess that no one in the governor's office understood the scope and magnitude of its problems. Over the years, dozens of programs, offices, bureaus, divisions, and agencies had been cobbled together into America's largest state agency. The underlying challenge that made social services agencies so difficult to manage was the proliferation of well-meaning federal and state programs, each with its own narrowly defined eligibility requirements, funding sources, and reporting deadlines. In many instances, federal and state programs duplicated, intertwined, and partially overlapped. Because Florida's HRS had the most comprehensive jurisdiction of any social service agency in America, it was the country's biggest nightmare to manage.

In the late 1980s, under Governor Bob Martinez, Greg Coler, the secretary of HRS, had launched a major initiative to develop state-of-the-art computer technology to coordinate and conquer this myriad of programs, eligibility, and reporting. Food stamps, welfare, child support, adoption, Medicaid, child welfare, and other family service programs would all be decoded for a client from a caseworker's desktop computer at the touch of a button. That was the goal. The federal government had a great interest in this demonstration project and agreed to pay most of the cost. After months of requests for proposals, bids, protests, and litigation, the development contract had been given to Ross Perot's company, EDS. There followed additional months of delay and cost overruns, as developing the decentralized capability proved more difficult than anticipated. In the end, EDS prevailed upon Coler to abandon the revolutionary decentralized system, change the specifications, and allow a mundane, centralized mainframe system to be installed. In theory a "big box" in Tallahassee would connect to every HRS office and desk statewide. The work of every office and caseworker could theoretically be reconciled, monitored, overseen, managed, and reported from Tallahassee. That was the new goal. But the actual result proved a nightmare, which we had inherited, along with continuing litigation between EDS, the State of Florida, and the federal government.

Greg Coler, the mastermind of the mess, had long since resigned under threat of indictment for allowing the specifications to be modified without rebidding the entire project. EDS was also cutting and running. They were trying to hand over a "completed turnkey" operation of the automated system to the department. Unfortunately the "turnkey" was a turkey. The system was full of bugs and broke down regularly. With each decision, the state blithely stumbled forward toward another disaster. Once the software was designed, the mainframe had to be bought to house it. Once the mainframe was bought and programmed, a region had to be put online to test the software and mainframe. Once the first region was put online, the other regions had to be added to justify the cost of the mainframe and software. Each region that was added slowed the mainframe down. Once a region was loaded onto the mainframe, caseworkers had no option but to use it because they had gone "paperless." They had to enter their cases onto the mainframe to generate the benefits expected by the clients.

Backed-up caseworkers were permanently logging onto the mainframe so that their backlogged cases would not lose their place in the waiting line. Every caseworker statewide was waiting on the Tallahassee computer, while their clients waited in lines that stretched out of the building and into the street. In the parlance of Uncle Remus, the HRS computer was a Tar Baby. Like Uncle Remus' Tar Baby, it was extremely "sticky," and if you touched it, you couldn't turn loose. The harder you tried to get loose, the more you became smeared with tar. Each month, hundreds of thousands of new data entries were being processed on the largest nonmilitary computer in the world. Hundreds of millions of dollars worth of food stamps, welfare checks, and other benefits were being automatically mailed out from Tallahassee by the mainframe. Ill-trained workers were putting in erroneous data and cursing the resulting erroneous output. The consultants who had taken EDS's place had crisis teams permanently camped out by the ailing central mainframe computers. EDS blamed IBM, which had supplied the hardware. Litigators for the State of Florida were withholding payments to EDS for failure to meet contract specifications. Federal litigators were threatening to sue the state for failure to oversee the expenditure of federal dollars. EDS was suing the State of Florida for nonpayment. The new mainframe consultants were threatening to walk away from the entire project. Caseworkers were fearful that a service meltdown would bring down the entire system.

In accordance with hallowed bureaucratic tradition, Lawton and I were only told there was a problem with the "Martinez Computer," and that progress was being made in reducing the inherited backlog. Everyone at HRS had forgotten his or her previous involvement in the project. Nobody let us in on the fact that the computer was a ticking time bomb, however, or that if it exploded the entire agency would be engulfed in the chaos that would ensue. Calamity finally struck. Without bothering to inform EDS, the state, or the feds, the computer itself decided to help the people waiting in the lines. The computer apparently made a unilateral decision to send out benefits to all. Medicaid cards, food stamps, and checks were distributed to everyone and anyone. Hundreds of thousands of recipients were delighted. Needless to say, not a single recipient reported his or her ineligibility or overpayment. The next month, the computer did it again. Again, no one said a word.

As the third month rolled around, someone at HRS happened to notice the discrepancy. The post office was returning undeliverable benefits to the computer. Clients had moved, gotten jobs, or died. Some people had begun to worry about the unexplained largess from Tallahassee and were sending benefits back. A room near the computer was filling with boxes loaded with the computer's undeliverable and returned gifts. News this big has a shelf life of minutes, and the press found out about it at approximately the same time we did. All hell broke loose. It had all the makings of a TV sitcom. No one knew who had authorized the allocations. Fingers pointed every which way. No one knew how much had been erroneously mailed out. Estimates were in the hundreds of millions of dollars. Lawton and I were besieged by the press, the legislature, and the feds. "What did you know?" and "When did you know it?" were the operative questions.

Insider-Outsiders to the Rescue

Lawton's solution was straightforward. The secretary of HRS and his deputies responsible for the computer were relieved of their duties. I was appointed acting secretary of HRS, with instructions to do whatever it took to straighten the mess out. This was not the first time I had wrestled with social service agencies. In fact, I had been part of the original legislative reorganization that had launched the original HRS in the early 1970s. Then, it had seemed a simple plan: Consolidate the Tallahassee headquarters of our many independent, uncoordinated, warring social service agencies, while leaving the actual delivery of services decentralized.

We were trying to achieve two things: centralized coordination and decentralized management. Unfortunately, instead of coordination, what we accomplished was a conflict between the program specialists in Tallahassee and the operations specialists in the local communities. As a member of the Florida Senate, I had tried unsuccessfully to straighten out the ongoing conflicts. Behind each headquarters program specialist was an advocacy group intent on preventing any relaxation of the standards it had lobbied to mandate. For nearly twenty years, these specialists had been tugging back and forth against each other at the department. By the time of the 1990s computer fiasco, we were no closer to our original objective than when we began. It was clearly time to start over. Using medical terms, the problem at HRS was chronic bureaucratic constipation. Tallahassee just could not let authority or control pass through to community managers. My challenge was to flush out the obstructions and the obstructionists as well. This meant cleaning out the top-heavy Tallahassee bureaucracy.

Fortunately, in the early months of our first term, I hired an experienced executive, Bob O'Leary, who had worked as an agency head for Governor Blanchard in Michigan. I housed O'Leary at HRS headquarters where he worked with Greg Farmer, Ben Watts, and others as part of an informal team, which undertook one-of-a-kind projects like privatization and crisis management. The Tallahassee managers of the "big box" weren't going to provide any solutions. They had liked and championed the disaster from the start. I asked for resignation letters from over thirty Tallahassee managers. With assistance from O'Leary and Ben Watts, I began sorting through the HRS management team, accepting many resignations, reassigning some, and firing a few. O'Leary became known at HRS headquarters as the "Angel of Death." I invited the directors of the HRS regions to come to Tallahassee to help fix the place. These regional directors managed hundreds and in some cases thousands of employees. They ran mental health facilities and juvenile centers. They supervised benefit caseworkers and abuse investigators. They directed the service delivery system in every community of the state, often overcoming the Tallahassee bureaucracy's meddling. They were human computers who coordinated the menu of federal and state programs, as well as the requirements and reports from their desks. Several seasoned Tallahassee managers from outside HRS joined the HRS regional directors, including Ben Watts, the secretary of transportation, and Jim Zingale, the secretary of revenue. Longtime Tallahassee insiders, they kept the regional directors and me from getting tripped up by the Tallahassee and Washington rulebooks.

With this unique team of Inside-Outsiders as advisors, the regional directors (Outside-Insiders) set about trying to actually make HRS functional for the first time since the early 1970s. That meant fewer centralized controllers and more decentralized control. Three separate management systems had evolved at the department. In theory, all three reported to the secretary. There were the centralized Tallahassee program managers, managing statewide mental health, statewide children services, statewide welfare, statewide juvenile justice, statewide child welfare, and such. There were regional directors in the several regions managing all local services such as local mental health, local children services, local welfare, local juvenile justice, local child welfare, and so on. *Finally*, the secretary also had a staff of fifty in his headquarters' policy office that could reinstruct either program managers or regional directors on behalf of the secretary. With three groups of managers all directing, everyone was giving directions and no one really directed anything. Long before, I had decided that the regional directors, who were in the community and closest to the clients, should be in charge. So my choices were clear. First, eliminate the secretary's policy office. Second, shrink down the Tallahassee program offices so that they could *only* coordinate the work of the regions. And third, finish shifting responsibility/authority to the regions, the regional directors, and their local boards of directors.

I was secretary of the Department of Health and Rehabilitative Services for 120 days. During that time, we not only fixed the problem with the massive computer, but also took the first steps toward decentralizing the equally massive agency headquarters. In most cases, this did not involve actually firing the employees, but transferring them back out to districts and local offices where they were desperately needed. By the time I left, we had eliminated the secretary's policy office, and also eliminated two entire layers of senior management from the Tallahassee bureaucracy. This in turn had meant that we could also send the staff support for these eliminated managers—300 in all—back to the districts. When the personnel departed, what remained was two totally empty Tallahassee office buildings, plus truckloads of office furniture and equipment, which was also shipped out to district offices. Finally, we tripled the inspector general's staff.

As of this writing, Florida's troubled Department of Health and Rehabilitative Services no longer exists. It has finally been decentralized, and is now the Department of Children and Families. Decentralization was accomplished by organizing "privatized" nonprofit Community Based Corporations (CBCs), which now provide human services under contract with DCF. At long last, the person making the decisions and delivering the services resides in the same community as the person needing the services. Tallahassee has been taken out of the management role, except for specific functions (e.g., the child abuse hotline and protective investigations) which remain a state responsibility. Decentralization has not been easy. Washington has been involved every step of the way and federal waivers have been required. Lawton Chiles and I took the first steps. Jeb Bush finished the structural reorganization with the privatization effort, which predictably was controversial and chaotic. Charlie Crist, to his credit, brought in Bob Butterworth, former longtime attorney general of Florida, as secretary of DCF. Butterworth, understanding the need to rebuild credibility within DCF, immediately established a policy of transparency and candor with the courts, the press, and the legislature. When mistakes were made, instead of stonewalling, Butterworth insisted on immediate investigation and openness. In the disastrous Foster Care program, instead of continuing the policy of removing children from troubled homes, Butterworth instituted a new policy of providing services in the home, putting the parents on probation, and keeping families together, except in cases of obvious danger to the child. After almost two years, Butterworth retired, having transformed the culture of DCF and created a new level of respect for the agency. Again to his credit, Governor Crist appointed another Democrat, George Sheldon, to succeed Bob Butterworth as secretary of DCF. Sheldon, who served as Bob Butterworth's deputy, is a former legislator whose experience with the troubled history of DCF goes all the way back to drafting the statutes which authorized the predecessor agency in the 1970s. Under Sheldon, the policies begun by Butterworth have been accelerated. Foster care caseloads are being dramatically reduced without increasing the risk to children, and DCF is being recognized nationally for its dramatic improvement.

Making Sense of Growth Management

Environmental concern in America got a big boost in the 1960s with Rachael Carson's book, *Silent Spring.* Toxic pesticides, herbicides, and industrial chemicals with long-lasting residues had become widespread. For years, these poisons had been killing birds, wild animals, fish, plant life—and even humans—without arousing any great public outcry. DDT was the first great alarm, as entire species of birds were threatened with extinction. However, it soon became apparent that DDT was not the sole culprit. Other widely used pesticides, like parathion, were even more toxic. Other studies showed that individual species could not be considered in isolation. Instead, the concept of interdependence was becoming widely accepted. All species, including humans, were finally coming to be seen as part of an all-encompassing ecosystem.

In Tallahassee, this new understanding was first expressed by a new environmental advocacy group, C-70, which introduced a specific package of reforms in the 1970 legislative session. This subsequently led to broader reforms like the Growth Policy Project, Environmental Land and Water Management Act, the Local Government Comprehension Planning Act, and the Growth Management Act. Florida's primary new environmental regulatory agencies were the Department of Environmental Regulation and the five regional water management districts. Each of these new laws, as well as each new enforcement agency, was predictably seen in agriculture and the rural areas as big government encroaching on individual liberty, and the battle lines were quickly drawn. As an active citrus grower who was also helping pass the new environmental laws, I was once again outside the lines. Many of these Florida reform efforts began while Lawton Chiles was a Florida senator, but they were not passed as new legislation until after 1970. By that time, Lawton was a member of the U.S. Senate, and deeply involved in development of the Clean Water Act, the Clean Air Act, and the new federal enforcement agency, the Environmental Protection Agency, or EPA. Since I had been in the thick of Florida's earlier environmental battles, Lawton asked me at the outset of our partnership to assume responsibility for bringing coherence to Florida's parallel efforts to manage growth while also protecting the quality and quantity of Florida's water.

This resulted in several separate but related efforts. The first step was our decision that Florida's five growth management agencies must begin functioning as a single entity on issues involving growth management. These were the Departments of Transportation, Community Affairs, Commerce, Labor, and Environmental Regulation. Although the Department of Natural Resources was a cabinet agency, its secretary asked to be included in the new growth management group. This appeared to be simple, but it actually proved to be complicated because it meant each of these agencies could no longer function as an advocate for its own individual interest group. The Departments of Transportation, Commerce, and Labor had traditionally viewed their roles as growth stimulators. On the opposing side were the Departments of Environmental Regulation, Natural Resources, and Community Affairs, which were responsible for planning, natural resource protection, and balancing growth and concerns for the environment. These opposing roles of growth stimulation and natural resource protection were spelled out in the statutes creating the agencies, and pushed with single-minded intensity by the interest groups that constituted each agency's de facto constituency. Cities and counties would plan for future development to move in a direction that would minimize environmental damage, while at the same time, the Department of Transportation planned new highways that conflicted with the plans of the cities and counties. Invariably, development moved in the direction of the new roads. Nobody considered working together. Agency heads, reflecting the views of the interest groups that were their constituencies, argued that their statutory responsibility prevented compromise. Knowing that development would follow highways, the Department of Environmental Regulation took great pride in filing suit to stop each new highway. Traditionally Florida's governors had not taken sides in this interagency anarchy, although all the combatants were answerable to the governor. In effect, Florida had a growth policy for each interest group, and left it to the courts to sort out the conflicts.

Lawton and I adopted a radically different approach. To begin with, we recruited secretaries for the growth management agencies who understood the big picture and were willing to work as a team to limit growth to the carrying capacity of Florida's rivers, lakes, beaches, wetlands, and the natural systems that depended on them. We decreed that there would be no more lawsuits between growth management agencies. To insure teamwork, we negotiated a written agreement between the heads of the respective growth management agencies and my office. This agreement, which we all signed, spelled out what we were trying to accomplish, what each agency's job was, and how we would resolve disputes. Any dispute not settled by the agencies would come to me for resolution. There would be no appeal.

Our growth management secretaries were some of the finest people who ever served in state government. Bill Sadowski, secretary of the Department of Community Affairs, took a leave of absence as managing partner of the Miami office of Akerman, Senterfitt, one of Florida's leading law firms. Bill, a highly respected former state legislator, totally transformed the Department of Community Affairs and its relationship with local government. He was tragically killed in the crash of a state aircraft, and his death took much of the pleasure out of life, for me and for Bill's other friends and colleagues. Frank Scruggs—my former law partner from Steel, Hector, and Davis, with a commanding intellect and an eloquence that could bring tears to your eyes—was our secretary of Labor. His pioneering efforts transformed this department from a hopeless bureaucratic muddle into an agency that actually helped unemployed workers with retraining and finding new jobs. As we became involved with welfare reform, the revitalized Department of Labor played a key role.

Ben Watts, a West Point–trained civil engineer, was our secretary of Transportation. Under Ben's leadership, Florida's DOT was totally decentralized, making it more responsive, transparent, and efficient. Road builders—whether Democrats or Republicans—agreed that Chiles's eight years brought less favoritism and political interference than at any time in the history of DOT. Carol Browner, our secretary of the Department of Environmental Regulation, was a fearless and knowledgeable advocate for Florida's environment. Carol went on to become secretary of the EPA under President Bill Clinton, and has now been appointed by President Obama as assistant to the president for energy and climate change. Her successor, Ginger Wetherell, a respected former state legislator, emerged as a leader in our unique program of Ecosystem Management. Greg Farmer, my former congressional staff director and close friend, left an important corporate position in Washington to become Florida's secretary of commerce. Greg totally transformed Florida's approach to economic development, leading the effort to abolish the Department of Commerce, transforming it into Enterprise Florida, Inc., a private nonprofit corporation. Greg also utilized this model of privatization in abolishing the Division of Tourism, replacing it with Visit Florida, Inc. Both of these nonprofit corporations are actually public-private partnerships, replacing state bureaucracies with private sector management techniques. Their boards of directors are drawn equally from the private and public sectors, and the private sector puts up a major part of the money to fund their budgets. Greg left us to become assistant secretary of commerce for tourism in Washington. Ultimately, Greg's efforts led to the privatization of this federal function.

Recruiting and coordinating this outstanding group of leaders was one of the most important and satisfying accomplishments of the Chiles years. All of us appreciated the fact that Lawton never backed down, and supported our efforts from the first day. His only joking comment was that the more Carol, Bill, Greg, Ginger, and I trampled on the perks of his powerful friends, the fewer invitations he got to go turkey hunting at their ranches.

Making Sense of Water Management Districts

Recognizing that growth management would never make sense until water managers had to take into account the needs of the environment, Lawton also put me in charge of coordinating policy for Florida's water management districts. All of these were the responsibility of the governor, although each had its own governing board. During our eight years, board membership was balanced, with environmentalists having at least as much influence as developers. Every person appointed by Lawton to a water management district board was personally interviewed, to assure each appointee understood our policy and was committed to enforce it. Stated simply, our goal was to manage Florida's water resources so as to assure sustainability, or sufficient water for Florida's natural systems.

The key was to assure "minimum flows and levels" and manage water consumption to assure that streams and lakes—and the ecosystems which depended on them—were not overwhelmed by rampant growth. The term "minimum flows and levels" described the minimum standard mandated by the Florida legislature in 1972, and generally ignored ever since. A lawsuit had been brought in the '80s to enforce this standard, as lakes and rivers had begun drying up. Florida's courts had affirmed that the law meant what it said, but the result was more of the same—nothing was done. Water managers took the peculiar position that no one knew how to establish minimum flows and levels, and therefore they were burdened with an unenforceable law. The awkward reality was that their governing boards had traditionally been either developers or vanity appointees who had been kept in a state of voluntary ignorance of Florida's statutory policy. Florida's de facto "policy" for twenty years had been to accommodate development based on political power, rather than protecting environmental systems. During our eight years, a modest number of high prestige board members who weren't committed to our agreed goals were not reappointed. This entire effort was intense, controversial, and involved politically powerful people. Lawton never flinched in his support.

The Strange Story of Ecosystem Management

In 1993, Lawton and I finally succeeded in merging Florida's overlapping and competing Department of Environmental Regulation and Department of Natural Resources, creating a new Department of Environmental Protection. At our request, the organizing statute mandated the development of an ecosystem management approach. This was the beginning of one of the most significant innovations of our entire eight years in office. The basic idea was to scrap the traditional disjointed, uncoordinated regulatory approach and develop "place-based management." Under this approach, hydrological and ecological connections were given priority, instead of jurisdiction based on political boundaries. A good example is the dilemma of the manager of a state park that includes a spring. He is responsible for protecting the spring, yet the recharge area for the spring is largely outside the park boundaries. The land is owned by hundreds of landowners, and land use permitting (e.g., development, dumping, pumping, etc.) is regulated by cities, counties, private utilities, water management districts, or no one at all. In reality, the park manager cannot protect the spring unless he receives cooperation from landowners and regulatory authorities outside his park boundaries.

In addition to place-based management, the other radically new proposal was to replace the existing adversarial regulatory culture with a cooperative approach. We called this "common sense regulation." Citizens needed to take more responsibility for Florida's environment. Without the full involvement of landowners, businesses, and ordinary homeowners, it is folly to expect that government alone can protect Florida's natural systems. To induce cooperation instead of litigation, we refocused the permitting process on results. What government needs is better protection of air and water. What we do not need is government trying to tell businesses, farmers, and homeowners how to obtain the results. To induce cooperation and citizen responsibility, government had to find ways to be more cooperative, less bureaucratic, and less intrusive. Place-based teams were formed when environmental agencies joined with citizens and landowners. The phosphate industry embraced "team permitting," and actually provided more protection to natural systems than they would have through the normal regulatory approach. Under the Clean Marina program, marinas volunteered to clean up their facilities in exchange for being labeled a "Clean Marina." There are many other success stories, particularly around Florida's major springs. During its short existence, Ecosystem Management was popular amongst citizens, landowners, universities, and the business community. Other states requested presentations, and a couple of other countries sent experts to review this new approach. Pam McVety, an experienced and respected environmental manager, was responsible for transforming Ecosystem Management from a theoretical proposition to a practical reality. Under the able leadership of Ginger Wetherell and Pam McVety, the Department of Environmental Protection won a number of awards for Ecosystem Management, including being a finalist for the Kennedy School of Government and the Ford Foundation Award for Innovations in American Government.

Ecosystem Management was just starting to gather momentum when Jeb Bush took office and cancelled the program. The only thing that survived was a Springs Initiative based on our place-based team at Ichetucknee Springs. The program's demise occurred at a critical point, because our next step would have been to link the place-based management teams with local government comprehensive planning. The goal was for local citizens to take responsibility for their natural systems, and voluntarily make changes, not only in how they manage their lands, but also in how their communities protect these lands.

The irony is inescapable. Here we had a successful, popular program getting government off the little guy's back and reducing regulation, while improving environmental protection. It was more conservative than anything Jeb did, except cut taxes. What went wrong? There are many dimensions to the decision of which programs to eliminate. I think the deciding factor was the failure of Florida's environmental interest groups to step up and list Ecosystem Management as a priority. These people are my friends and supporters, but their Tallahassee representatives could never get comfortable with a nonadversarial team approach. Perhaps they thought it reduced the leverage they had under Florida's traditional practices. In any event, environmental regulation went back to business as usual.

The Coming Train Wreck

Our efforts to achieve coordination between state agencies and water management districts, complex as they were, only dealt with part of the problem. The remainder had to do with coordination between water management districts and local governments or water supply authorities. Unlike state agencies and water management districts, these local government entities are independent from the governor and the only way to get cooperation is to pass a law requiring it. The political power in Florida—the home builders, developers, construction trade unions, and the banks that finance them—is all on the opposite side.

It took three years, but finally, in 1997, we passed legislation that made the most significant changes in Chapter 373 F.S. since its passage in 1972. One of my biggest regrets is that we were unable to prevail on the most critical policy debate of all. Politically, it was not possible to give *appointed* officials (water management districts) power to override decisions by *elected* local governments. The result was that, incredible as it may seem, water management districts continued to be required to grant permits to withdraw water for new developments and new golf courses, even when it was clear from the evidence that there was not enough water for the new development without drying up our lakes and rivers. As of the date of this writing, legislation has been passed requiring local governments to identify new sources of water before granting permits to withdraw water. There is much confusion, however, and it appears at present that many of the proposed "new" sources will, in fact, be nothing more than the withdrawal of "excess" water from Florida's rivers. Since studies have not yet determined the minimum water needed to sustain Florida's ecosystems, nothing has changed. In fact, because of the slowdown in growth resulting from the current financial crisis, the situation is actually becoming more critical: In 2009, the legislature began systematically repealing key elements of Florida's system of environmental regulation. When growth resumes, development will be even more out of control. This is Florida's impending train wreck.

Lawton's Last Hurrah—Joe Camel Meets the He-Coon

Florida's lawsuit against "Big Tobacco" is the stuff of legend. It ended in 1997 with a historic settlement. The tobacco industry agreed to pay the State of Florida a sum in excess of $11 billion as compensation for taxpayers' money spent over decades taking care of Florida's indigent and uninsured citizens who were suffering from tobacco-related lung cancer and related illnesses.

Over the years, the tobacco controversy had gradually increased in intensity, as lawsuit after lawsuit by countless individual plaintiffs was filed. From a litigation standpoint, the problems were immense. The threshold issues involved the industry's insistence that tobacco was not addictive, and that if it was addictive, the tobacco industry had no reason to know this. In addition, for an individual, the difficulty of proving that smoking had caused his or her illness proved immense. Cynicism was the order of the day. For every dollar the tobacco industry spent defending lawsuits, it spent many more on ads linking smoking to masculinity (The Marlboro Man), and then to attractiveness in females (You've Come a Long Way, Baby). Gradually, internal industry documents appeared, making it clear that top management had known for years that smoking was addictive, and that smoking was connected to a measurable increase in the incidence of lung cancer. At some point, it had become clear that even the surgeon general's warning printed on each pack of cigarettes had been a double-edged sword. On the one hand, it was a direct warning that smoking caused cancer. On the other hand, it gave credence to the legal defense that smokers had knowingly assumed the risk, and were thus responsible for their own injury.

That part of the tobacco story had made headlines for years. In state after state, juries had awarded multi-million-dollar verdicts, only to have them overturned in appellate courts. Then another dimension was added, as it became increasingly clear that the industry, through saturation advertising campaigns with cute cartoon characters like Joe Camel (complete with a cigarette dangling from his lower lip) were purposely aimed at getting more children to start smoking. The dilemma of the tobacco industry was simple: If your product is lethal, you are going to be regularly killing off your best customers. This dilemma was supported by the arithmetic, which went something like this: Every day, 3,000 smokers were dying and 2,000 more were quitting. In order to stay in business, the tobacco industry had to find 5,000 new smokers each day. It was as simple as that. Once he understood the real story of

Joe Camel, Lawton became enraged, and a totally different story began. This story had a legislative subplot in addition to the ever-present litigation theme. Both of these were overlaid on a bare-knuckle back room political brawl with no rules and no referees. Having been a member of the Florida Senate's Doghouse Democrats, in opposition to Senate president Dempsey Barron, I knew something about backroom political brawls. This one topped even that. As one observer put it, this was a lobbyist Olympics.

W.D. and the Mother of All Conspiracies

It began just as the Senate was about to recess for lunch, toward the end of a legislative session, with a secret amendment which came directly from Senator W. D. Childers' computer. Childers offered it as a "friendly" amendment to Senator Howard Foreman's noncontroversial Medicaid bill which just happened to be pending on the Senate calendar. In the end-of-the-session crunch, the explanation of the amendment by Senator Childers was all-purpose and generic: "This just cleans up a couple of glitches in the law." According to Steven Bosquet, a member of the press who happened to be observing, Senator Foreman looked surprised, but made no objection to the Childers amendment. Senators were distracted, and the bill passed unanimously along with numerous other uncontroversial bills.

Senator Foreman was not the only person surprised by the Childers amendment. Guy Spearman, the knowledgeable and tenacious lobbyist who represented tobacco among other clients, had taken the usual end-of-session precaution of assigning a staff member to read last-minute amendments as soon as they reached the Senate clerk's office. Despite its obscure wording, the amendment had to do with liability of third parties (i.e., the tobacco industry), under Florida's Medicaid statute. Seeing this, Spearman immediately faxed the amendment to attorneys at Covington and Burling, the nationally known law firm which represented Spearman's tobacco clients. Their response was immediate: the Childers amendment was potentially lethal and must be delayed until it could be fully analyzed. Spearman went directly to the office of the Speaker of the House, where Speaker Bo Johnson left the podium to talk with him. Spearman informed Johnson of the urgency of the situation and asked that the Foreman bill, with its amendment, be delayed for twenty-four hours to allow his lawyers time to evaluate its potential impact. Johnson gave a friendly, vaguely reassuring response. What Spearman and his henchpersons did not know was that Johnson, the Speaker, and Peter Rudy Wallace, the chairman of the House Rules Committee, were both parties to the Childers conspiracy. The next day, while Spearman's lawyers were still analyzing the Childers amendment, the Medicaid bill, complete with the Childers amendment, appeared at the top of the Special Order calendar and passed the House unanimously. Soon thereafter, the amended Medicaid bill received approval from the governor's staff and became the law of Florida.

The "glitches" that the Childers amendment had cleared up were those provisions that had previously made it impossible for the State of Florida to sue the tobacco industry. In layperson's language, here is what had occurred: First, in the event of a suit by the state of Florida against the tobacco industry, the defense of assumption of risk would not be applicable. Second, because of the large numbers of Medicaid and welfare patients involved, individual damages did not have to be proved. Statistical calculations were acceptable in proving damages. Third, each individual company's share of the total damages could be calculated based on market share. Without a word of debate, Florida's law had been changed to allow the state to sue the tobacco industry for the hundreds of millions of taxpayer dollars it had paid out in medical treatment of uninsured and indigent victims of tobacco-related diseases. Senator Childers, with a straight face, maintained at first that he was the innocent victim, and that some anonymous villain had slipped the amendment past him. This story might have been plausible, except that within days, the *Wall Street Journal,* having been tipped off by Childers' friend and attorney, Fred Levin, broke the real story. The *Wall Street Journal's* report was basically accurate, except that Fred Levin's version of the story stated that the Childers amendment had slipped past, unnoticed by Guy Spearman and other tobacco lobbyists. In fact, Spearman later told me that the only place he had been caught off guard was in not realizing that the Speaker and chair of the Rules Committee were both included in the conspiracy.

To people familiar with the Florida legislature and its rules and procedures, this had been the Mother of All Conspiracies. Finding an uncontroversial bill with a topic germane to the Childers amendment was, in itself, a major challenge. Getting the bill positioned at the top of the Senate Special Order calendar during the closing days was even harder. Recruiting the Speaker, rules chairman, and other co-conspirators in the House who were willing and able to move the Senate bill with the Childers amendment, without leaking the news of the conspiracy, was almost unthinkable. To cap things off, in the absence of this conspiracy, there was no way an amendment with this amount of substance could have escaped the scrutiny of the governor's staff, who operated free of the chaos and confusion of the closing days of the legislature. In fact, the Childers conspiracy had included members of the Senate and House; Governor Chiles and Attorney General Bob Butterworth had signed off in advance; and worst of all, the fingerprints of a trial lawyer were all over it.

The fingerprints on the Childers amendment were those of Fred Levin. At a national conference of trial lawyers, he had heard a discussion of the Mississippi lawsuit against the tobacco industry, and the formidable technical problems involved. Back home, Levin had looked at Florida's Medicaid statute and realized how simple it would be "by changing a few commas and semicolons" to minimize these problems. Levin developed a plan, which he took to his friend, Childers, who arranged a breakfast with Lawton Chiles at the governor's mansion. Chiles immediately approved the idea of trying to amend the Medicaid statute, and demanded total secrecy. Levin was surprised at the intensity of Chiles's feelings, particularly his anger at the industry's cynical use of the Joe Camel character to make tobacco more tempting to children. From this point forward, Harold Lewis, a member of Chiles's staff, assisted Levin and Childers. Dexter Douglass, Chiles's general counsel, was involved, as was Bob Butterworth, Florida's attorney general. Levin began recruiting a "dream team," consisting of some of Florida's top trial lawyers, while Childers put together the plan for passage of the necessary changes in Florida's Medicaid statute. In an unprecedented move, the dream team would cover all the litigation costs, and their fee would be contingent on success. If the tobacco industry won, the suit would not cost the state of Florida any money.

There was a downside to the conspiracy. Passage of the Childers amendment had embarrassed many respected legislators, in addition to some of Tallahassee's most experienced lobbyists. They argued that it had been a breach of the duty of candor which legislators owe to the institution and to each other. Whether or not this was true, many legislators had clearly been caught napping. These legislators, encouraged by a large group of lobbyists, came back to Tallahassee the next year vowing to repeal the Childers amendment. This made it harder to sustain Lawton's position. Individual legislators who had voted in favor of a suit against the tobacco industry were pressed hard by tobacco lobbyists to reverse their position as soon as the next session began because of their outrage over the trickery involved in passing the Childers amendment. In a bizarre effort to clear his name, Senator Childers announced that he would vote in favor of repealing his own amendment. Chiles, disillusioned by the obvious power of the tobacco lobbyists and sensing an impending defeat, sought to enlist his longtime friend, Mallory Horne. Over the course of his long legislative career, Mallory had the unique distinction of having been House Speaker, and later Senate President. As a legislative strategist, he was second to none. At first, Mallory declined to be involved. Pressed by Chiles for the reason, Mallory told Lawton he was naive to think he could win a fight against Big Tobacco. Legislators knew they could vote against Chiles without fear of adverse consequences. Lawton responded by authorizing Mallory to assume the role of "enforcer."

At the start of the session, the repeal effort had strong momentum. Horne's first action was to quietly let it be known that legislators voting for repeal would no longer be considered the governor's friends. According to Mallory, many legislators, including first-timers, had grown accustomed to the idea that they could vote against Chiles without suffering any adverse consequences. Horne's warning quickly became reality, as the governor's new budget pointedly omitted items favored by legislators supporting the tobacco industry's effort to repeal the Childers amendment. Despite Horne's tough new rules, legislation to repeal the Childers amendment quickly passed the House. Later the Senate also voted to repeal, but the vote was much closer. Predictably, Chiles vetoed the repeal bill. The question now was whether both houses of the legislature could muster a two-thirds majority to override Lawton's veto. In the House, the veto was overridden. In the Senate, however, the situation was different. Based on the previous vote to repeal, it was unclear whether the votes were there to override the veto. Lawton's challenge now was not so overwhelming: A two-thirds majority was required to override a veto, so Chiles and Mallory Horne only had to convince fourteen out of forty senators to vote to sustain his veto.

The Strange Debate on the Veto Override

Throughout this period, the lobbying pressure was incredibly intense. Both the tobacco industry and the governor's office made it clear they intended to take no prisoners. Two Democrats, Senators George Kirkpatrick and Charles Williams, said they would vote with the tobacco industry to override the veto. It was also known that one Republican, Senator John Grant, would vote with Chiles to uphold the veto. Senator Ginny Brown-Waite, a Republican, and Senator Pat Thomas, a Democrat, had both voted with the industry to repeal the law, but Mallory felt they might be persuadable. Childers, as always, was a wild card. He had already voted at least once on each side, and there was no way to predict what he would do next. Mallory's assumption was that having been "shown the light" by the tobacco industry, Childers would vote to override the veto. The main target of both sides was Thomas. When I had been a member of the Florida Senate, Pat and I had been a part of the same delegation. We had run for office in several of the same counties, and had also been seatmates in the Senate for six years. He represented his constituents honestly and effectively. I cherished his friendship. In a pressure cooker situation like this veto override, Pat would typically make an art form out of what appeared to be indecision. It was not unusual for Pat to swing from firmly undecided to leaning yes and then to leaning no, giving no clue as to his true intentions. On the day of the actual vote, he would often contrive to be the last undecided vote. Over the years, this tactic had magnified his leverage on issues as varied as new roads, new prisons, and judges, all of which were critical to Pat's rural Panhandle counties. Mallory, who had also served at various times in the same delegation with Pat, understood his unique ways as well as anyone could. The 1995 session had come to a close with neither side moving to bring up Lawton's veto for an override vote. Mallory told the old story of the fearful patient, watching the dentist prepare to drill, who suddenly grabbed the dentist's private parts and said, "We don't want to hurt each other, do we?" According to Mallory, at the conclusion of the 1995 session, each side had the other by the private parts, and nobody could afford to make a move.

As the opening date of the 1996 session approached, the scene resembled a game of high-stakes poker. Pat Thomas and Ginny Brown-Waite were still publicly committed to vote with the industry on the override, but Mallory had reason to believe that, for personal reasons having nothing to do with politics, both were having second thoughts. The industry must have sensed the same thing, because a decision was made to go forward in the opening days of the 1996 session. Under Senate rules, vetoes were referred back to the original committee of jurisdiction. Senate rules were unclear, however, about how or when a veto override could be taken out of the committee and put on the floor for a vote by the full Senate.

During the interim, a request had been made for a ruling by the Senate president, Jim Scott, a pro-tobacco Republican who favored overriding the veto. During the opening week of the 1996 session, before Chiles's forces had had a chance to rehearse speeches or prepare a final debate strategy, Senator Scott ruled from the podium that vetoed legislation could be withdrawn from committee and brought directly to the floor anytime the Senate was in session. This ruling, a surprise, was followed a week later by a motion from the floor by Senator Kirkpatrick to withdraw the tobacco bill from committee and override the governor's veto. Mallory Horne and Dexter Douglass, joined by Chief of Staff Linda Shelley, her deputy, Dan Stengel, and Harold Lewis could do nothing but watch the debate on television. At one point, as tempers rose on the floor of the Senate, Dexter Douglass, ever the fighter, wanted Lawton Chiles to go on the Senate floor and personally appeal to wavering senators (as a former member of the Senate, Lawton had floor privileges). Mallory Horne felt strongly that the tactic might backfire, with senators resenting what would be seen as strong-arm tactics. Harold Lewis sided with Douglass, while Shelley and Stengel sided with Horne. In the end, Horne's side prevailed.

Mallory sent a note to Pat Thomas, asking him to step off the floor and talk. Mallory's recollection is that Thomas, obviously under emotional stress, said that his prior commitment to the tobacco industry weighed heavily on him, and he intended to vote to override Lawton's veto. Mallory concluded that this was not a tactic to gain leverage, but a sincere statement. According to Mallory, Lawton's response was also sincere. He was deeply offended, and immediately sent Thomas a handwritten note saying he hoped that after all they had been through together, their friendship weighed as heavily as Pat's commitment to the industry. According to Mallory, Pat Thomas came back off the Senate floor with tears in his eyes and told Mallory to tell Lawton he would vote to sustain Lawton's veto.

The debate was close to a conclusion, but the outcome was still unclear. Neither Brown-Waite nor Thomas had taken the floor. Suddenly Brown-Waite rose and sought recognition. She began by describing the personal anguish of watching helplessly as her father, a lifelong smoker, died from lung cancer. She ended with the following statement: "I'm fed up with the tobacco industry, and I'm not going to support them anymore. I want to be proud of this vote." As she concluded, there was silence. Then Senator Childers took the floor and said, "It's over. It's over! The governor wins!" He then made a unique, entertaining, and profane speech, in which he caustically assured other senators that, although many of them had scolded him during the debate for his breach of the duty of candor, he would not identify those other SOBs who had known in advance about the amendment (he was cautioned by the presiding officer that the proceedings were being carried on live television, but continued without pausing). After assuring the SOBs that their secret was safe with him, Childers finally concluded with a statement that if the tobacco veto was brought back for a vote, he would "probably vote" to sustain the governor's veto.

The debate was clearly over. Senator Thomas had advised the industry he intended to support the governor. There was no need for a vote, which would have put every senator on record. Senator Kirkpatrick moved that the Senate adjourn, and that was the end for Joe Camel. Although the rules would have allowed the veto override to be brought up again, everyone realized that, as a practical matter, the votes were "probably" not there to support an override.

Prior to the passage of the Childers amendment, Fred Levin's "dream team" had begun the background research for Florida's lawsuit against the tobacco industry. According to Bob Kerrigan, who had been chosen, along with Bob Montgomery, as lead counsel, if the Childers amendment was defeated, they had little more than an ancient common law theory of liability to support their position. Now, however, the odds in favor of the state of Florida's lawsuit improved dramatically. That afternoon, one of the tobacco companies announced that it would no longer contest the lawsuit. It appeared for the first time that there might be a realistic chance to win the lawsuit, or at least reach a settlement. At an impromptu celebration that same evening, Pat Thomas said that his decision to oppose the tobacco industry had resulted in large part from listening to his wife, Mary Anne, who, like Lawton and Rhea Chiles, had been furious with the tobacco industry for using the Joe Camel character to induce children to start smoking.

Much like the legislative debate, the suit against the tobacco industry was unparalleled in its intensity. Every issue was contested. The defense lawyers, realizing that Lawton's team was financing the massive pretrial effort out of its members' own pockets, purposely took advantage of every technicality. The stakes were high because other states were looking to the Florida case as a precedent. Members of the trial team, all of whom were accustomed to being in the spotlight, found it difficult to divide the pretrial responsibilities. With some prodding from Lawton, it was agreed that lead counsel at trial would be Bob Montgomery of West Palm Beach, and Bob Kerrigan of Pensacola. They coordinated with the respected lawyer Parker Thomson of Miami, who had been retained by Attorney General Butterworth as special counsel.

The conclusion of the lawsuit was as unorthodox as its beginning. In a Palm Beach courtroom, jury selection had begun. In another room, settlement negotiations had also begun. Tobacco industry representatives were negotiating with Bob Butterworth, Parker Thomson, Bob Kerrigan, and Bob Montgomery, representing the State of Florida. Also at the table for the final negotiations were Lawton and Rhea Chiles. They insisted that the billboards with the Marlboro Man and Joe Camel be taken down, and that a separate trust fund be established—with funding from the tobacco industry—to support an antismoking campaign targeted at teenagers. Finally, after intense negotiations that continued until the early morning hours, a settlement was reached. Florida's success became the model for an unprecedented national settlement.

Early in Lawton Chiles's career, he had embarked on a long-shot thousand-mile walk, which had been a symbolic protest against the corrupting influence of big money in Florida politics. He and Rhea often said this initial campaign not only changed Florida politics, but also influenced Lawton, making him see the importance of siding with ordinary citizens against the power of big corporations and big government. Throughout his career, he pursued this uphill struggle. How fitting that his final battle would be against odds just as great as those he had faced in the beginning. The other thing Lawton's final battle demonstrated was that there are still politicians like Pat Thomas and Ginny Brown-Waite, who upon seeing a leader willing to lay it on the line as Lawton did, can be depended upon to do the right thing.

The 1998 Governor's Race

The Campaign from Hell

Looking back, the entire drama of my 1998 campaign was foreshadowed by the clumsy way my candidacy was announced. It was as if the curtain suddenly came up before the lights had been dimmed or the audience had been seated. This bizarre development occurred less than halfway through the second Chiles-MacKay term. It was in August, 1996—twenty-seven months before the 1998 election. In addition to my regular responsibilities, I was also serving as chair of the Miami Oversight Board. I was also Florida campaign chair for the Clinton-Gore team as they campaigned for reelection in November 1996.

The political scene in Florida was chaotic. Since the 1994 gubernatorial campaign, Jeb Bush had reinvented himself as a politician who was concerned about the needs of all Floridians and was a person of substance and knowledge. To his credit, Jeb had spent little time sulking. He had organized a think tank called the Foundation for Florida's Future. The Foundation was professionally staffed, with Jeb as its chair. Articles and commentaries appeared, championing an ideology that called for reduced taxes, smaller government, school vouchers, privatization, and freedom from regulation. Using the foundation as his base,

Jeb spoke regularly across the state, achieving visibility unprecedented for a person with no record, experience, or credentials. He also authored a book—with help from a professional writer—purporting to set forth his views. All in all, it was a highly effective pre-political campaign, totally preempting other potential Republican candidates. From 1994 on, Jeb Bush became the de facto Republican nominee. My supporters were concerned that Jeb was campaigning on a full-time basis, while I was continuing to bury myself in the trivia of trying to make government work. A number of my friends suggested that if there was ever a time to "rise above principle" and start campaigning, this was it. It was illegal to raise money or actually campaign before qualifying as a candidate, although it was possible to open an exploratory account to cover preliminary expenses before making a formal announcement.

By mid-1996, Senator Bob Graham was rumored to be interested. After having been governor, he was said to be finding the U.S. Senate slow and frustrating. A number of Graham's close friends were also friends and confidants of mine. It was an awkward situation. Third parties who purported to be emissaries, but might have been independent entrepreneurs, suggested a deal where Bob Graham would resign from the U.S. Senate and declare his candidacy for governor. If this were to occur, Chiles would then appoint me to the U.S. Senate to serve out the remainder of Bob Graham's unexpired term. Jeb's campaign and rumors of Bob Graham's candidacy placed me under intense pressure. I either had to raise money to pay for a political campaign, or skirt the law, start campaigning, and pretend nothing was happening. I filed papers with the Elections Division of the Office of the Secretary of State, making it clear that I intended to open an exploratory campaign account. Actually announcing my candidacy was a long way off—or so I thought. Abruptly and unexpectedly, though, the curtain lifted.

Someone in the Elections Division called the *St. Petersburg Times* and the *Miami Herald*, both of which ran stories that I had announced for governor. There was no way I could deny it now. Three days later, the AP wrote a profile of Jeb Bush in which it noted that Jeb did not intend to rely on public financing, and thus did not intend to abide by the limitations on contributions required by the campaign finance law.

The article went on to say that Bob Graham was the only Democrat who could defeat Jeb. So much for my exploratory campaign.

The Democratic Primary

For fourteen months, until November 1997, I was the only announced candidate from either party, so the press focused on my quarterly financial reports as a way of handicapping my prospects. Strangely enough, this situation was just what I needed to make me concentrate on organizing a campaign and raising money.

At the Florida Democratic convention, a straw ballot in which I was listed as a candidate alongside Rick Dantzler and Keith Arnold—both respected members of the Florida Senate—had me receiving 82 percent of the vote among Democrats. President Clinton broke with tradition and attended my fundraiser in December 1997, although I was not yet the Democratic nominee. As a result, I ended 1997 with more money than anyone anticipated. Jim Pugh, one of America's largest builders and managers of apartments, who lived in Winter Park, had agreed to chair my campaign. He and my longtime friend and political advisor, Ted Phelps, devoted a major part of their time for several months to help get my campaign off to a solid financial beginning. We had no campaign manager, and paid staff consisted of only those persons essential for scheduling and financial reporting, while everything else was done by volunteers. My friends over the years, including Greg Farmer, John Edward Smith, Sandy D'Alemberte, Jim Apthorp, Duby Ausley, Jon Moyle, Walter McLin, Sam Dubbin, and others were functioning as a steering committee. They were joined by Jay Stein, CEO of Steinmart, from Jacksonville, Dr. Phil Frost, founder and CEO of Ivax Pharmaceuticals, from Miami, and other friends from the Clinton-Gore team. Also on my steering committee were Steve Pajcic, Ira Leesfield, and Chris Searcey, leading Florida trial lawyers. Polls had me leading Jeb Bush by a margin of forty-three to forty, and no other Democrat polled over 20 percent. Despite a very awkward beginning, my campaign thus far had been a success. I ended 1997 having raised $1,750,000, in fifteen months.

One issue that caught me totally off guard was the lack of agreement on a theme—or plotline—for my campaign. After seven years in office, Lawton and I were close to achieving our goal of replacing rigid, rule-driven state bureaucracies with community-based partnerships. With this decentralization, we were reducing the role and size of state agencies. Unfortunately, we had never been able to convert this non-ideological concept, which we called "Reinventing Government," into a twenty-second bumper sticker slogan. Although editorial boards were generally supportive, the working press simply wouldn't write about what we had accomplished or the importance of continuing this effort. I was convinced that I could energize Floridians about the need to limit growth and turn control of Florida back to the local community, but many people in my campaign felt strongly that I was being defined as a national Democrat, and that Jeb's ideological slogans were achieving some resonance. After some intense internal arguments, we agreed to conduct a poll to determine the public's views at the end of 1997. The answers that came back were contradictory, ironic, and frustrating.

Voters' memories of the severe cutbacks in the early '90s were sufficiently vivid that few people wanted to risk interfering with Florida's growth-related prosperity, which was only then back in full swing. Partly because of the success of our reforms, people were not particularly interested in further discussions about government reform. Eight years of reinventing government was sufficient for most voters. As one of my advisors put it, we had exceeded the voters' attention span. I was further exasperated that voters seemed not to be concerned about Jeb Bush's ties to developers and that much of his funding was coming from them. His all-purpose message, calling for less government, lower taxes, and privatization, was generally well received by the electorate. "New" Floridians, who flooded into the state in the 1980s and 1990s, were too new to Florida to be interested in arguments about growth, reinventing government, and protecting ecosystems. Any idea that might conceivably lead to an increase in taxes was dead on arrival. With a famous name, a two-year head start, unlimited funds in his campaign, and no record to defend, Jeb's ideological program reflected the same themes being spelled out by the Republican message machine in Washington.

Unlike previous campaigns, where voters had resonated to the centrist, nonideological ideas Lawton and I had put forward, I found myself more and more identified as a national Democrat.

The Willie Logan Revolt

Early in 1998, a particularly nasty dispute broke out in the Democratic caucus of the Florida House of Representatives. Willie Logan, the first African American in Florida history to have been selected as Speaker designate, was deposed by his Democratic colleagues and replaced as Speaker designate by Ann MacKenzie, a respected Broward County legislator who happened to be white. Logan was finishing his course work for a Ph.D. at the University of Florida, and was not willing or able to fulfill the traditional responsibilities and expectations the members had for the Democratic leader. Instead of being the headliner at his colleagues' fundraisers in legislative races from Miami to Pensacola, Logan had been busy with his educational obligations.

The black caucus felt, however, that Logan was a victim of racial discrimination, and asked Lawton and me to intervene in this process. We declined, arguing that the governor's office should stay out of internal legislative politics. While this was the right position for us to take, it set off a firestorm in Florida's black caucus. We were accused by Congressman Alcee Hastings—who himself had been impeached when serving as a federal judge—of being Good Old Boys with a "plantation mentality." For Lawton, the allegations were particularly unpleasant. For me, in the second year of a campaign for governor, they were disastrous. A number of my longtime friends, the leadership of Florida's African American religious and political communities, came to my defense, but Logan's supporters continued to argue that my refusal to intervene was evidence of racial prejudice. The Willie Logan crisis was eventually resolved in April 1998, when Vice President Al Gore personally interceded on my behalf. The leadership of Florida's NAACP and a cross-section of Florida's black political leadership endorsed me. The cost was ninety days of frustration and distraction at a critical time in the campaign and, despite the endorsements, the loss of many black supporters who still thought I had a role in Logan's removal.

While the Willie Logan controversy was playing out, my campaign encountered other significant distractions. Murmurs of concern from the party's old guard began to surface in the press. These were the Democratic lobbyists for law enforcement, firefighters, and prison guards with whom I had collided in my earlier efforts at pension reform. They were joined by the leadership of AFSCME and other public sector unions who had opposed the Chiles-MacKay efforts to reform unduly restrictive civil service rules. Ironically, the "special interests" opposing our efforts to make government more efficient were mostly public sector unions.

Although I could not prove it, I strongly suspected that these same Democratic union leaders and other Democratic leaders opposing reform were, in fact, the "unnamed critics" who were arguing that I couldn't win against Jeb. At the same time, liberal ideologues were arguing that neither Rick Dantzler, Keith Arnold, nor I—the announced Democratic candidates—could win, because we weren't sufficiently liberal. Some were rumored to still be trying to recruit another candidate to run in the Democratic primary. These last rumors turned out to be true. David Lawrence, the publisher of the *Miami Herald*, confirmed that he had been thinking about the Democratic nomination. This led to a critical *Herald* column by Carl Hiaasen, entitled "Publisher Loco." Although Hiaasen did not endorse Dantzler, Arnold, or me, he made it clear that this fight within the Democratic Party establishment was not a good place for an outsider to start a new political career. I was relieved that Lawrence, whom I had respected and considered a friend, did not get in the race.

Members of the Broward legislative delegation were rumored to be among those dissatisfied with my candidacy. This could have meant serious trouble, since Broward County was by far the biggest Democratic county in Florida. Fortunately, I had strong friendships in the Broward party leadership, and they stayed by my side. Dianne Glasser, at a meeting of the Broward County Democratic Executive Committee, announced that any Broward legislators who did not support me would themselves have opposition in the Democratic primary. Finally, an informal meeting of the self-appointed Democratic Party elders was held in Tallahassee. Steve Pajcic, whose candidacy for governor had been crippled by this same kind of Democratic Party meltdown, attended on my behalf. Pajcic's arguments prevailed, and the rumors of a party insurrection finally came to a halt.

Brass Balls

After the Willie Logan fiasco, the leadership of Florida's black community became heavily involved in my campaign. Nobody thought that blacks would support Jeb Bush, but there was a concern that many would simply stay home on election day. I was enthusiastically supported by many of Florida's African American clergy, who insisted that I appear at their Sunday worship services to be endorsed from the pulpit. The leader of Florida's 1,000 AME churches, Bishop Phillip Cousins, was particularly enthusiastic, and insisted that I appear for his endorsement at the annual AME statewide conference at Disney World.

My friend, state representative Alzo Reddick of Orlando, who was well known and respected as a statewide African American leader, accompanied me. The event began with a formal reception. More than 1,000 pastors were in attendance, accompanied by their wives. Alzo and I, together with Mabel Butler, an African American county commissioner, and Betty Carter, a white supervisor of elections, were the only politicians in attendance. Alzo and I arrived thirty minutes late, only to discover that we were still an hour early. We were immediately escorted to our places, approximately 500 persons back from the front of the receiving line. A majestic choir was singing, and nobody was in a hurry. Mabel and Betty, notorious free spirits, immediately sized up the situation and decided to go have a couple of drinks, leaving Alzo and me to hold their places in line. An hour later, just as the reception line began moving, Mabel and Betty reappeared. Clearly they had been having more fun than Alzo and I. As they rejoined us, Mabel was in the midst of an emotional dissertation about her admiration of Lawton's courage: "He's got brass balls! That's what I like: big brass balls!"

Suddenly, the choir finished its final number, and it was just Alzo, Mabel, Betty, and me with 1,000 AME pastors, their spouses, and Bishop Cousins in a huge silent hall. The pastors and their spouses nearest to us, fearing a bolt of lightning, scattered like a covey of quail. There we were, all by ourselves. Making gestures indicating a swinging pendulum, Mabel delivered her concluding line: "That's what I like: A man with brass balls so big that they go clank, clank, clank, when he walks!" Later, Lawton told me that when he met with Bishop Cousins, he had said that although Mabel's terminology was not commonly used in theology, he personally thought the Old Testament prophets probably went clank, clank, clank, as they walked.

My Most Disastrous Mistake

My most disastrous mistake of the campaign was the decision to select a professional campaign manager from outside Florida, instead of asking one of my longtime supporters to lead the campaign. Although Greg Farmer was not available, Julie Fletcher, Samelia King, and Loraine Ausley were. Any one of them was capable of taking over the operation that had been constructed by Jim Pugh, Ted Phelps, and me.

The new campaign manager, Doug Heyl, had previously managed statewide campaigns in Tennessee and New Jersey. He was highly recommended by Bill Clinton. He was interviewed by Jim Pugh and Ted Phelps, who said they could work with him. Based on this, I made the decision to hire Doug, although we had not actually met. Only later, after he had moved to Tallahassee and organized a full campaign staff, did I discover that his exclusive interests were paid media and fundraising. I could not convince him that the network of dedicated Chiles-MacKay volunteers were essential to my campaign plans. It was not a question of Doug's competence, but simply the incompatibility of our ideas. I was torn between my personal impulse to fire him immediately or following the consensus of my advisors, and letting him stay long enough to see if his system would work. Not making an immediate change was my second major mistake. Doug's system might have worked for another candidate, but it was totally repugnant to me.

April and May 1998 were the most miserable months of my entire career. Committing myself entirely to the logic of the professionally managed media campaign, I spent two months, eight hours a day, "cold calling" a list of Democratic contributors. The phone call effort was supported by two staffers. One staffer was dialing the next call while I talked, and the second was tallying the results. There was a paid consultant who came in each week to make sure I stayed "on task." Ironically this was the same system that had totally disgusted Reubin Askew, causing him to abandon his 1988 effort to succeed Lawton Chiles in the U.S. Senate. At the end of sixty days, I had supposedly solid commitments totaling $2.5 million. As it turned out, tallying campaign commitments was exactly like counting votes in the Congress. A "firm" commitment for a future contribution was like a "leaning yes" commitment in a congressional whip count. Commitments were reliable on those days when the campaign was going well, but they often disappeared entirely when things went bad.

On June 30th, Rick Dantzler and I agreed to run as a team. Rick had been my most serious Democratic challenger, and this enabled me to shift my entire focus to the general election. Rick had been a strong Chiles-MacKay supporter and a respected leader in the Florida Senate, with a reputation as a serious thinker who cared intensely about the environment. He and his wife, Julie, are classy, courageous people. If we had been elected, Rick and I would have continued the teamwork that Lawton and I had established.

Although the telephone fund-raising campaign was a success, the cost of two months of relative invisibility for my campaign while I phoned potential supporters for money was devastating. For the most part, the people on the "cold call" list were people I had never met, although all of them had been, at one time or another, major contributors to other Democratic campaigns. I learned that many of them represented corporations that did business with state government, and had values and priorities that differed from mine. Many of them were explicit about what they expected in exchange for their contributions. Some were so cynical that they let it be known they were contributing to both sides, just to cover their bets. In order to succeed, I had to resist the urge to tell prospective donors to go to hell, stick to the professional fund-raiser's script, and not talk about issues that motivated me. I lost fifteen pounds in sixty days, solely from the stress of fund-raising by telephone. I also lost my enthusiasm. I was strongly tempted to do what Reubin Askew had done in 1988 and simply quit rather than try to raise money and campaign in a manner I didn't believe in. Instead, Doug Heyl and I finally agreed that things weren't working out, and he moved on. I was fortunate that Robin Rorapaugh, also an experienced campaign manager, was available. Robin immediately began incorporating the Chiles-MacKay grassroots network into the campaign. I felt better. The worst was over.

At the outset of the campaign, I had assumed I would be running a traditional incumbent's campaign. Lawton Chiles and I had laid out a platform seven years earlier, had largely stayed with it, and had accomplished much of what we had promised. There was a budget surplus, instead of the deficit we had inherited. We had been one of the first states in America to reform our welfare system, reducing Florida's welfare caseloads by more than 50 percent. Our growth management agencies, environmental agencies, and water management districts were following a coherent set of policies for the first time in Florida's history. Government was less bureaucratic and more businesslike. We had, in fact, begun reinventing government, although we had never been able to convert the concept into a bumper sticker slogan. I should have realized how much Florida had changed from the narrowness of Lawton's 1994 victory over Jeb. During the seven years we had been in office, Florida, like the rest of the southern states, had been steadily becoming more Republican and more ideological. My situation was analogous to that of Al Gore two years later. I had been Florida's best lieutenant governor, just as Gore had been America's best vice president. In both situations, we had been the "inside men," and our work had been largely invisible.

From the outset, Jeb Bush campaigned on ideological national Republican themes. The voters were not concerned that Jeb was a developer, or that much of his campaign financing came from developers. Jeb was talking about less government, lower taxes, gun owners' rights, and keeping government from interfering with freedom, and those were the issues that had traction. I had successfully faced ideological opponents throughout my career, arguing that experience, competence, and the ability to work cooperatively to deal with real-life issues should trump ideology. This race was different, however. Although we were competing for the office of governor of Florida, the issues were being defined nationally. My professional consultants were accustomed to this, but I was uncomfortable in a race that was primarily about ideology.

The combination of the fiasco over Willie Logan, the infighting among the Democratic old guard, and our own ineptness had cost our campaign dearly. On July 20th, the Mason-Dixon poll showed us down twenty percentage points. Roughly half of my $2.5 million in "firm" commitments became worthless the moment this poll was announced. That was the bad news. The good news was that after letting Jeb Bush and his foundation get away with almost four years worth of feel-good "compassionate conservatism," the Florida press finally began to focus on his political program and what it would mean to the state and to Floridians.

From a campaign standpoint, Jeb's education platform was controversial. To his surprise, his proposal for vouchers was not well received. I attacked it immediately as unconstitutional, and the press hammered it as an untested ideological proposal. Jeb was on the defense for the first time in the campaign. I was suddenly feeling reinvigorated. Jeb stumbled further when he proposed that the state grade schools solely on the basis of FCAT test scores and withdraw some state funds from low scoring schools while rewarding high scoring schools. The press criticized this plan as simplistic, and a potential disaster for poor families whose children constituted the largest proportion of those in the low performing schools. Jeb's FCAT plan also ignored that failing schools are almost always rural, or in predominantly minority, socially troubled neighborhoods. These schools confront a much greater challenge than schools in wealthy white neighborhoods. I argued that this kind of ideological purity might work in theory, but made no sense when applied to public schools. I asked voters what would happen if Jeb's FCAT plan was applied to hurricane recovery. Michigan and Indiana would get "As" and a bonus, because their programs, on the surface, seemed to thwart hurricane damage, when in fact, neither state had ever experienced a hurricane. Florida, on the other hand, would get an "F" each year, even though we have the best hurricane response in America. Under Jeb's plan, after a couple of bad hurricanes, people would be given vouchers to assist them to move out of Florida. By Jeb's logic, this would force Florida to stop having hurricanes. I began enjoying the campaign and hoped Jeb's next plan stirred up as much controversy as this one.

An Affair to Remember

In July 1998, President Clinton was at the height of his popularity. Like every other Democratic candidate running for governor, I wanted President Clinton to appear on my behalf. Conventional wisdom was that the president's limited time would be best spent where the candidate's odds were most favorable. Clinton's staff advised him Florida was a lost cause. Because of our friendship and my work for him, Clinton rejected their advice and agreed to come to Florida. This show of support was critical, since his appearance would mobilize Democratic voters and mean as much as a million dollars for my campaign.

Unfortunately, just as I began calling big money donors for contributions to the presidential dinner with Clinton, the president testified before a grand jury investigating the Monica Lewinsky affair. It was the worst fundraising experience of the campaign. I ended that day with commitments of $20,000, and two outrageously funny Monica Lewinsky jokes. It went downhill from there. The night of his grand jury testimony, President Clinton spoke on national television, apologizing for misleading the nation. That was August 18th, and my presidential event was scheduled for September 10th. Clinton was being criticized from all sides, and many Democratic leaders were among his harshest critics. I was advised to renounce my association with Clinton. I opted to stick with the president, but many of my supporters abandoned me when I did. It was the best thing that could have happened to Jeb. One well-placed observer commented that Bill Clinton's calamity, by distracting

Florida's press away from Jeb's candidacy, probably saved his education proposals from being hammered into oblivion.

As the time of the presidential dinner drew near, some supporters appreciated that I had not abandoned Clinton. Money began to come in, initially in a trickle, and then in a flood. On August 27th, a Mason-Dixon poll of Florida voters showed that Clinton's favorable ratings were higher than before the scandal. But the same poll revealed that I was not closing the gap against Jeb. The conclusion was obvious. For an entire month, the Clinton megadrama had preempted the more modest drama of my campaign. Voters were not following the campaign in Florida. On the first day of September, I did an interview with CNN. The opening questions were generally favorable and easy to answer. Then the interviewer noted that Clinton's Florida visit would be his first away from Washington since the scandal had broken. He asked two questions:

How will the president be received?
What will the visit do to your chances?

The realistic answer to both questions was the same, and CNN knew that as well as I did. The realistic answer was: "Who knows?" But I took the question seriously and observed:

I am head of the Democratic ticket in Florida, and Bill Clinton is coming to raise money for the Florida Democratic Party. I certainly don't condone his personal actions and I have been greatly embarrassed by the whole matter. On the other hand, Bill Clinton has been a very good president and a great friend of Florida. He has been by our side on everything from hurricanes to tornados, fires and floods—to such important matters as base closures. I am pleased he is coming to Florida to help Democrats to be competitive. He will be enthusiastically received.

Labor Day weekend, the same question continued to hound me. The good news was that seven television crews interviewed me. The bad news was that all the questions were essentially the same: "Don't you think President Clinton's coming to Florida will hurt your campaign?"

Like it or not, my campaign had become a sideshow to the Clinton-Lewinsky drama unfolding in Washington. Every day the fiasco persisted meant that my campaign had lost one day of coverage by the state news media.

On the morning of September 11, the Republican-dominated Congress put the entire Starr grand jury report on the Internet. In the ensuing hysteria, rumors were rampant that Clinton might be forced to resign. Democrats were flaking off like flies. There was one small bright spot. Unbeknownst to most non-Internet readers, Larry Flynt, the pornographer and publisher of *Hustler* magazine, had offered a reward of $1 million to anyone providing proof that specific congressional leaders were in fact engaging in the same moral depravity of which Clinton was being accused. This led to the quick resignations of Speaker Newt Gingrich and appropriations chair Bob Livingston, both of whom were involved in clandestine affairs with congressional staffers on their payrolls. Flynt deadpanned that he didn't mind Washington's rampant immorality: Without immorality, he wouldn't have been rich enough to offer the reward. What offended him was the obscene hypocrisy that was also rampant in Washington.

In rural North Florida, with its high concentration of fundamentalist Christians, there was not much point in campaigning while the impeachment sideshow was going on. South Florida, however, was a different story—at least among the condo commandos. Accustomed to the gritty politics of big cities, they were unfazed by the scandal. As far as they were concerned, Monica Lewinsky had probably been a setup, and Clinton's only mistake was getting caught in the trap. On Friday, September 18, I attended a big event in south Palm Beach County organized by Merril Stumberger. It was appropriately named "Condomania." In the excitement, I was introduced as "the next governor of New Jersey," and nobody noticed—it was just like old times.

Media Strategy

Having opted not to abide by the limitations of Florida's campaign finance law, Jeb had raised unprecedented sums for his media campaign. A significant part of this was corporate money contributed as "soft money" to the Republican Party and money contributed to so-called "independent expenditure" groups. Despite the distractions of the Clinton impeachment, I had raised significant money—at least by historic standards—and had also qualified for matching funds under Florida's campaign finance law. Many corporations, wishing to hedge their bets, had also contributed to the Democratic Party, so I also had some soft money available. Finally, Florida's teachers mounted a major independent expenditure campaign against Jeb's school voucher proposals. Starting in September and continuing until election day, Jeb ran a saturation media campaign, seeking to define me in negative terms.

The common theme of the ads was "MacKay's not my Buddy." The people in the ads purported to be law enforcement, firefighters, and blue-collar workers, saying my program would lead to more government and higher taxes and would hurt ordinary citizens. Jeb's negative television barrage was augmented by the mass mailing of a "scare letter" to senior citizens that portrayed me as being against Social Security and Medicare. It was a tough few weeks. People were joking about the risk that my own dog might bite me. Jeb's paid television ads were overlaid on the nightly news, or "free media." After two campaigns with Lawton Chiles, I had learned a great deal about how to use free media effectively. The best free media comes from carefully orchestrated crowd events. During the final weeks of a campaign, media coverage is assured. From the candidate's perspective, live shots of real people are much more effective than paid ads, and are played over and over. If the crowd event actually comes off as planned, it conveys a sense of excitement and momentum. If the event goes awry, the busted play also makes the nightly news.

As the last two weeks of the campaign approached, my campaign was running short of funds, and we were in danger of being overwhelmed by Jeb's paid media. With our limited paid television augmented by our effective free media campaign, however, we were actually gaining ground. Polls showed the gap beginning to narrow. Jeb's media people covered their fannies with comments that they "had always known this would be a tight race."

The Last Two Weeks

Tuesday night, October 21st, was the final debate, moderated by Tim Russert. As in earlier debates, Jeb stuck to his ideological script. His position was that Florida needed less government regulation, more freedom, and lower taxes. In response, I argued that Jeb's ideological theory simply did not fit the realities Florida faced. Florida already had low taxes, and Lawton and I had reduced Florida's regulatory burden by more than half. I alluded to Jeb being a developer, whose campaign had been financed by developers, realtors, home builders, and other groups interested in stimulating growth. My position was that, with increasing environmental stresses and water shortages, the one thing Florida didn't need was a developer as governor. Wednesday's press reported the debate as pretty much a tie. Neither side had scored any major points. That meant I had missed a major opportunity, and Jeb had avoided a potential "He-Coon" embarrassment.

Thursday, October 23rd, featured a well-attended rally by teachers in Pinellas County, followed by a Pasco County fish fry hosted by my friend, Clyde Hobby, with 600 people in attendance. Pinellas County, on Tampa Bay, is predominantly urban, while Pasco, immediately to its north, still had significant rural areas and rural traditions. Both events had energy and excitement, and generated good positive media. Our paid television ads, augmented by television paid for by Florida's teachers, continued hammering on Jeb's FCAT and school voucher proposals. Feedback was that we were carrying the debate on these issues. Friday, I stopped by Tallahassee to have my clothes altered because of continued weight loss. I looked gaunt enough without ill-fitting clothes. Sunday, October 25th, the *St. Petersburg Times* and the *Ft. Lauderdale Sun Sentinel* endorsed me. Then it was five churches, two afternoon rallies, and two and a half hours attending a night rally at the Mt. Olive Baptist Church in Ft. Lauderdale. Mt. Olive's pastor, Dr. Mack King Carter, was a friend who had known my family during his youth in Ocala. He had recruited Jesse Jackson to appear on my behalf, and the huge church was packed. Jackson gave a carefully nuanced endorsement, making it clear he cared much more about Mack King Carter than Buddy MacKay. By that time, the TV cameras had left, so it didn't matter.

Monday, October 26th, I was exhausted. This was supposed to be a down day, but it turned out someone in Orlando had put together a hasty, ill-timed endorsement by a Puerto Rican Democratic club. If I had been in my right mind, I would have vetoed the idea, but instead, I went ahead. The event was sparsely attended and poorly organized. My last minute attempt to graft a Puerto Rican plank onto my standard stump speech was a disaster. The speech was too long, and the crowd was too small. The television commentator ended his piece: "It's beginning to look like it's all over."

Friday, October 30, Jimmy Buffet gave a free outdoor concert in West Palm Beach, endorsed me with enthusiasm, and pointed out the importance of the work I had done in bringing together the historic Everglades restoration agreement. That night, President Clinton attended another Palm Beach fund-raising dinner and raised an additional $350,000 to help pay for my final television blitz. The Florida Voter poll showed the gap at eight points. It may have been all over, but nobody on our side was giving up.

Saturday, October 31, I took part in neighborhood walks with Lawton and his FDLE security detail, plus local law enforcement and several television camera crews. Our entourage was so intimidating that most people were afraid to open their doors. Fortunately, a beautiful young mom with two young children recognized us, opened the door, and embraced Lawton and me. It was spontaneous, unrehearsed, and emotional, and it was all over the evening news.

Sunday, November 1, the Sunday before election day, was set aside for a totally different kind of campaign. This was where the immense influence of African American churches became apparent. Accompanied by Addie Green, a well-loved state senator, I was whisked from church to church in West Palm Beach. In each instance the worship service was interrupted as soon as we appeared. While I was being escorted to the pulpit, parishioners were being reminded of the importance of going out to vote on Tuesday. Lawton Chiles and I had appointed more minority judges and agency heads than any governor in Florida history, and I was fighting for fairness in funding for schools in minority neighborhoods. When I got to the pulpit, there was a glowing endorsement. From 10:30 to 1:30, Addie and I visited nine different churches.

Sunday night was the "Hillary Event" organized by women, aimed at women, and headlined by Hillary Clinton. The event itself was in St. Petersburg, where it drew the largest crowd of the entire campaign. In addition, it was simulcast at a big crowd event in Century Village, a huge retiree community (and Democratic stronghold) in south Palm Beach County. As usual, the condo commandos in Century Village did it their own way. There, the Hillary Event was not for women: it was for seniors. Their theme was "This Is Not the Last Hurrah!" For the campaign plane, unfortunately, Sunday *was* the last hurrah. It broke down, and I missed the Hillary Event entirely, along with the political reporters traveling with me.

The traditional statewide fly-around is on the last day before the election. The campaign had chartered the largest plane we could afford. Lawton and Bob Graham came along. The whole idea was to get on TV in every media market. Between stops, individual interviews were scheduled with each reporter traveling with us. My press secretary, Susan DeLido, maintained constant eye contact with me to make sure I stayed on message. The reporters were determined to get me to talk about all the things that had gone wrong in the campaign, and Susan was fiercely determined not to let them succeed. The last story before the election was not going to be about self-pity.

Thirty years earlier, in 1968, as a young volunteer, I had attended a statewide meeting in the final days of LeRoy Collins' ill-fated campaign for the U.S. Senate. The memory of Collins' speech that day is still fresh in my mind. Earlier, at the request of President Lyndon Johnson, Collins had served as a mediator in the intense conflict between Martin Luther King Jr.'s embattled forces and the segregationists who opposed them. In 1968, faced with the photo of his walking alongside Martin Luther King Jr. over the Edmund Pettus Bridge in Selma, Alabama, Collins was in an untenable political position in Florida. He was going to lose for all the wrong reasons. And everyone knew it. He spoke of the importance of being on the right side of history, and expressed deep gratitude to his friends and supporters for rallying around him, and never leaving him feeling unsupported or alone.

The parallels are not exact. I do not mean to imply that my untenable position came about from a heroic stance, like that of Collins. There is another important point, however. After thirty years in public life, I was in a final campaign and things had turned out badly. Part of it was my fault, but even with a perfect campaign, I would have had an uphill race. Absent a miracle, I was not going to win, and everyone knew it weeks in advance of election day. Suddenly, almost spontaneously, hundreds and then thousands of Floridians joined my family and stepped up to be at my side—to be identified with me even in defeat. My son, Ken, took two weeks off and served as my travel aide. Other family members and friends rallied around me. They provided an emotional lift that carried me through the final frustrating days of the 1998 campaign. Many said it was as important to them as it was to me. I don't know whether that was literally true for them, but it meant everything to me.

I ended up raising and spending $12 million. This included soft money contributed to the Democratic Party, but not the significant independent expenditures of the FTP/NEA, the professional association representing Florida's teachers. This was a new record for a Florida Democrat, but it was a modest sum when compared to Republican fund-raising. According to Tom Slade, chair of the Florida Republican Party, by opting out of the fund-raising limits of Florida's campaign financing law, Jeb and the Republican Party raised and spent $30 million. I lost the race by ten percentage points.

The Morning After

I spent the rest of the week calling and thanking friends and supporters, many of whom had given all their discretionary time and money to support me. It was hard to avoid the feeling that I had let them down. The most difficult part was reading the papers and realizing that some of my supporters had been playing both sides and were now jockeying for position in Jeb's new administration. On the positive side, I was no longer a security risk and thus was suddenly free from the constant necessity of a security guard. Steve and Ann Pajcic generously offered their secluded Amelia Island home, and Anne and I took our first vacation in more than a year. I had a few weeks remaining before the end of the term and it was necessary that I start looking ahead. I had incurred significant debt in replanting frozen citrus groves, and I still faced the reality that I needed employment. Fortunately, there were several interesting opportunities available.

My friend, former governor Dick Riley, was U.S. secretary of education. He asked me to consider becoming assistant secretary for higher education. I was also interested in a vacancy as assistant secretary of the Department of Interior, under former governor Bruce Babbitt. This would have potentially allowed me to continue to push for Everglades restoration in Washington. I was also interested in developing a coherent federal position on sustainable development and resource conservation, which logically should have been done at the Department of Interior. Vice President Al Gore shared these interests. I went to Washington and discussed these possibilities with the vice president, as well as Secretaries Riley, Babbitt, and White House staff.

Sandy D'Alemberte, as president of Florida State University, was interested in organizing a regional research consortium composed of FSU and other respected universities like Mississippi State and Auburn. While in Congress, I had been one of the organizers of the Business–Higher Education Partnership, and Sandy encouraged me to think about undertaking this project.

During this same time, Reubin Askew had called the director of the program on politics at the Kennedy School at Harvard, and I was offered the possibility of a year's sabbatical as a visiting fellow. Anne and I went to Boston on December 11 to discuss this possibility. After a fast Friday of interviews at Harvard, Anne and I had a leisurely Saturday. At the Boston Museum of Art, we happened to see an exhibit of the impressionist Claude Monet. We also saw the Gardner Museum, with its gorgeous interior garden. For the first time in years, we were simply tourists, with leisure like everybody else, and no security guards.

Missing in Action

When we returned to our hotel, our day of leisure had vanished. The manager had the expression of a worried mother whose teenagers finally returned home after disappearing for several hours. She had been called by the office of the governor of Massachusetts, and then visited by the state police who had been searching for us all afternoon. Nobody had told her I was anything other than a tourist, but now she had been made to believe that we had gone missing on her watch, and that she was somehow responsible. At her insistence, I called the Massachusetts state police.

Lawton Chiles had died that afternoon from an apparent heart attack, and while Anne and I had thought we were enjoying the first day of our new lives as unguarded, unescorted citizens, I had actually become governor of Florida. I had been missing in action on my first day in office. Worse yet, the highly trained state police of Massachusetts had not been able to locate me. I had been hiding in plain view. To make up for their apparent incompetence, the Massachusetts state police loaded us into one of their official cars, muscled their way to Logan Airport with lights and sirens at full blast, bumped a couple of bewildered passengers from a flight awaiting departure to Atlanta, and ostentatiously accompanied us onto the plane. Other passengers averted their eyes. It was unclear whether we were prisoners or celebrities.

Arriving at Atlanta's Hartsfield Airport, the same ceremony occurred in reverse. When the door opened, passengers were instructed to remain seated. Not wanting me to go missing on their watch, Georgia state police entered the plane and escorted Anne and me out before anyone else was allowed to disembark. We were then extracted from the terminal by a side door to a waiting car, where we roared off across the busy tarmac to the separate private aviation terminal. There we were bundled onto a waiting aircraft from Florida's official fleet, and hustled off to the head of the line of aircraft awaiting departure. The weather was bad, and it was a white-knuckle flight. Anne worried that Florida might be the first state to lose two governors in a single day. Arriving in Tallahassee shortly before midnight, we were met by our son, Dr. John MacKay, and a security detail from FDLE. We went directly to the capitol where I was sworn in as governor by my friend, Supreme Court Justice Charlie Wells, with my son, John, and Anne as witnesses. It was almost midnight. There were no ceremonial cannons.

That was only the beginning of my security problems. As governor, I was no longer the responsibility of the Florida Highway Patrol, who had somehow managed to protect me for eight years with a single security guard. Now, I was the responsibility of the Florida Department of Law Enforcement (FDLE), which operated a command post and communication center occupying the entire basement at the governor's official residence. Predictably, their position was that Anne and I should immediately move into the governor's mansion, so they could properly insure our safety. Rhea Chiles, who was moving out, had problems enough without Anne and me as houseguests, and we decided to stay where we were.

Like Lawton Chiles eight years earlier, I took the position that FDLE should simply leave me alone. Like Lawton, I had to compromise. In my case, this meant FDLE providing round the clock security at our residence. Our neighbors had become accustomed to my coming and going at odd hours, but even to them, this arrangement was excessively weird. After two days and nights of agents sitting in cars in front of our house, Anne and I invited the agents to come inside. This meant sharing the house and had many of the characteristics of being under house arrest.

Funeral Thoughts

I was sitting on the dais at the funeral of Lawton Chiles. Facing me in the front row were some of Lawton's closest friends, who also happened to be some of America's most powerful political persons—Vice President Al Gore, Senator Sam Nunn, Senator Pete Domenici, and a host of other dignitaries from Washington and Tallahassee. It was a sad time, but Rhea was determined to make it a celebration of Lawton's extraordinary life. Funerals don't usually have themes, but in this case, Lawton himself had set the stage. At his inauguration, he had spoken of bringing back Camelot, and he often framed his challenge in terms of a quest. I found myself thinking about the real story of Lawton Chiles and LeRoy Collins, Reubin Askew, Bob Graham, Fred Karl, Sandy D'Alemberte, Steve Pajcic, Jim Redman, and others with whom I had served; not the glorious story of Camelot, and fighting fire-breathing dragons, but mundane stories of taking on the most powerful people and institutions in society, occasionally winning, occasionally being beaten down, and then fighting another day.

In my own case, I had celebrated my thirtieth anniversary in Florida politics with a resounding loss to Jeb Bush. Knowledgeable people said I knew more about Florida government than any other elected official, but my political salesmanship was said to be like that of the dentist specializing in root canals ("This is going to hurt like hell, but you'll thank me in the long run").

My personal view is that Lawton Chiles was an improbable combination of King Arthur and Don Quixote, the eccentric knight whose enduring symbol was the broken lance, which had been fractured by a blow from the blade of a mindless windmill. In politics, there are lots of windmills. The all-powerful wind is money, which turns the blades. Regardless of the rhetoric, the political wind is invariably at the service of the rich and powerful. A person without major personal wealth seeking to challenge an incumbent has to be willing to tilt at windmills. Both Lawton's historic walk across Florida and also his defeat of Big Tobacco were times when he beat the windmills. His consuming passion as governor was his concern for children, one of the groups that, in the politics of money and power, tends to be left behind. He did more to help Florida's kids than any other governor. I was proud to have been part of that, and spoke about it at the funeral. Other politicians spoke, telling humorous stories, but also remembering the years of Lawton's service in Washington and Tallahassee. My role had been more Sancho Panza than Lancelot. I found myself thinking of Panza's line in *Man of La Mancha* when Aldonza, the prostitute whom Quixote fancied as Dulcinea, his queen, indignantly asked why he kept on committing himself to Quixote's eccentric crusades: To me, Sancho Panza's response said it all: "I like him. I really like him."

Political scientists measure the impact of a political career in diverse ways, many of which have to do with how much was accomplished. Much of this has to do with timing and circumstances beyond human control. From my perspective, Lawton Chiles, with his career-long battle against the corrupting influence of big money and his equally steadfast priority on the needs of children, was one of Florida's most influential leaders. I really liked him. More than that, I admired what he stood for, and will always be proud to have been associated with him.

Three Weeks as Governor

During my "term," measured in days, my main concern was to assure a smooth, cooperative transition for the incoming administration. This was an important tradition in Florida politics. Governor Bob Martinez and his wife, Jane, had been especially gracious to Lawton and Rhea and Anne and me, and I felt it was important to Lawton to continue the tradition. The only decision of importance during my three weeks in office was the matter of pardoning women who had been convicted of murdering their husbands before the so-called Battered Spouse defense had been recognized under Florida law. Before his death, Lawton had asked that all such cases be reviewed. I pardoned all those women for whom the defense would have been applicable, provided they were sufficiently stable that their freedom was not a threat to public safety.

I attended the inauguration ceremony. My only function of any importance was to assure that the National Guard cannons were not pointed at the incoming governor. At the end of thirty years in public office, I was once again Citizen MacKay.

A Return Trip to Washington

Special Envoy to the Americas

After my abbreviated term as governor, President Clinton asked me to be his special envoy to the Americas, where my primary responsibility would be to follow up on Clinton's commitment at the Miami Summit to create the Free Trade Area of the Americas and begin changing the historic relationship of the United States to Latin America. This offer appealed to me because of its potential for all the countries of the Americas, but especially for Florida. Miami would have been the logical trade capital of the Americas, like Brussels in the European Union.

Presidents Roosevelt and Kennedy had originally articulated the vision of a hemispheric free trade area. In both instances, the response in Latin America had been enthusiastic, but the initiative had failed due to lack of follow up by the United States. In 1990, the vision had been revived by President George H. W. Bush and had been brought into sharp focus by President Clinton at the 1994 Miami Summit of the Americas. The result of the Miami Summit had been an agreement signed by thirty-four elected presidents, committing to a ten-year timetable to negotiate the Free Trade Area of the Americas (FTAA). Mac McClarty, who had been President Clinton's first chief of staff, had served as special envoy for four years, and his efforts had been well received throughout the hemisphere. As I introduced myself throughout Latin America and the Caribbean, I was repeatedly told that this was the first time elected leaders in Latin America had ever felt they had a voice inside the White House.

Concerned that I might find myself an outsider in a bureaucratic turf battle, I had discussed the situation with Madeleine Albright, secretary of state, and Sandy Berger, national security advisor, before agreeing to accept the appointment. Both of them confirmed the difficulty of managing all the ongoing conflicts in our historic East/West relationships, while also giving priority to an emerging new set of North/South relationships in the Americas. Our history of gunboat diplomacy in the Americas had gotten worse with the illegal and ill-guided adventures of the CIA in the twentieth century. Each country had its own resentments, many of which were well founded.

The key to the new relationships was mutual respect and long-term commitment, neither of which was assured without continued White House pressure on the various U.S. agencies. The fact that President Bill Clinton had committed the U.S. government to the FTAA did not mean that influential federal agencies with constituencies opposing free trade (e.g., organized labor, agriculture, and the EPA) were going to voluntarily cooperate. The name of the game was passive aggression, a game played with consummate patience and skill in Washington's bureaucracies. In Congress, there was aggression, but no passivity. The Congressional Hispanic Caucus, whose constituencies had much to gain from free trade, had been badly burned by organized labor for voting in favor of NAFTA. The same was true, to a lesser degree, throughout the Democratic Party in both the Senate and the House. Because of the stresses of the recently concluded impeachment battle, no one at the White House was enthusiastic about talking to the Congress about Latin America, so I became jokingly known as the president's special envoy to the Congress. Many of my friends from my years as a member of Congress were now in leadership positions in both chambers, so it turned out that I was uniquely qualified. I was received with warmth and respect and was able to negotiate effectively, even in areas of strong disagreement.

Following the advice of Mac McLarty, I traveled extensively throughout Latin America and the Caribbean, meeting presidents, foreign ministers, and chambers of commerce. On my own initiative, I also began meeting with leaders of women's rights, civil rights, labor, and environmental groups, and I coordinated with U.S. Attorney General Janet Reno in her efforts to achieve better cooperation between the various judicial systems in Latin America and the U.S. system. Particularly in issues of drug enforcement, the inability to coordinate on deportation of criminals was crippling the hemispheric effort. McLarty's observation was that in Latin America, personal relationships are extremely important, and I felt our new relationships should include leaders of civil society, instead of being restricted to those persons interested only in business and trade. President Clinton encouraged this broadened and expanded concept of the role of special envoy. Invariably, as a conversation with a president or foreign minister concluded, the same question would come up: "Except for my local ambassador, I don't know anybody at the State Department or the White House. If I run into real problems, can I call you?" Usually there would be a follow-up phone call within a short time, just to see if I was serious. I had ready access to Madeleine Albright and Sandy Berger, and when an issue was critical, I had access to President Clinton. I sent the president a brief memo each Friday, summarizing my activities for the week. Each Monday morning, the memo was back on my desk, with handwritten comments from the president. Copies of my memos with the president's response went to Albright and Berger. It was an amazingly simple and effective management structure.

Fair Elections: Hugo Chavez and Al Gore

By chance, I happened to be scheduled to speak at a trade conference in Caracas, Venezuela, shortly after Florida's botched vote count in the 2000 presidential election. Hugo Chavez had recently been elected president of Venezuela, a country with a history of election fraud. The Venezuelan contest had been declared free and fair by numerous outside observers, from the Carter Center to the Organization of American States. America's election, on the other hand, had apparently not been observed by anyone, especially not by Florida's secretary of state, Katherine Harris, who was in charge of assuring that elections in Florida were fair. Even after my bizarre experience in the 1988 election, nobody had ever bothered to make sure Palm Beach County's voting machines could count ballots correctly.

The first indication that something might have gone awry in the vote count in Florida came when Pat Buchanan, the conservative populist, received 2,000 votes in Palm Beach County. Buchanan's reaction was astonishment. Either something was wrong in Palm Beach County, or else he had been cheated in the remainder of Florida, where he had done miserably. Numerous voters in Palm Beach County complained that the columns of holes in the middle of the "butterfly ballot" did not make it clear which hole corresponded to which candidate. Thus, thousands of voters had apparently punched more than one hole—one for each guess. Thousands more voters had punched the wrong hole. Then there was the problem of the hanging chads, where the ballot paper, although punched, did not fall free, so that the machines failed to register the vote. All of this happened in precincts that were typically among the most reliably Democratic in Florida. The final frustration, for me, was that the hanging chad problem occurred in the same precincts and on the same voting machines that had undercounted my votes in the U.S. Senate race against Connie Mack ten years earlier.

As I was in Venezuela, suffering through the tongue-in-cheek offers of Hugo Chavez and Fidel Castro to send observers to assure the fairness of the U.S. recount, Al Gore was in the process of being deprived of the presidency, even though his nationwide vote exceeded that of George W. Bush by 500,000 votes. If this had happened in Latin America, people would have stormed the barricades. In the United States, however, George W. Bush took office peacefully.

Raging Grannies and Trade Negotiations

At the conference of the World Trade Organization (WTO) held in Doha, Qatar, a ten-year round of trade negotiations had been agreed upon. Trade negotiations under the so-called Doha Round proceeded in parallel with the hemispheric free trade negotiations under the Miami FTAA agreement. The first of the Doha negotiations, held in Seattle in 2000, set the pattern for all further trade negotiations. Prior to Doha, trade negotiations had been private affairs. Only trade specialists were invited. Other "civil society" groups interested in issues impacted by trade, such as labor, human rights, pollution, and poverty, were summarily excluded. At Seattle, these groups, joined by anarchists, thugs, and other frustrated civil society organizations, proceeded to picket, demonstrate, and seek to disrupt the negotiations. What started as peaceful, half-humorous demonstrations quickly turned violent. The national press carried images of people in bunny costumes and little old ladies (Raging Grannies) being carted off to jail, while downtown Seattle was in flames.

I became accustomed once again to being picketed. My most vivid memory is the 2000 annual meeting of the World Bank, held in Washington, D.C. When it became clear that civil society protestors were targeting the meeting, the entire city of Washington was shut down, except for "essential" federal workers. Just as the meeting was about to convene, a loaded dump truck that appeared to be involved in an "essential" government project backed up to the front entrance of the World Bank and dumped its full load, which turned out to be a huge pile of fresh horse manure. As I walked past the crowd of picketers, several called out to me. They were members of my church, Washington's Church of the Savior.

On the surface, the unresolved trade issues deadlocking the FTAA and the Doha Round of WTO negotiations are not complex. America's indefensible agricultural subsidies threaten to bankrupt family farmers in Latin America and around the world. The official position of the United States was that we were prepared to eliminate agricultural subsidies, but only when the rest of the hemisphere reciprocated with proportionate across-the-board tariff reductions on nonagricultural imports. In my view, these issues would be simple to resolve if the political will was there. Ironically, two of the major sticking points involved protected Florida commodities—citrus and sugar. The real roadblocks that finally brought the FTAA negotiations to a frustrated halt were not trade issues at all, but fundamental disagreements over nontrade social issues. In other countries, these are the issues that are referred to as "civil society concerns." Plainly put, when George W. Bush became president, his administration took a rigid ideological position that precluded linking civil rights, child labor protection, environmental standards, collective bargaining rights, and other social issues to trade negotiations.

This is eye glazing, and after a dozen or more fairly unsuccessful attempts to explain it to members of Congress, I turned to a real world example. The contrast between the European Union and the FTAA explains it all. In the EU, the rich-country organizers from Western Europe agreed to open their common market to their poor neighbors. No country can join the EU, however, until it has adopted agreed standards on social issues like law, civil rights, environmental protection, and other civil society concerns. Each country applying for membership is given an agreed period of time to implement the necessary reforms, plus financial assistance during the transition period. Once a country becomes a member, its citizens have the right to seek work anywhere within the EU. By contrast, the Bush administration took the position that trade issues with Latin America should be separated entirely from civil society concerns. Peeling away the political rhetoric, the Bush position reflected the demands of the U.S. Chamber of Commerce, whose members steadfastly refuse to accept responsibility for the well being of anyone beyond their stockholders and (to a limited extent) their employees. Under this limited conception, the FTAA, if completed, would still leave the United States and Canada as islands of wealth surrounded by token democracies plagued with corruption and unable to protect either their citizens or their environment from exploitation. Under these circumstances, their citizens' best road to a life of dignity and respect will continue to be producing illegal drugs, or immigration—legal or illegal—to the United States.

The Obituary of the FTAA—Death by Neglect

The FTAA is dead. The Bush administration in its first years refused to help Argentina, which was then our closest ally in Latin America, when it suffered a financial crisis due to international financial instability. This contrasted with Clinton's support for Mexico under similar circumstances and reinstated our reputation in Latin America as an unreliable partner. It had the same impact on trade negotiations in the Americas as walking away from our European allies in the "go it alone" era of Cheney, Rumsfeld, and Wolfowitz. Instead of a close ally, Argentina is now an adversary; instead of becoming our counterpart in the FTAA negotiations, Brazil is leading an effort to strengthen Mercosur, a regional trade bloc that will play the EU and China against the United States; the rest of Latin America has given up on free trade with the United States, with the exceptions of Chile, Peru, Colombia, and the tiny countries of Central America. For most of America, the quiet death of the FTAA is not seen as a matter of great importance. For Florida, however, it represents a little-understood loss of great magnitude. The FTAA would have transformed Florida, putting it in the geographic center of a hemispheric free trade area that would have dwarfed the EU by comparison. Latin America—excluding the western tip of Ecuador— lies east of North America, and the shortest trade routes by air and sea would be through Florida's ports. Miami, with its Latin culture, would have been the trade capital of the Americas.

What difference would it have made? Just look at Los Angeles and Seattle, which have been economically transformed by trade with Japan and Southeast Asia. Thousands of highly paid, nonpolluting jobs have been created. The economic expansion has expanded the tax base, so that schools and other services are being provided without raising taxes. International trade does not compete with tourism, agriculture, or retirement. Finally, adding this new sector would help stabilize Florida's traditional boom and bust economy.

A Recovering Politician

I have now experienced more than a decade as a recovering politician. To my surprise, it has been one of the most interesting and satisfying periods of my life. First, I spent four years as a part-time adjunct professor at the University of Florida's Levin College of Law. Working with students at that level of motivation and capacity was exhilarating. I am sure I learned as much as they did. My effectiveness was measured by a process of confidential student evaluations, where I came out far better than at the polls!

While still teaching, I became certified as a mediator in Juvenile Dependency—the judicial process that ensues when a child must be removed from a family for his or her own safety. The child must be protected while the parent goes through necessary rehabilitation or mental health stabilization. Many times, placing the child with relatives is not possible, and state-managed foster care is the only alternative. The problem is that foster care entails disruptions and risks of its own. Kept for a prolonged period in a nonintimate setting and moved from one foster home to another, a child will lose the ability to trust or bond with people. So a new theory is developing that foster placement should be a last resort—not a first option. Better to leave the child at home or with relatives if his or her safety can be assured. I became certified as a Dependency Court mediator and helped organize a pilot project in the five counties of the Fifth Judicial Circuit. Our premise is that, by utilizing nonadversarial mediation in lieu of traditional court hearings, we can better assure the cooperation of the parents, eliminate the necessity for formal court proceedings, and reduce the delay in reuniting children with their families. Secondarily, whenever possible, we can divert children from the risks of foster care. While the results are not final, they have thus far exceeded our expectations, substantially reducing the length of foster care stays and the expense of adversarial court proceedings. Other judicial circuits are adopting our program. Working with privatized locally controlled case managers and volunteer guardians ad litem has been one of the most gratifying experiences of my entire career.

My other gratifying volunteer endeavor has been serving on the board of directors of Southern Legal Counsel, a nonprofit public interest law firm which represents persons who are handicapped, homeless, mentally ill, or otherwise subject to discriminatory treatment. Being indigent, such people are often unable to find lawyers to protect their interests, although the Florida Supreme Court and the Florida Bar aggressively promote volunteer, or pro bono, services for the poor. Southern Legal Counsel, more than thirty years old, does not accept funding from Congress or the Florida legislature because the defendants in its lawsuits are often local, state, or federal bureaucracies or law enforcement. Its funding comes from foundations, private contributions, and the legal fees allowed by the courts. I am currently serving as chair of the board of SLC, and find myself increasingly proud of this intrepid group of fearless, highly specialized civil rights lawyers. Led by our senior lawyer, Neil Chonin, our most important lawsuit will be a challenge of the adequacy of legislative funding for Florida's public schools.

Thinking about Florida

Looking Back: Florida's Fairy Tale

During my time in public life, the story of Florida has been a fairy tale told to newcomers. The theme, which many people have come to believe, is that life in Florida is not complicated like life "up North." The weather is mild, the scenery is beautiful, and somebody else keeps things clean—just like Disney World. For a long time, the fairy tale seemed to be coming true. In 1968, when I was first elected, there were fewer than 5 million Floridians. Over the past forty years, our net growth has averaged 1,000 new residents per day, year in and year out. Equally dramatic has been the expansion of tourism. In 2007, Florida attracted more than 80 million tourists. In this fairy tale, just as in Cinderella's, when bills come due, there is always a handsome newcomer who rescues her, and they live happily ever after in his high-rise condo on South Beach.

During this same period, there have been other stories, told by people like John DeGrove, the respected academic whose growth management theories were put into practice under Bob Graham, Nat Reed, the private sector leader whose vision for Florida inspired generations of politicians in both parties, and Marjory Stoneman Douglas, the senior citizen who showed how to lead with nothing but brains, sheer courage, determination, and persistence. These stories, based on reality, were more complex and many Floridians found them too intense. Since the election of Reubin Askew, no candidates except Askew, Bob Graham, and Lawton Chiles have been able to be elected governor based on reality. To make matters worse, compromise was increasingly portrayed as less than honorable and a new fantasy, ideological purity, was becoming accepted in lieu of bipartisan, nonideological problem solving.

The twenty-first century brought the conflict between Florida's fairy tale and the realities of everyday life in Florida into sharp focus. For the first few years, business was booming, but even as the boom accelerated, Floridians were looking at new look-alike cities being built all around them, while also seeing their existing roads wearing out and their schools becoming overcrowded. Existing lakes were going dry, and water restrictions were becoming a fact of life. At the same time, consumptive use permits were still being issued to withdraw millions of gallons of water each day to water the new golf courses being built for people who weren't even here yet. Residents were hearing new terms like "infrastructure backlog" and "off-balance sheet liabilities" and coming to understand the implications of continuing to live in a land of political make-believe. The handsome newcomer with the supposed big bankroll had come and gone, but ordinary Floridians were not living happily ever after. In fact, the cost of living was going up because the costs of growth were being passed along to existing residents.

Lawton Chiles and I made several efforts to introduce reality into Florida's fairy tale. Like our ill-fated effort at tax reform, our effort to require identification of new sources of water before issuing permits for water withdrawal vanished without a trace. By the conclusion of our eight years, Florida politics had become sharply divided along ideological lines. As my 1998 campaign showed, discussing reality had become more difficult than ever. In the new century, amendments have passed requiring local governments to identify sources of water to meet anticipated future water needs. It is common knowledge, however, that even with these changes, Florida is still behind the curve. As documented by Cynthia Barnett in her compelling book, *Mirage*, with the exception of the Tampa Bay region, there has not even been a serious effort to achieve water conservation.

Floridians would be fortunate if the impending water shortage were the only unresolved issue left over from the 1990s. There is also Citizens Property Insurance Company. What started as a modest effort to backstop the private insurance market has morphed into the State of Florida becoming the biggest insurer of new coastal construction. Worse yet, according to experts, policies are being written at premium levels far below what would be needed to reflect the actual risk. At the outset, everyone was told that there would be a remote possibility that a catastrophic hurricane might cause losses exceeding the reserves of the state-backed company, even with reinsurance. In that event, the statute authorized the State of Florida to sell bonds backed by an assessment against all casualty insurance policies in force in Florida. What began as a remote possibility is now a probability.

What does this mean to an ordinary Floridian? Simply put, if Florida should suffer a catastrophic loss from a hurricane like Katrina, Citizens Property Insurance Company will prove to be just another mirage. In theory, bonds sold by the State of Florida will cover the loss. The *proceeds* of the bonds will be used to rebuild beachfront homes destroyed by the hurricane(s), but the *cost* will be borne by every homeowner in Florida—even those whose homes are in the low-risk interior. The assessments could cause homeowners' insurance rates to increase by 50 percent or more and would continue over the lifetime of the bonds. In today's market, where the lessons of the subprime fantasy are still being learned, who would knowingly invest in such bonds? What if—God forbid—Florida should be struck with a second major hurricane?

Florida made the cover of *Time Magazine* in its issue dated July 10, 2008. The feature article, entitled "Is Florida the Sunset State?" alleged that over a broad range of issues, Florida's political leadership is still dodging the tough decisions, insuring easy reelection, and endangering the state's huge potential. *Time's* article was ignored by Florida's leadership, as was a subsequent article in the *New Yorker* in its issue of February 9, 2009, entitled "The Ponzi State." What happened to the original Mr. Ponzi—and more recently to his successor, Mr. Madoff—is that the growth on which the scheme depended evaporated. In 2009, for the first time since World War II, Florida had no net increase in population. Experts say growth will resume when the current recession abates, but the consensus is that Florida's historic growth pattern will be permanently reduced. Like it or not, reality has intruded into Florida's fairy tale.

Looking Forward: When All Else Fails

Florida is not America's only fairy tale state. California is on the verge of bankruptcy, with a significant number of its legislators prepared to allow the state to default on its obligations rather than abandon their ideological purity. The lesson, for Floridians as well as Californians, is summarized by the old adage: "When all else fails, read the directions."

For Floridians, the first of these is that tax reform does not have to be ideological, and that politicians proposing it are not necessarily liberals. Jim Smith, John McKay, and Jack Latvala, all of whom are respected Republicans, have shown that. Particularly in Florida, where the exemptions for the rich are larger than the tax base, it is possible, by eliminating loopholes, to give a tax *reduction* to the vast majority of Floridians while still increasing the revenue available for schools, roads, and other basic government services. A second important direction is that water is not an isolated concern, but the leading edge of Florida's growth issue. As Marjory Stoneman Douglas pointed out years ago, unlimited growth without concern for Florida's fragile environment is unsustainable. Simply put, Florida's constitution should provide a guarantee that growth and development will not be allowed to exceed the limitations of our environment. If any proposition can meet the definition of conservative, this is it. Finally, Floridians should not give up on Lawton Chiles's lifelong crusade to minimize the undue influence of special interest money on Florida's future. Recent campaigns, where millions of small contributors were mobilized using the Internet, promise to offset the seemingly permanent influence of soft money and other corrupting practices of the last century, and candidates from both parties should see to it that Lawton Chiles's career-long crusade for campaign finance reform is not abandoned.

I love Florida, and remain optimistic about its future. The unresolved issues I have outlined are not insurmountable, although it would be less painful if they could be addressed before we have a catastrophic hurricane or run out of water. I have no doubt that Florida will have a new generation of leaders like Askew, Chiles, Graham, Pajcic, Mills, Jim Smith, Curt Kiser and others—Democrats and Republicans alike—with whom I have been privileged to serve. A new consensus must emerge, one that will enable Florida's new leaders to deal with reality and make the necessary tough choices so that growth and sustainability become compatible. For the Florida story, that would be a happy ending indeed.

Acknowledgments

Throughout my career, my brothers and sister have been major encouragers and participants. Alfred MacKay, professor of philosophy and subsequently dean, provost, and acting president of Oberlin College, took semesters off on two separate occasions in order to participate full-time in my political campaigns. George MacKay and his wife, Eloise, raised money, organized campaign events, and hosted campaign staff as houseguests for weeks at a time. And Elizabeth MacKay Fisher, after encouraging me to keep the journals of my political adventures, employed a freelance editor who reviewed my material and started me thinking seriously about organizing a memoir.

My sons have literally grown up with politics, and each in his own way has been an active participant. Ken, a successful businessman, has contributed time and money on numerous occasions, served as a personal aide, and helped me hold things together during the last furious weeks of both winning and losing campaigns. John, a medical doctor in Tallahassee, was available night and day for emergencies that went far beyond those normally encountered by physicians. Ben, a gifted teacher at Stanton College Prep, a magnet school in Jacksonville, sustained me intellectually with his ideas and insights. Andy, the youngest, started as a teenaged volunteer, or "grunt," and quickly emerged as my resident computer expert.

Anyone who has been a member of Congress or a statewide elected official knows the importance of a trusted senior manager, a person who can balance the conflicting demands of politics, policy, and personal life. Over the years, I was fortunate to be associated with a series of hardworking, talented managers, starting with Greg Farmer and Samelia King, and then Nancy Cowart, Julie Fletcher, and Jean Sadowski. In Washington, during my time as special envoy to the Americas, my chief of staff was Frank Sanchez, who now serves the Obama administration as assistant secretary of commerce for international trade. While working with me, Frank's deputy was Sharon Leggitt, who managed to hold our office together in the midst of the turbulence of the White House.

Those persons who were there when it all began have a special place in my heart. In Ocala, this group started with my law partner, John McKeever, and included Jim Williams, my friend and mentor in politics and business, and Jim Blocker, Ed Anderson and Mal Duggan. In Gainesville, the list was eclectic, starting with Bill Cross, who managed my early campaigns, and including Cornelia Hannah, Rosa Williams, Ron and Deanna Carpenter, Dr. Gerry Schiebler, Louise Maloney, Jean Chalmers, and Phil and Barbara Emmer. "Eclectic" may not be the correct word, but there were times when my Gainesville supporters— although committed to me—would refuse to meet together in the same room. In the turbulent politics of Miami, John Edward Smith, Janet Reno, Mel Maguire, and Sam Dubbin were always there for me. Tallahassee is the political center of Florida politics, and there, my political efforts have all begun with Duby Ausley, Jim Krog (now deceased), Sandy D'Alemberte, and Jim Apthorp. Between them, this group understood as much about what was really going on as anyone in Florida. After handicapping my chances (slim to none), they would invariably opine that they had "been down with lots of sinking ships," and they might as well keep the tradition alive. In the Orlando area, my most generous supporters and friends were Jim and Alexis Pugh. Across the state, there was a brave band of nonideological Republicans who supported me, like Nat Reed and Whit Palmer. I have no way to express the depth of my gratitude to the countless other volunteers across the state of Florida who gave generously of their time, enthusiasm, and resources to support me and the causes I became involved in.

Of all my adventures, none has encompassed more agony and ecstasy than attempting to write this, my first book. I first owe a debt of gratitude to my friend, Rick Edmonds, the talented and respected former editor of *Florida Trend* magazine, who, having lived through some of my crusades, offered to show my stories to the editors of the University Press of Florida. Fortunately for me, Rick also agreed to help in putting the material into a format suitable for publication. Equally important were the recommendations of the University Press of Florida's editors, and particularly the detailed critique of David Colburn and the suggestions of Susan MacManus. Meredith Morris-Babb, the driving force behind the entire process, has been a pleasant taskmaster.

Finally, Anne, the light of my life, who stayed out of the spotlight and made the personal sacrifices necessary to assure that our sons were raised in the stability of a loving home, while also campaigning for me and supporting me, even when she disagreed with my positions. She has been the main force in putting this manuscript together, occasionally having to physically restrain me to prevent the destruction of her beloved laptop.

Index

Figures (illustrations) are indicated by *f* after the page number.

Chiles, Rhea, 120, 122, 128, 130, 131, 199, 222; Lawton's funeral, 222–23

Chiles-MacKay administration: Apalachicola-Flint-Chattahoochee River dispute, 156–58; budget cuts, 140–41; children, concerns of, 175–78; Clinton connection, 158–60; education accountability, 147–48; environmental issues, 153–56, 182–83; executive branch agencies, 140; first term, 139–41; Hurricane Andrew, 160–64, 161, 162; inauguration ceremony, 139; "Joe Camel" tobacco litigation, 189–99; MacKay as acting secretary of HRS, 178–81; political scandal, 171–72; reinventing government efforts, 144–47, 153; revenue crisis, 140–41; revenue dilemma, 144; school overcrowding, 150–51; staffing issues, 140; tax reform, 141–42

Chiles-MacKay campaign in 1990: as adventure, 5; beginning of, 121–22; budget issues, 125; campaign headquarters, 122–23; campaign strategy, 129–31; fund-raising letters, 124–25; health issues, 120, 127–28; North Florida, 135; parallel fundraisers, 125–27; polls, 129–30, 136; press interviews, 129; recruiting Lawton, 119–21; "reinventing government" theme, 131; South Florida, 135–36; victory speech, 137

Chiles-MacKay campaign in 1994, 104f, 166–70; campaign finance reform, 166; Democratic Party internal struggles, 169

Chonin, Neil, 233

Christian, Floyd, 23, 24

Christian fundamentalists, 89; creationism issue, 134–35; impeachment issue (Clinton), 214

churches, 12–13

CIA, 81, 82, 83, 112, 226

Cities in Schools program, 132

Citizens Property Insurance Company, 237

citrus farming, 8, 9, 10, 101f, 120

civil defense, 160–61, 164

Civil Rights Act (1965), 63

civil service reform, 146

civil society: NAFTA ignoring, 171; special envoy to the Americas, 227; in trade negotiations, 229, 230

Civil War, 90–91

Class of '82 Budget Group, 72

Class of '82 weekly budget briefings, 74–75

Clean Air Act, 182

Clean Marina program, 187

Clean Water Act, 182

Clinton, Hillary, 159–60, 218

Clinton, William Jefferson: balanced budget, 75; campaigning for MacKay, 212–14, 217; campaign manager recommendation, 208; DLC, 168; DLC platform, 169; EPA secretary, 184; FEMA, 163–64; impeachment scandal, 1; Lewinsky affair, 212–14; love of campaigning, 164–65; Mexico supported, 231; presidential primary, 158–60; reinventing government reforms, 146–47; tax increase, 169

Clinton campaign in Florida, 159, 164–65

Clinton reelection campaign chair in Florida, 201

Cluster, Ed, 18

CNN interview, 213

Cold War, 82

Coler, Greg, 175–76

college attendance, 8

collegial political culture, in Congress, 109

Collins, LeRoy: awareness of, xiii; endorsement from, 113; as exceptional, 2, 111, 218–19; as reformer, 16, 42, 223; U.S. Senate campaign, 218–19

committee hearings, congressional, 67–68, 70–71

Communists, 83, 84

Community Based Corporations (CBCs), 181

community-based decentralized system, for state government, 144–45

comptroller, office of, 23

computer technology in state offices, 175–78

condo commandos: birthday party on NPR, 132–33; Clinton supporters, 159; governor's race (1990), 135; governor's race (1998), 171, 214, 218; photo, 104f; U.S. Senate race (1988), 112–13; vertical counties, 60–61

Condomania event, 214

condo politics, 60–61

Congress, U.S.: "bed wetters," 69–70; campaign, 63–66, 84–86, 99f; Central America policy, 80–84; conclusion, 91–92; district staff, 67; district work periods (recesses), 67–68, 71; fate of idealism in, 92; finer as-

Department of Labor, 183
Department of Revenue, 54
Department of Transportation, 183
deportation of criminals, 227
desegregation: apprenticeship programs, 25;
    College of Law, 11; military, 11; UF campus,
    11–12
developers, water management districts,
    185–86
Dire Emergency Supplemental Appropriation
    Bill (1984), 75
Disney World AME conference, 207–8
displaced persons, 83–84
district work periods, 67–68, 71
Division of Emergency Management, 164
Dixie County: courthouse insiders, 34–35;
    sheriff's race, 45–46; voter fraud, 175
DLC (Democratic Leadership Council), 159,
    168
Dobson, James, 122
"Doghouse Democrats," 39, 191
Doha Round, 228–29
Domenici, Pete, 73, 222
Doughty, Polly, 40
Douglas, Marjory Stoneman, 3, 105f, 155, 238
Douglass, Dexter, 193, 196–97
dropout rates, 24
drug enforcement, 227
drug smuggling, 47
Dubbin, Sam, 113, 203, 242
Duggan, Mal, 242
Dukakis, Michael, 113–14, 117
Dukakis debacle, 113–14
Dunn, Edgar, 39
Dunwoody, Mac, 12
Dyckman, Martin, 4, 27

ecosystem management approach, 186–88
Edmonds, Rick, 243
EDS, 176, 177
education, MacKay's: college, 10; public
    school, 10. See also public education;
    University of Florida College of Law
education accountability, 147–50
Education Accountability Commission,
    148–50
educational reform, 23

education budget, 142–43; dedicated revenue
    sources, 142
education commissioner, 23
education funding, tax policy and, 55
Education Reform Commission, 150–51
election of 2000, fairness questioned, 228
Eleventh Commandment, 14
El Salvador, 82, 83–84
Emergency Management, 160–64
Emmer, Barbara, 242
Emmer, Phil, 242
energy grid, 30, 42
Enterprise Florida, Inc., 185
environmental concerns: C-70 group, 182;
    Cross-Florida Barge Canal issue, 3–4,
    77–79; Department of Environmental
    Regulation, 140; early love of unspoiled
    nature, 9–10; fragile environment and
    growth, 238; Green Swamp, 153–55; growth
    management, 182–85; regulatory agencies,
    182; water management districts, 185–86
Environmental Land and Water Management
    Act, 182
Environmental Protection Agency (EPA), 182
ERA (Equal Rights Amendment), 37, 43–45,
    48
European Union, compared to FTAA, 170–71,
    230
Everglades, defense of, 3, 220
Everglades Agricultural Area, 155
Everglades Forever Act, 155–56, 217
executive agencies, reduction of, 22

families and children, in social service
    reform, 38
family enterprises, 7–9
Farmer, Greg, 66, 71, 85, 124, 179; governor's
    race (1998), 203, 208; privatizing efforts,
    185; as secretary of commerce, 185; as
    senior manager, 242
FBI, 89, 172
FCAT (Florida Comprehensive Assessment
    Test): controversy over, 149; Jeb Bush's
    plan, 211–12, 216
Federal Elections Commission, 115
Federal Reserve, 74
FEMA (Federal Emergency Management
    Agency), 163–64

"Fidel Castro Defense," 174
firefighter unions, 146
Firestone, George, 31, 38, 39
First Presbyterian Church, Ocala, 12–13
Fisher, Elizabeth MacKay, 241
fish fries, 49–50, 52, 216
Flag Day, 86–87, 100f
flat world remarks, 134–35
Fletcher, Bob, 127
Fletcher, Julie, 66, 208, 242
Florida: current challenges, 235–39; fairy
    tale of, 235–36, 238; former position in
    South, xii; loss of FTAA, 231; as symbol, xi;
    uniqueness, xi
Florida Association of County Commission-
    ers, 130
Florida Chamber of Commerce Foundation,
    141–42
Florida Council of Churches, 135
Florida Defenders of the Environment, 3–4,
    80
Florida Department of Law Enforcement,
    47, 222
Florida Education Funding Program (FEFP),
    30, 41
Florida Farm Bureau, 37, 44–45
Florida Highway Patrol, 42, 52, 222
Floridan Aquifer, 77, 153–55
Florida politics, MacKay's characterization
    of, 2–3
Flowers, Gennifer, affair, 159–60
Flynt, Larry, 214
FMLN (Farabundo Martí Liberation Front),
    83, 84
Foley, Tom, 120
foreign automobile dealers, 115
Foreman, Howard, 191
Fort King Presbyterian, 13, 89
"forum shop," 26
foster care, 181, 232
Foster Care program, 181
Foundation for Florida's Future, 201–2
Frank, Pat: as Doghouse Democrat, 39, 53;
    political career, 40
Franklin County, 51–52
Frederick, Bill, 144–45, 152
Frederick Commission, 145, 151–53
freedom of the press, 36–37

free market theory, 149
free trade: agricultural subsidies issue, 229;
    deficiencies of agreements, 171; opposition
    to, 85, 226; WTO negotiations, 228–30
Free Trade Area of the Americas (FTAA),
    225–26; Clinton pledge, 165; European
    Union compared, 170–71, 230; MacKay's
    role, 2; obituary, 230–31; significance,
    170–71
Friends of the Everglades, 3
Frost, Phil, 203
Ft. McCoy, 18
Ft. Myers, 137
FTP/NEA teachers' association, 219
fund-raising: Askew on, 111; deadline in
    governor's race (1990), 136; Fifty Five
    Club, 126, 127; governor's race (1990),
    119–20, 125–27, 133–34; governor's race
    (1998), 203, 204, 209; as important qualifi-
    cation, 59; Martinez's tactics, 119; "Pay to
    Play," 119–20; presidential straw ballot,
    158–59; Punta Gorda event, 134; ticket
    book method, 126; U.S. Senate race (1988),
    109; U.S. Senate race, 59; Washington
    lobbyists, 65
fund-raising letters, 124–25
funeral home, family-owned, 8

Gainesville: campaigning in, 19; Ocala's rival,
    19; office staffing, 40; supporters acknowl-
    edged, 242
Gainesville League of Women Voters, 40
Gallagher, Larry, 84–86, 112
Gallagher, Tom, 85
gambling, 14
gangs, in South Dade County, 163
Garin, Geoff, 136
generation of leaders, 3
George MacKay and Company, 8
Georgia, 157, 169
Gephardt, Dick, 120, 168
Gettysburg Address, 90
Gibbons, Sam, 16, 67
Gingrich, Newt, 109, 214
Glasser, Dianne, 206–7
Godwin, Jean, 67
Gold Coast, 60–61
"Golden Age" of state government, 3, 27

tion campaign, 119, 130; services tax fiasco, 53–54, 110, 119; staff appointees, 140

Masaryk, Tomas, 87

Masaryktown, 86–87, 100*f*

Mason-Dixon polls, 120, 129, 211, 213

Massachusetts state police, 221

media consultants, 130

media industry, taxes and, 54

mediator in Juvenile Dependency, 232

Medicaid: costs of growth, 144; economic slowdowns related, 15, 55; education funding versus, 142; as point of vulnerability, 55; tobacco industry liability, 191

Medicare issue, 132

Meek, Carrie, 40

Meek, Kendrick, 42, 143

Merkle, Robert "Mad Dog," 114

Mexico, 171

Mexico City, 82

Miami: Crazy Joe Carollo, 172–75; diversity as an asset, 165; as a foreign country, xiii; Hurricane Andrew, 161–64; private sector, 163; as trade capitol of Americas, 165–66, 225, 231; voter fraud, 175

Miami-Dade County, 60

Miami-Dade Emergency Management, 161–64

Miami Herald, 3, 175, 202, 206

Miami Oversight Board, 201

Mica, Dan, 111, 112

Michel, Bob, 109

Mildner, Harry, 132–33

Mildner, Pauline, 132–33

military personnel overseas, absentee votes, 114–15

military service: of reformers, 3, 16; U.S. Air Force, 11

Mills, Jon, 53, 54, 100*f*, 168

Minnesota, 73

minorities, on charter schools, 145

Mirage (Barnett), 236–37

Mississippi, 76

Miss Liberty, 87, 100*f*

moderates, 109–10

Moffitt, Lee, 53

Montgomery, Bob, 106*f*, 198

Moody, Jim, 72

moonshine industry, 49

Moreland, Don, 48, 51

A Most Disorderly Court (Dyckman), 27

Moyle, Jon, 203

Mt. Olive Baptist Church (Ft. Lauderdale), 216

Muhree family, 47

NAACP, 35, 205

NAFTA (North American Free Trade Agreement): Clinton on, 165, 169; deficiencies, 171; European Union compared, 170–71; Hispanic caucus, 226; labor vote, 167, 169

NARFE (National Association of Retired Federal Employees), 90

National Guard, Florida, 139–40, 161, 162, 224

National Public Radio (NPR), 132–33

natural resource protection, 183

Neal, Pat, 39

Nelson, Bill, 110, 119, 120, 121, 129

Newmans, Joe, 49

New Orleans, 164

newspapers, in Taylor County, 36–37

Nicaragua, 80–84

No Fault Automobile Insurance, 29–30, 41, 42

North, Oliver, 80–81, 84–85

North Florida: compared to South or Central Florida, xii–xiii, 20; governor's race (1990), 135; MacKay's early votes, 22; nature of, 20; Speaker of the House contest, 21–22; "traditional values," 18, 19; U.S. Senate race, 112; view of Washington, 63

nuclear attack threat, 161

nuclear buildup, 65–66

Nunn, Sam, 53, 73, 135, 168, 222

Obama, Barack: Browner in administration, 185; Mitchell as envoy, 2

Ocala: as big city to rural counties, 36; church matters, 12–13; compared to Daytona Beach, 12; family business, 8–9; Gainesville's rival, 19

occupational specialists, 25

O'Leary, Bob, 179

"One Fool at a Time," 114–15

O'Neill, Tip, 63

Operation Greenpalm, 172–73

Orlando Marriott World Center, 137

Ortega, Daniel, 82, 84

Osborne, David, 131, 145, 169

Buddy MacKay was governor of Florida after Lawton Chiles's death, and served Chiles for eight years as lieutenant governor. He also served Florida in the U.S. House of Representatives, and was elected to the Florida House and Senate from 1968 to 1983, serving six years in each house. This is his first book.

A former editor at the *Philadelphia Inquirer*, Rick Edmonds is the media business analyst for the Poytner Institute.